Learning to Succeed in Science

Bloomsbury Gender and Education

Series Editors:

Marie-Pierre Moreau (Anglia Ruskin University, UK)
Penny Jane Burke (University of Newcastle, Australia)
Nancy S. Niemi (University of Maryland, Eastern Shore, USA)

The **Bloomsbury Gender and Education** series publishes rigorous, critical and original research exploring the relationship between gender and education in a range of institutional, local, national and transnational contexts. Books in the series will cover a range of issues, themes and debates of key interest in contemporary societies and will be relevant to an international and diverse readership. The series will contribute work that speaks to key contemporary themes, debates and issues and to theoretical, methodological and empirical concerns in the field.

Themes explored across the series will include attention to gender in relation to schooling, tertiary education and lifelong learning, digital and social media, educational policies and practice, gendered and sexual violence, and gender identities and sexual orientation. As such, the series is an essential resource for academics and researchers working in fields including gender and education, sociology and gender studies, as well as those interested in gender issues and social justice more broadly.

Advisory Board:

Anita Kit Wa Chan (Education University of Hong Kong, Hong Kong), Marilia Carvalho (Universidade de Sao Paulo, Brazil), Claudia Cervantes-Soon (Arizona State University, USA), Julia Coffey (University of Newcastle, Australia), Debbie Epstein (University of Roehampton, UK), Helen Fisher (University of Roehampton, UK), Jessica Gagnon (University of Portsmouth, UK), Akane Kanai (Monash University, Australia), Elina Lahelma (University of Helsinki, Finland), Nicky Le Feuvre (University of Lausanne, Switzerland), Uvanney Maylor (University of Bedfordshire, UK), Julie McLeod (University of Melbourne, Australia), Heidi Mirze (Independent Researcher, UK), Lauren Misiaszek (Beijing Normal University, China), Barbara Read (Glasgow University, UK), Jessica Ringrose (UCL Institute of Education, University College London, UK), Vanita Sundaram (York University, UK), Carol Taylor (University of Bath, UK)

Also available in the series:

Gender in an Era of Post-truth Populism: Pedagogies, Challenges and Strategies, edited by Penny Jane Burke, Rosalind Gill, Akane Kanai and Julia Coffey

Academic Women: Voicing Narratives of Gendered Experiences, edited by Michelle Ronksley-Pavia, Michelle M. Neumann, Jane F. Manakil and Kelly Pickard-Smith

Learning to Succeed in Science

Stories of South Asian Women in Britain

Saima Salehjee and Mike Watts

BLOOMSBURY ACADEMIC

LONDON • NEW YORK • OXFORD • NEW DELHI • SYDNEY

BLOOMSBURY ACADEMIC
Bloomsbury Publishing Plc
50 Bedford Square, London, WC1B 3DP, UK
1385 Broadway, New York, NY 10018, USA
29 Earlsfort Terrace, Dublin 2, Ireland

BLOOMSBURY, BLOOMSBURY ACADEMIC and the Diana logo are trademarks of
Bloomsbury Publishing Plc

First published in Great Britain 2023
This paperback edition published 2025

Series design by Charlotte James
Cover image © Jonathan Knowles/ Getty Images

A catalogue record for this book is available from the British Library.

A catalog record for this book is available from the Library of Congress.

ISBN: HB: 978-1-3502-3215-0
PB: 978-1-3502-3219-8
ePDF: 978-1-3502-3216-7
eBook: 978-1-3502-3217-4

Series: Bloomsbury Gender and Education

Typeset by Deanta Global Publishing Services, Chennai, India

To find out more about our authors and books visit www.bloomsbury.com and
sign up for our newsletters.

This book is dedicated to Ruth, Sian, Rhian, Oscar and Rosie and the rest of Mike's extended clan.
And Saima dedicates the book to her wonderful parents, extraordinary supportive sister and her nephew and nieces: Arsalaan, Haaniya, Samia and Sana.

Contents

List of Figures

List of Tables

Series Editors' Foreword

Contemporary debates concerned with the global urgencies of addressing inequalities point to the topicality and social significance of the field of gender and education. The intersection of gender and education is a buoyant site of scholarly and political mobilization occupied by a multitude of ontological and epistemological positions, theories and methodologies. Key themes shaping the field range from schooling, tertiary education and lifelong learning, digital and social media, educational policies and practice, gendered and sexual violence, gender identities and sexual orientation, the politics of representation and *truth*, the relationship of gender equity to environmental justice, embodiment and difference, and knowledge production. However, this is not an exhaustive list, and gender and education as a field relates to multiple historical, contemporary and intersectional issues of our times.

This research series is concerned with publishing rigorous and original research, which critically engages with contemporary debates about gender and education as they unfold in a range of institutional, local, national and transnational contexts in, across and between the spaces that are often hidden from view through complex geopolitical and inequitable global relations. Indeed, these debates include critical attention to the problematic of spatial and geopolitical relations, which are attached to categorizations in their many troubling forms. Intersectional and international perspectives are a central tenet of the series to broaden, provide depth and extend the field of gender and education in all of its complexities. Engaging with insights from across gender and education studies – including theories of intersectionality that provide a critical lens on gender and its relationship to other identity markers, positionalities and systemic inequalities – the series engages societal debates and theoretical developments within the field. It invites a growing understanding of the intersections between and across different structural and political forces that shed light on gender inequalities.

Linked to its feminist ethos, the series is a home for monographs and edited volumes authored by emerging and established scholars concerned with gender inequalities and social justice as they pertain to intersectional aspects of gender and education in a broad range of social and institutional contexts. This intersectional and international outlook is also a strong feature of the editorial team. The editors are based in the UK, the United States and Australia, with a strong commitment to generating knowledge from positions of inter/national, institutional and/or positional marginalization and/or difference, and the series benefits from the insights of our outstanding editorial board including researchers from across the world.

The series is intended for a readership composed of academics and postgraduate research students, as well as feminist practitioners and activists from across the world with an interest in gender and education and, more broadly, social justice. In particular, we hope that it will appeal to academics whose work is broadly located in the field of gender and education and with a subject background in education, sociology, gender studies or in other social science or humanity subjects; to students enrolled on these programmes; and to practitioners based in schools, higher education and non-governmental organizations.

The nature of science and who can take up an identity as a scientist is a central concern of the sociology of gender, education and social justice. Work in this field tends to either focus on the ontologies and epistemologies of science and their implications for equity or on *women in science*, considering macro-social issues such as the leaky pipeline and/or girls' and women's experiences of science as a subject and a career. *Learning to Succeed in Science: Stories of South Asian Women in Britain* bridges this gap. The book raises important ontological questions about the nature of science and success, while also foregrounding the experiences of South Asian girls as they study science and consider a career in STEM. *Learning to Succeed in Science* explores South Asian girls' negotiation of a science identity without compromising on the complexities of navigating science trajectories in relation to intersections of identity, power and structural inequalities. Far from the neat, linear stories that characterize neoliberal discourses of success, the book also points to pedagogical approaches likely to yield positive science identities among minoritized groups as well as those who do not share such identifications.

Prof Marie-Pierre Moreau, Anglia Ruskin University, United Kingdom, Prof Penny Jane Burke, University of Newcastle, Australia, Prof Nancy S. Niemi, University of Maryland, United States

Acknowledgements

Saima and Mike would like to thank all of the women who have participated in the research studies we report here. We are enormously grateful for their time and energy in talking to us over time. We are particularly indebted to Geeta Ludhra for early discussions on the themes of the book – thank you Geeta.

Saima is thankful to her extraordinary University of Strathclyde mentors and School of Education laboratory support staff. Special thanks to the Head of the School of Interdisciplinary Studies and the research team at the University of Glasgow for their support and encouragement in completing this book.

Mike would like to acknowledge colleagues in the Department of Education at Brunel University London for their long-suffering patience as he prioritizes writing over many of the routine chores he should be doing.

1

Setting the Scene

There is a temptation to start this book with talk of ladders.

The book is about studying and living in the body of science, and we are not the first to suggest that, as one increases knowledge and understanding of science, she or he climbs a *science ladder*. It gives the sense that learning science is incremental and hierarchical, beginning with basic conceptual building blocks, and that one ascends the rungs to reach ever higher levels of expertise and sophistication. There are numerous anecdotes of established scientists maintaining that a student is in no position at all to *do real science* until they have achieved at least a doctoral degree, a PhD. After that *entry-level* rung has been reached, the next stage of the ladder awaits until one arrives at the dizzy heights of being a research scientist, leading a research team, making an outstanding discovery and/or, ultimately, winning a Nobel Award for science.

Second, this book is about success and, again, the *ladder of success* is a well-established metaphor. The route to success is a process of climbing, rung by rung, towards the upper reaches of acclaim. While there may be the odd snake to slide down, as in the game of snakes and ladders, the mantra is always to *pull oneself up*, climb back on the ladder and begin the ascent over again. Third, there are parts herein where we consider social mobility, the possible upward rise (or fall) through social strata, something that is often called *climbing the social ladder*.

In his classic book *Metaphor and Thought* (1993), Andrew Ortony makes the case that *all* thought is metaphorical; we perceive, interpret and talk via metaphors – it is simply how we see the world. We certainly make use of metaphors in this book, although it must be said that we do refrain from making use of ladders for reasons we explain in a moment. There are, though, three key metaphors that we do use, sometimes referring to them as models. The first is the idea of *diffusion*. In the context of science, diffusion simply describes the ways that the small particles of matter intermingle. The sense is that, if we have a glass of water and add in drops of red dye, then over time the particles in the red dye will diffuse throughout the glass to give an even and consistent spread of colour. The particles of the dye move in between the particles of water and spread out through the container. Scientists use this description, too, to discuss how a smell, an aroma, a perfume, say, can spread throughout a room because the particles of the perfume move and diffuse between the particles of air in the room. Even if the perfume is open at one end of a room, it will eventually diffuse throughout the room and be detected by a keen nose at the other end.

We use this model of diffusion to discuss the spread of culture. This may not seem anything like a perfume or dye, but we see the spread happening in a similar manner. So, for example, we appreciate that science has very special ways of looking at the world, has very specialist ways of labelling, describing and explaining natural phenomena. It can give the appearance of being a massive, largely impenetrable, body of knowledge that is accessible only to the highly trained afficionado. However, we see similarities with an open bottle of deeply scented cologne that wafts and penetrates throughout a room over periods of time. So, it is really not uncommon to encounter the use of science terms in everyday situations and contexts, be that a kilocalorie rating on the side of a packet of food; a gluten-free announcement on the same packet; a cumulus nimbus cloud in the sky; precautions against viral infection; the role of inoculations against disease, the functions of insulin in diabetes, discussions of carbon emissions in global warming; the causes of acid reflux; buying an electric car; the uses of gene therapy; using a touchscreen smartphone; talking of time in terms of nanoseconds; the workings of soaps and shampoo; and a myriad of other examples. That is, many of the specialist terms within the body of science have percolated – diffused – throughout society and become intermingled with terms and expressions in everyday culture.

Our second metaphor is that of the *leaky pipeline*. This is a metaphor often used to describe the loss of women from careers in science, technology, engineering and mathematics – and arguably other fields before entry into, and certainly in reaching, senior roles (Goulden, Mason & Frasch, 2011; Resmini, 2016; Howes et al., 2018). The metaphor encapsulates the recognition that, at various steps along the way, structural sexism and racism in society – among other factors – can lead women, people of colour and other under-represented and historically marginalized groups to stumble or leave what could have been successful and influential careers in science. As we discuss in later chapters, we need to amend that metaphor and consider instead not a leaky but a *semi-permeable pipeline*. Permeability has two possibilities: first that, along the way, as described earlier, women drop out or leave the mainstream routes into education and employment within the sciences. However, being permeable also means that, second, women can engage with and, perhaps, enter and join those mainstream routes, even after a slow or hesitant start or later in life. Across OECD countries, around 40 per cent of workers currently participate in job-related training (World Economic Forum, 2019). So, for example, retraining programmes into industry or health services, into manufacturing or environmental roles, will contain clear elements of science that form part of entrants' reskilling and qualification. We recognize that this may well not be *rocket science*, the highly specialized work of the research scientist. It is, nevertheless, an engagement with science that generates and constitutes a science-based working life. It forms part of what we term *women's science lives*. This inward flow to the pipe is a major plank of employment training and lifelong learning and is certainly to be seen in most governmental aspirations to re-educate and re-equip the workforce in order to enhance a science-literate and technological society.

Our third key metaphor is the act of *wearing culture* as if one was choosing and putting on clothes. This comes from the work of Anne Phillips (2010) and is a metaphor we have found useful in many ways. There is a clear sense, of course, that we can very seldom, if ever, fully *take off* or discard our culture or heritage and wander naked unto the arena. No matter how hard we might try, it is difficult to *reconstruct yourself* as an entirely new and different person, to become someone entirely novel without any reference or lingering vestiges at all of either the past or present. We do see, though, that there are various times and places where one might want to be fully immersed in a particular culture, to *wear it closely and heavily* while, on other occasions, one might want to move easily between quite different cultural groups and maybe wear one's culture loose and light. This is seen among some of the women participants we present throughout the book. There are occasions when they want to be fully immersed in their culture, revel in its rituals and practices while, on others, they enjoy slipping and sliding between cultural expectations, sometimes adopting other cultural norms to blend with a group, sometimes creating hybrid moments of witty duality, of clever *cultural crossover*. Examples of all these will be clear as the book progresses.

All metaphors have their limitations. As we have already pointed out, our view of science and science education is certainly not that of a ladder. It is true that some people are *at the top of their game* and do make significant contributions to knowledge and understanding of the universe. On the other hand, there are also those who would deny knowledge of even the most rudimentary features of science and how things work and want nothing to do with the world of science. They are not on the ladder and have no wish to be, even on the lowest rung.

Moreover, most important in our view, gaining knowledge and understanding in and of science is not a simple straight line, pointing forever upward. The route into science is not a single, unidirectional assault course. Science is actually a megalithic enterprise, and there is most certainly room for a vast number of people inside. There is so much of it, so many ways to become acquainted with science, that even the most celebrated of Nobel scientists will have command of only a tiny sliver of this enterprise. This leaves an enormous amount of science available for the rest of us. And there are so many possibilities for us to become conversant with, and successful in, those parts of science that appeal to us most.

Similarly, the idea of the ladder of success is misplaced. Like science, the nature of success is hugely multifaceted and means many different things to different people. Again, success is very seldom a straight line with equally spaced rungs or easily delineated *steps to success*. There are no *Three Steps to Heaven*, as Eddie Cochran's 1960s song would have it. Success depends on the task, the context, the person, the challenge, the setting and conditions, one's culture, the many ways in which success can be evaluated and measured. In much the same discussion as that of the nature of science, it is possible to view some people as enormously successful while others profess little or no success in their lives. But the grand bulk of people will understand and achieve success in one form or another and in many spheres of their lives. So, the book is about science and success and, as we make clear in the pages to follow, we see not one but many routes into science and not one but many forms of success.

We are science educators

It is a very pleasant position to be in, to be able to locate and position ourselves, our work, our missions in life in just two words, *science* and *education*. That said, it would be nicer still if we could neatly corner those two words, make manifestly clear to everyone exactly what they mean. Being exact, though, is not straightforward. While on the one hand we might have a real sense of what science is, as we have already intimated that, as soon as the lid is lifted slightly it becomes suddenly not one thing but many. Science is not just biology, chemistry, physics; it is also astronomy, biochemistry, cosmology, dermatology, entomology, fluid mechanics, geology – and that uses just the first seven letters of the alphabet. The word *science* also incorporates the work of scientists, the many organizations they work for, the processes they use during their work and the outcomes they develop from their endeavours. So, being science educators suddenly becomes rather more hazy than might first be suggested. Exactly what kind of science are we educated in and educating for?

And then there is education. The Latin roots of the word *educare* are really not much help here because contemporary uses of the word are broad and entangled. There are many ways in which education happens – in schools, in work, in play, in everyday life; via people, books, television, the internet; through clubs, churches, societies, communities; driven by examinations, government diktats, local policies, employment needs, personal agendas and so on. These are just a few of the many possibilities and so, like science, the word *education* is wonderfully multifaceted. Exactly what kind of education do we mean?

As science educators, we have both arrived at this point in time from quite similar but different routes. To introduce ourselves: Saima is a biochemist whose MSc thesis looked at the effect of lead toxicity on the levels of serotonin in albino Wistar rats; her doctoral research explored issues of individual science identity, particularly among young Asian women in a faith school. Her research work has continued in that vein. Mike, on the other hand, has a background in physics, particularly electronic systems, and his PhD studied teenagers' difficulties in understanding school physics. He enjoys research on science literacy and the general public's understanding of science. While we hail from different parts of science, we both have considerable teaching experience, at school and university levels as well as in informal, out-of-school situations. This allows us to set out our broad mission as science educators:

1. In tune with numerous governments and organizational policies, national and international, we see the need for greater public engagement with both science and technology. We see this engagement coming about through greater levels of science literacy and appreciation of science within the general population. *Science literacy* itself is not an easy term to define, but we attempt this later in the chapter, and it also crops up in many other places in the book. By mentioning the general population we are also signalling that we have interests that include, but go way beyond, what happens in school, colleges and universities.

2. We set off from the premise that all people have *science lives*. A person's science life is that part of their everyday life that touches – intersects and interacts with – science. For some people this might be a very large part: a good deal of their working life is involved with science as, for example, is the case for researchers, medics, clinicians, engineers, lecturers, laboratory assistants, environmental engineers, forensic scientists

and the like. For others, it may be very small, their science lives
consists simply of tending their garden, fixing a household appliance,
watching the BBC's *Blue Planet*, working on some domestic DIY
improvements, brewing home-made beer or making wine. There are, of
course, numerous people in between who are firefighters, paramedics,
agronomists, mechanics, health and safety officers, environmental
officers, amateur climatologists, nature watchers, freshwater fishers,
amateur astronomers, coral-reef scuba divers, those who are enthusiastic
ornithologists or protectors of turtle nesting sites – and a vast number
of other examples in addition. Having a science life – however small,
medium or large – means that we can also talk about people's science
identity, which we abbreviate to their 'Sci-ID'. Again, we discuss more
about these science lives and identities as the book progresses.

3. Our educative drive comes not just from the democratic need to emancipate
people towards greater appreciation of the science-based decision-making
that surrounds their lives but also to increase inclusion in science of
previously under-represented and minority groups within society by virtue
of their gender, culture, race, ethnicity or heritage. We lean on the original
Greek sense of the word *pedagogy* and relate it more to *walking with*,
leading towards and *guiding* than designing direct transmissive educational
instruction. In this book we take a view of pedagogy as a philosophy and a
praxis encompassing interpersonal, moral and ethical features, rather than
that the technical aspects of a teacher's work with students, and we aim to
create spaces for personal engagement, critical being and purposive change.
That is, while we are certainly not passive, we see ourselves at the behest of
those who are *becoming scientific* and increasing the scope of their science
lives and prefer *walking with* and *accompanying* them as they do so, rather
than forms of bad teaching or telling. In our view, engaging with science
– formal or informal learning about science – is not a simple incremental,
hierarchical or linear *building block* process. Rather, it is a complex, fluid,
personal and interpersonal enterprise that, in our contemporary world,
draws upon multiple literacies and multimodal approaches to accessing
and synthesizing concepts, facts, processes, information, affect and values
towards generating meaning and understanding. We go on to discuss these
literacies further as the book takes shape.

This leads us to something of a formula: where indeed would we scientists be
without formulae? It is actually a progression from our view of the diffusion

| Science in life | → | Having a science life | → | Developing a science identity | → | Expressing successes in science |

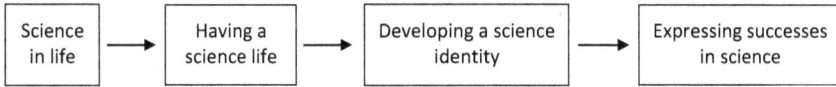

Figure 1 Development of science identity.

of science into everyday life to the growth of people's science lives to the development of their Sci-ID (Figure 1).

We have written extensively in other places about each aspect of this progression, usually articles in science education journals, but this is the first time we bring them together in one place. We are not suggesting it is inevitable, that just because science does percolate throughout society then all people will de facto have a science life, one that therefore generates in them a developing Sci-ID. We have also written about science *refusniks*, people who turn perniciously against science in all its forms and become avowedly anti-science. We have met those who twist science to become *flat Earth enthusiasts*, conspiracy theorists, deny the moon landings, become *anti-vaxxers* and the like. There are people, too, who innocently reject science as just too difficult, simply not for them, 'I'm not a science person', 'science is for boffins', 'scientists are nerdy' and so on. So, our progression is not for everyone. We take solace in the fact, though, that it does fit many people who, once they encounter some science, become increasingly engaged and indeed surprise themselves by enjoying what they are doing, be it the plant biology of gardening, the cosmology of stargazing, the geology of rock collecting, the ornithology of birdwatching, the ichthyology of freshwater fishing – and many, many more such examples. Science accumulates and becomes absorbing; science success accumulates and becomes self-fulfilling.

Building on the earlier points, the book focuses specifically on a group of women from south Asian backgrounds living in the United Kingdom of Great Britain and who relate to science both as science specialists and being science literate. So, we discuss, debate, analyse and present the science lives of more than fifty UK-based south Asian women driven to move away from a (1) market-driven, entrepreneurial, socially standardized (male, White and middle class) approach towards a (2) public engagement, science-literacy approach, one that promotes science education and science professions. Moreover, we (3) include people from socially diverse backgrounds embracing under-represented and minority groups, in our case, the UK-based south Asian women.

At this point, let us introduce just some of the participants in the book (Table 1).

Table 1 Six participants

	Place of Birth	**Self-Designation**
Amna	Pakistan	Stroke consultant
Bushra	England	Science student (GCSE)
Khadija	Pakistan	Schoolgirl secondary
Saarya	Italy	Teaching assistant
Sonia	Oman	Science educator
Tamze	Turkey	Science educator

While we have listed just six of our women participants here, there are many (many) more in the chapters to follow, and we will introduce this extended cast as the book progresses. To flesh out these first few names a little, please meet four of the women on the list. Each one has an extended *science life story*, but here we note just some initial aspects of their science lives.

> Amna is in her forties and is a stroke consultant. She was born in Lahore, Pakistan, and received a Bachelor of Medicine and Surgery (MBBS) from Pakistan. She was straightaway married to a Pakistani doctor. Soon after their marriage, she immigrated to England as her doctor husband was offered a post with the national health service (NHS). She was always seen as a doctor, even during her primary schooling. Because her family in her community were (and are) 'recognised as a family of doctors. When I was young, people used to say you are very intelligent, so you will – definitely – become a doctor, like your father.' In addition, Amna's father worked as an army doctor and as a child she moved from place to place to serve the army and, in turn, the public. So, her ambition to help people became deeply rooted in her childhood. Some family members (not her parents) gave suggestions that Amna becomes a dentist rather than a doctor largely because it is a 'shorter route', 'easier life' and gives a better home and work-life balance. But, she said, 'I thought – that's so boring.'
>
> Saarya, mid-thirties, is working as a laboratory technician in a central London school. She is the only child of Hindu Sri Lankan parents. She was born in Italy and immigrated to England with her mother when she was five-years-old – her father joined them eight years later. Saarya identifies herself as a hardworking, self-motivated and ambitious person – qualities that she says were 'embedded in the lives of her parents'. She 'hated' early science at school – she took accounting as her major and then studied applied science simply because she was required to choose another (minor) subject. At the

age of sixteen, however, she began to see herself as a 'science person' and eventually graduated in biomedical science from a prestigious London-based university with aspirations to become a secondary school science teacher in a West London school.

Sonia, a young woman (age undisclosed), is married with children of her own. She is currently undertaking a master's degree at a London university and is specializing in science education. She has otherwise been a college lecturer in Oman and says she came to science rather late in life – migrating from computer sciences and teaching college programmes in computer technology to a growing interest in broader issues in science, technology, engineering and maths (STEM) issues more generally. She reads avidly, especially around environmental matters and climate change, and sees her interests developing into 'education for sustainability' – not least to try to generate a better world for her children (and for others).

A recent arrival to the UK, Tamze is in her early thirties and was previously an established biology teacher in Turkey. She is now teaching science in a London school while she also undertakes a part-time PhD programme in science education. She has a strong Muslim background and is interested in examining the ways in which religious observance intersects with the study of science, especially in the everyday lived experiences of young Muslim women and girls. She came to science very early in life and says she has been a committed science person for as long as she can ever remember.

These brief pen portraits say both a little and a lot. They illustrate some of our preoccupations with origins, age and stage in life, with *becoming scientific*, with Sci-ID, with interests and aspirations, with obstacles and hindrances to successful achievement. We are interested, too, in what *moves* people in their science lives – those triggers and pressure points that act to transform young women like Saarya from 'hating science' to becoming a *science person* or transform women like Sonia from one career path to another. These stories hint at but cannot fully document some of the complexities of the lives these women have – and continue to have. However, more of them soon: along with many others, these south Asian women appear and reappear on numerous occasions throughout the chapters to follow. As is commonly the case, life is seldom simple and – as we intimate in these brief pen portraits – their lives are generally vivid, fascinating and multifaceted. This leads us to introduce a key theoretical thread through our writing, the interweaving interrelationships between large-scale social issues and small-scale lives: between intersectionality and personhood.

The intersectional and the personal

Intersectionality is a theoretical framework that argues for the importance of exploring ways in which different social divisions interrelate in the production of social relations. It is a theoretical perspective that investigates and interprets how multiple interlacing social factors such as race, sexuality, gender identity, ethnicity, religion, class, ability, socio-economic status, age and language can intersect as socio-cultural forms of power and privilege (such as heterosexism, patriarchy, sexism, racism, ageism, classism). These are dominant prevailing social forces that shape social realities.

In her 2008 article, Jennifer Nash takes a critical look at intersectionality and examines intersectionality from the perspective of those whose lived experience is one of multiple identities. Her essay 'Re-Thinking Intersectionality' puts forward four major issues and challenges to intersectional thought. Her first issue questions the lack of clear methodology in intersectional thinking, making the point that a strong methodology that examines *multiple subject positions* has yet to be proposed. Her second question concerns the theoretical importance of Black women as an intersectional prototype. Third, she questions the ambiguous definition of intersectionality. She asks, whose identities are intersectional? Is every identity an intersectional identity or only those of Black women? Finally, Nash asks about the coherence between the theoretical and the lived experience of multiple identities. In noting the complexity and messiness of identity, intersectionality needs 'to begin to sort out the paradoxes upon which its theory rests in the service of strengthening its explanatory power' (p. 14).

Our view is that we are all subject to intersectional forces in different forms; we all respond to them in different ways. We adopt the broad tenets of intersectionality throughout the book as one of our main theoretical backdrops and discuss this more fully in Chapter 2. In our work, though, we do respond to Nash's insightful questions and add four key ingredients to intersectionality as a theory, all four of which are uncommon *outliers* in discussions within the academic literature in the field.

Insertion one: Intersectionality is personal

Our first insertion is to make the argument that intersectionality can be personal. Much of the discussion surrounding intersectionality takes place at what Christian Chan and Adrienne Erby (2018) call the *macro-system level*, with particular emphasis on power relations among various social groups and strata and focusing on the multilayered oppression and exclusion of women of weakened social groups, especially in the labour market and in formal organizations (e.g. see the work of Styhre & Eriksson-Zetterquist, 2008). There have, however, been calls to drive this analysis down from the macro to the micro, in order to examine individual peoples' lives (e.g. by Hankivsky et al., 2017; Shields, 2008; Teranishi, 2007). It is what Vrushali Patil (2013) terms 'domestic intersectionality'. At this micro level, intersectional analysis reveals complicated identity negotiations of being, for example, young, a woman, student, daughter, scientist, as well as how these identities interact, nest and shift (Wells, Gill & McDonald, 2015). We add our own voices to this mix: our sense of this literature emboldens our commitment to developing a commentary on the nuances of lived experience in terms of a multiplicity of identities, the ways that intersectionality is made personal in the UK's multicultural society.

Insertion two: The culture of science

Our second insertion into the theory is to argue that science is itself a powerful *macro (social) force*. Science has both its own culture and is, at the same time, a significant part of our wider culture. As Lucy Avraamidou (2020a,b) notes, there have been a good number of studies that have used intersectional approaches for the purpose of examining how science impacts the intersections of, for example, race and gender. The formal culture of science involves not only specialized knowledge and skills but also values, beliefs, expectations, communicative codes, conventional actions (i.e. performing both practical and impractical experiments) and specific attitudes that are part of science culture (Aikenhead, 1996; Taconis & Kessels, 2009). Some, if not all, of these can be seen as active forces that intersect people's lives. As an example, Andrew Hoffman (2012) discusses the enormous accumulation of documentation within science circles concerning anthropogenic (man-made) sources of greenhouse gases. These have led to a build-up in the atmosphere, leading to a general warming of the global climate and to changes in the statistical distribution of localized weather patterns over long periods of time. Global climate change has become an accepted plank within the culture of science; science recognizes this as a powerful body of evidence. However, as intersectionality would have it, the impact of this cultural edict impacts different people differently. In this respect, Hoffman also reports a National Survey of American Public Opinion on Climate Change, where belief in climate change declined from 71 to 57 per cent over a period of time. He makes the case that people's opinions are based on their ideological preferences, beliefs, personal values and experiences, and these are influenced by their referent groups and immediate prevailing culture: 43 per cent appreciate the impact of science; 57 per cent heard it and rejected it. So, science may well be a major social force but is felt differently by different groups and individuals.

Combining insertions one and two: Science identity

These two intersections draw towards our framework of Sci-ID as an evolving ecological process that centres around powerful (macro) and personal (micro) forces. In this instance we explore and present the lived experiences as narratives of – often – underprivileged and minority groups of women. The relationship between micro and macro forces cannot be separated within the lived experiences of individuals. However, we believe this relationship is multiplicative and ongoing at the micro level. Our view is that the culture of science serves to promote widespread external and intersectional systems of macro social forces (such as gender and race). Therefore, our focus is on how individuals' micro forces make use of the culture of science to develop their Sci-ID – and is much less on how the macro social forces impact upon Sci-ID development. Consequently, we depart from common depictions of Sci-ID within science education literature, which places emphasis on the macro social forces shaping Sci-ID. For example, we retreat from the extensive work of Archer and her colleagues (e.g. 2010, 2013, 2016). They have used the idea of Pierre Bourdieu's *social capitals* in science education and derive their own term for this as a person's *science capital* – which covers 'science related qualifications, understanding, knowledge, interest and social contacts' (p. 3). This has been criticized for being too deterministic due to its over-reliance on the macro social forces (such as gender, race and social class) rather than showing much balance between the macro social forces and micro forces (critiques, for example, by King, 2000; Sullivan, 2002; Reay, 2004). Archer and her associates do lay the root causes of non-science participation largely outside of the girls themselves (Archer, DeWitt & Wong, 2014). They also, though, do acknowledge some personal agency – where students enjoy science but think of science as 'not for me' and as it becomes 'unthinkable' when it comes to taking up a career in science (Archer et al., 2010).

In our discussions throughout the book, there are (at least) three intermingling cultures under consideration: (1) our participants' culture of heritage, their *family culture* derived commonly from their own or their parents' countries of origin, (2) the *culture of the UK* and what that means as the

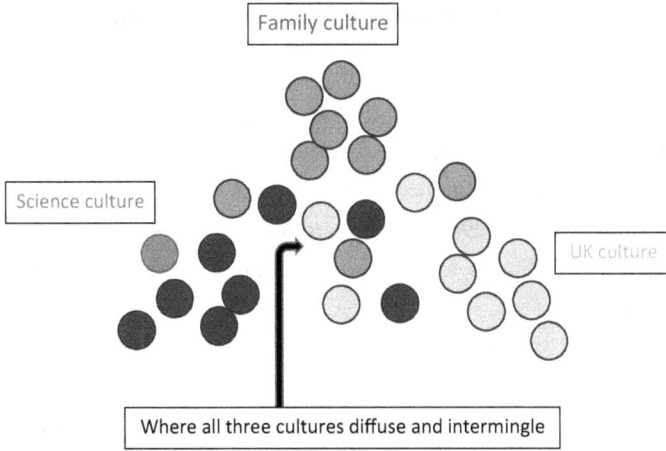

Figure 2 Diffusion of overlapping cultures.

country of residence, education and employment and (3) the *culture of formal science*, its practices and institutions. As we talk to the women in our studies – and as they talk to us – we can see the ways in which they create equilibrium in diffusing and blending these three cultures in forms that allow them to see their efforts as successes in science. It appears to be a balancing act, balancing between prevailing cultures while – in most cases – still holding onto (wearing) their original family cultural values and traditions (Figure 2). We discuss this further in chapters to come.

This brings us to our sense of *Sci-ID*. Our own perspectives on Sci-ID (Salehjee, 2017; Salehjee & Watts, 2018) owe allegiance to Jack Mezirow's (2009, 2018) transformative learning theory and Knud Illeris's (2014) further iterations of this work. In essence, it is that (1) identities are not entirely at the mercy of external influences, there is a *self-determining* core of stability, a form of micro force or personal agency that empowers people to accept or decline influences from the macro social forces; (2) the journey towards increasing stability in identity depends on a range of different factors, for example, age, experiences, relationships, events, triggers and so on. These have correspondence with immediate cultures including, in our case, south Asian family culture, UK culture, science culture and (3) one's identity depends on the preferential *weight* attached to those large-scale intersectional forces, to transformative experiences, to the (meso level) *social actors* in one's life (such as parents, peers, schools, teachers, churches, clerics, youth centres, youth workers, employment and employers). These preferences derive from that personal core of stability and are discussed more thoroughly in the following chapters.

Insertion three: Intersectionality needs a discussion of success

Our third insertion into intersectionality is a discussion of success – as we have pointed out, another difficult word to explain. Many studies of intersectionality, especially in the United States, have focused on gender and race discrimination but have paid much less attention to the success of Black or Asian immigrant women (Blake-Beard, 1999; Egan & Gardner, 1994; Fulbright, 1985; Spaights & Whitaker, 1995). So, as befits a book about success, this deserves greater consideration.

There are public successes and personal ones, large successes and small. Large public success is celebrated in numerous ways: for example, an Olympic gold medal, rave theatre reviews, a BAFTA award, a blue name plaque on a building, military medals, public honours such as an MBE or even a knighthood. Smaller, more private successes can be seen to be jogging a personal best time, finally publishing an article in print, winning a game of chess, scoring a goal, being appointed to that coveted job. To some extent, success is based on the notion of choice. Successful people have been able to maximize the outcomes of the choices they have made previously, and they also have a greater number and range of future choices open to them. They are seen to have made the *right* choices and have realized these in the *right* way so as to be seen as successful. Not all people can benefit from the choices they make and so they are seen to be less successful, or unsuccessful, in their efforts: fewer choices mean fewer opportunities to enjoy success. The notion of *success* then is a contested one and can be interpreted in various ways – certainly way beyond success, say, in school examinations and academic qualifications.

Success can be measured in different ways. One approach is to look at the processes involved in an activity rather than the eventual outcomes. So, success might come through a more streamlined or more efficient way of working so that the kitchen floor is just as clean as ever but simply took less time and effort; the same grade was reached in a test, but the student found a smarter way of learning. Another approach is to change people's perceptions and understanding of what success means in a certain area. When musicians create a new form of music, they need to bring their audiences along with them, enable them to appreciate the success of their new musical style over time. Third, of course, is to measure success against established objectives, where external observers and the actors themselves can see the extent to which goals have been achieved.

There is a broader question though: How do we measure success in life? What constitutes a successful life? For some, it is the money that counts – the salary, the direct bonus payments and rewards. More money equals more success in life. Billionaires are probably successful people by definition. Richard Ryan and Edward Deci (2000), though, argue differently. They see self-determination as key – a view that portrays successful people as those who can be proactive, make their own way in life. Individuals with this kind of intrinsic motivation tend to regard their careers, for example, as interesting and joyful. They can use their talents to fulfil their ambitions and often have a high level of control over what they do and how they work. And, in this sense, control is important: where work-life, career, everyday living is controlled by more powerful others, it can have a dispiriting effect, be demotivating, people have fewer opportunities and cannot easily see success in what they do. So, perhaps success is 'owning my own home', 'having my own place'. Success is giving up smoking or alcohol, 'owning my own body'. Success is helping family and others, 'owning my loved ones'. This line of discussion trades on a debate between neoliberals and social determinants. For example, Simon Bradford and Valerie Hey (2007) refer to 'success' as part of a neoliberal discourse where a 'person's psychological capital' draws on 'practices of self-esteem, confidence and self-belief' (p. 600). Success in this mode is measured by self-achievement.

There is a values approach, too, to success: 'Am I living by the values and standards that I set myself?' 'Am I law-abiding and do I generally maintain standards of honesty and integrity?' 'Am I conscious of my carbon footprint and concerned for the environment?' 'Do I give to charities and participate in community activities?' 'Do I care for others and have positive relationships with family and friends?' 'Do I have a good work-life balance?' 'Do I value satisfaction in what I do over material gain?' 'Have I done something significant with my life?' 'Can I feel proud of my achievements?' These are difficult, personal, measures. Shalom Schwartz's (2009) theory of values has been widely used in this respect because the proposals he sets out for self-enhancement have resonated with patterns of relationship across some seventy different cultures. This gives credence to his idea that values guide choices, decision-making and actions, and it is these values that people use to judge success.

Combining insertions one, two and three: Science identity and success

A key element of our book is that we focus on success not barriers, nurturing and supporting Sci-ID at the micro level. Yes, of course there are myriad intersecting hindrances to young women's achievements in the world, let alone the world of science. However, our chosen direction has a strength-based focus in keeping with the sentiments of Marcia Devlin (2009), who encourages the adoption of a positive stance when attempting to understand why, for example, some indigenous Australian students manage to succeed, despite the barriers they face. This leads us to look at building personal strengths, overcoming challenges, persevering through difficulties, showing resilience against resistance. So, more than just talking about the nature of success itself, this book is about successful women. Here we introduce a term much discussed in the literature and supporting our micro level personalized understanding of Sci-ID around women and success: *the nature of personal agency*. According to David Bakan (1966), 'Agency manifests itself in self-protection, self-assertion, and self-expansion' (p. 15). Discussions of agency have a very long history: the extent to which we can set out, determine and assert our own actions when faced by the tide of events in life and the actions of others – well intended or otherwise. In her 2009 book, Sandra Hanson describes the plight of African American girls in the United States as they express interest in science and calls it *Swimming Against the Tide*, the girls mentioned in the book try to maintain their own motivated agency in the face of the discouragement that they experience all around them. We return to the issue of agency in greater detail in Chapter 2; here we make only general comments by way of introduction. Anthony Giddens (1991) and Ulrich Beck (1992, 2002) have argued that an increasing emphasis on individualization and choice has accompanied industrial and economic changes taking place around the world, social changes in tune with what they call *late modernity*. Weakening and breaking old-fashioned, traditional, social structures over time has resulted in people having more personal agency, greater self-design and opportunities for individual performance. These days, people's lives are less determined by, for example, gender and class – not least because education is strongly influential in the processes of *de-traditionalization*. Not everyone would agree with this line of discussion, of course, and the suggestion that (young) women, for example, are now somehow free from the constraints of gender and class has been disputed and described as a myth (Baker, 2010).

Can women give expression to their success stories through their own personal choices and agency? The answer to that question must be both no and yes. No one is an independent sovereign *atomistic* island untouched by life in the surround, free-standing and in full control over her destiny. Nor are they wholly lacking in agency to the point they are simply helplessly adrift on a social tide, entirely at the mercy of circumstance. In our past work (Salehjee & Watts, 2020) we have argued for an 'ecological' model of Sci-ID emphasizing agency and self-identity developments wherein the individual grows and develops as an entity within the possibilities offered by the surrounding environment and prevailing macro social forces. People are not only shaped by their environments but also actively shape their own immediate circumstances, therefore shaping their success in science lives, too. That is, biographies of personal self-determined life trajectories including life successes and life failures must be constructed within prevailing social norms and frames of reference. We can depict this as a continuation of Figure 1, as science in life leading to having a science life to developing a Sci-ID next expressing personal successes in science.

Insertion four: Intersectionality critique, science identity and success

The fourth insertion we make is to remedy some of the negativity commonly attached to intersectionality. Others have raised it, and in this book, we critique intersectionality using the intersections of two lenses: Sci-ID and success.

Intersectionality as a theory and methodology provides inclusivity of minoritized women's lived experiences through 'vagueness and open-endedness ... which may be the very secret to its success' (Davis, 2008, p. 69). This is achieved by capturing the complexity of relationships among multiple social groups and within a specific social group to reveal interlocking systems of oppressions (McCall, 2005; see Chapter 2) to unveil the 'lived experiences' of individuals. We align our criticism with Alice Ludvig's (2006) critique on haziness towards the use of intersectionality in theory and practice, in asking exactly 'who defines when, where, which and why particular differences are given recognition while others are not?' (p. 247).

That is, we agree with Kathryn Russell's (2007) views on the presence of inconsistency and unreliability in emphasizing one social characteristic over another, such as centring class over gender and race and so on, and how their interconnections are presented. There is over-reliance, in our view, on external powers, macro forces and oppression, where intersectionality is seen to generate 'knowledge ... from and about oppressed groups, ... and reveal how oppression is constructed and maintained through multiple aspects of identity' (Collins, 1990, p. 7). Sara Salem (2018) believes that class, gender, race and social class macro forces are interlocking and tied to global power relations at the macro social level. Similarly, Sherene Razack's (2005) uses the term of interlocking – rather than intersecting – forces when discussing the interconnection between systems of oppression. She sees a system of oppression where such interlocking forces 'keep several balls in the air at once' (p. 343).

Most researchers using an intersectionality framework suggest that each structural inequality needs to be analysed separately and simultaneously in order to avoid a 'single story of oppression' and capture the breadth and depth of intersectionality as storied by individuals (e.g. Belkhir, 2009; Bowleg, 2008). But then, such analyses (separately and simultaneously) fail, in our view, to include the experiences of success and their development of Sci-ID – those which have been achieved as women of colour. Sometimes success is viewed as the purview of only a handful of privileged members of an oppressed group (e.g. Harris, 1990). However, our stories capture those who are beginning scientists, those in professional roles and those who are striving and/or aspiring to succeed in science.

Stories of success are important for several more reasons. First, without them, the unveiling of the lived experiences of women of colour, those who possess strong Sci-ID and are successful in various aspects of their (science) lives, would make for a very incomplete account and leave only tales of oppression and subjugation. Therefore, we need to give powerful importance to success stories and not simply repeat a range of *stories of oppression* in order to meet our aim of supporting minority groups in succeeding.

Second, we want to unseat some *taken for granted* positions. Colour, class, culture, gender, age and ability are not of themselves *given* as barriers to success. There is something of a spirit of celebration in our collected stories that looks to challenge the assumptive world of intersectionality.

Finally, while we agree with Umut Erel, Jin Haritaworn, Encarnación Gutiérrez Rodríguez and Christian Klesse's (2010) view that

> intersectionality . . . [is] an analysis that is critical of power relations and appears to us as the precondition for understanding the effects, relationships and interdependencies of power and domination. (p. 64)

A postcondition for us would be to extend our understanding and exploration of effects, relationships and interdependencies of power and domination not only at a macro level but also at the micro level. This postcondition requires voicing the experiences of women of colour and of their Sci-ID by focusing on not just oppressions but also successes.

That is, our reading of intersectionality literature leads us to:

(i)   focus on the positive sides of the lived experiences to a far greater extent than any negative experiences.
(ii) rely more on micro social force descriptions and much less on macro level understanding, acceptance and reliance. Our focus on success aims

to counteract 'intersectionality as a synonym for oppression' (Carastathis, 2016, p. 305).

(iii) stress the exploration and presentation of Sci-ID to give greater authority to individual women of colour. We do this to define and present their recognisable similarities and differences, their challenges and privileges.

(iv) focus on successes (positive experiences) and would also present challenges, hurdles and barriers (negative experiences) which were witnessed by women of colour and narrated by them.

In summary here, there are bound to be readers who bridle at our need to meddle with intersectionality in these four ways and our unwillingness to acquiesce faithfully to the original formulations of the theory. We are, however, unhappy with the idea that the theory be used solely, for example, as statistical categorizations of sections of society in relation, perhaps, to race and gender. While there is every essential need to undertake critical analyses of major social structures, with their multiple forms of privilege and of oppression, there is also a need to understand the context of individual developmental processes. While much of intersectionality is antithetical to this individualization and is more commonly concerned with generalities and norms in an effort to explain overarching behaviours and processes, we see it as a productive success of the theory that can be used in a more focused way. As Moin Syed and Alex Ajayi (2018) point out, intersectionality is best described as a humanistic theory and, as such, is a 'soft' rather than a hard, predictive, theory. In this sense, then, it is amenable to shifts and changes both in scope and interdisciplinarity.

So, as we make clear in the following chapters, our focus in this book is on the personal agency of south Asian women and on ways in which they find spaces and direction to give expressions to their individual Sci-ID – and the importance they attach to success. In doing so, we tend to privilege the personal emotions over the social (Dixon, 2012). By exploring interrelated dimensions of social and cultural identities, intersectionality aims to expand diversity (Smooth, 2013) between and within identity categories. In this introductory chapter, our principal questions are: How do south Asian women position themselves between three strong cultures – the cultures of science, UK and South Asia? And, how do the relative *weights of culture*, and corresponding social forces, interact in their science lives? We look to answer this further into the book and our discussion draws on our current research (Salehjee, 2017; Salehjee & Watts, 2018; Ludhra, 2015), which is very much work in progress. Before we explore these issues further, we look first at the term south *Asian*, the ways in which south Asian communities have arrived and taken root within the UK. We then discuss some of the literature highlighting identity, specifically Sci-ID.

The term *south Asian*

The category *Asian* is also both very broad and contested. In Britain, *South Asian* refers specifically to the communities having ancestral connections with India, Pakistan and Bangladesh. Analysis of the most recent census in the UK, completed in April 2021, is not yet available to us and so – as we write – we must fall back on the census of 2011 for informative data. So, for example, according to that 2011 Census, overall, there are three million south Asians in the UK, and their population is increasing rapidly. Of that 5.3 per cent of the population, Indians made up the largest of the south Asian minority ethnic groups (2.5 per cent of the population), followed by Pakistani (2 per cent) and Bangladeshi (0.8 per cent) (Census, 2011). South Asians in the UK are predominantly Buddhist, Hindus, Muslims or Sikhs, with the majority (two-thirds) of British Asians being Muslim. The majority of the south Asian heritage Muslims in the UK are from Pakistan (43 per cent), Bangladesh (16 per cent) and India (8 per cent) (Census, 2011). Consequently, Pakistani and Bangladeshi Muslims constitute the youngest age profile in comparison to all the other migrant categories in the UK. Interestingly, most of these young Muslims have been born in other countries and migrated to the UK before the age of sixteen. Needless to say, there exist a series of paradoxes at play in attempting to picture the outcomes of these migration patterns.

Throughout the book we refer to *south Asian women* even though we understand *south Asian* to be an extensive term that in itself encompasses many diverse groups. According to Brown and Talbot (2006), any division among south Asian communities is not straightforward – not least because a number of British south Asians with Indian subcontinent ancestry were born in other British colonial countries such as Mauritius, Kenya and Uganda. Moreover, Paul Ghuman (2011) notes, these might include East African Asians who came to the UK via Tanzania, Kenya or Uganda or even people from Mauritius. Sarita Malik (2012) discusses how, within everyday discourses, the term *Asian* is synonymously aligned with the word *Indian*, and this is particularly noticeable when discussing Sikh and Hindu communities. Moreover, between and within each south Asian group, there exist further differences of gender, class, caste, race, language (including regional dialects) and religio-cultural beliefs, to name but a few. These differences may be influenced by the geographical roots of families from India or Pakistan, as Ghuman's (2011) and Avtar Brah's (1996) research, in particular, discusses the importance within these groups of family heritage and cultural values.

In this book, the phrase *south Asian women* (or *girls*) does not therefore position women within a homogeneous category, not least because the homogeneity of women is similarly an area critiqued by Black feminists. We take up our position alongside Kalwant Bhopal (2010) who maintains that south Asian woman should be seen as 'a starting point from which to focus on the varied lives of women who share a migratory background' (p. 1).

Migration and integration in the UK

Ceri Peach (2006), for example, has given a very clear and detailed picture of the migration patterns from the Indian subcontinent to the UK, in particular charting the movement of peoples after the formation of India and Pakistan in the aftermath of the British Empire in 1947. In 1971, East and West Pakistan became Pakistan and Bangladesh. Early research during the 1970s on the experiences of south Asian women in the UK (Wilson, 1978; Brah, 1979) has tended to present them in essentialized ways, as passive victims of 'traditional' and 'patriarchal' families (Puwar, 2004; Wilson, 2018). To some degree media representations continue to echo such discourses, where Muslim women in particular are seen to be oppressed by Islam as a 'sexist religion' (Bulbeck, 2010, p. 496). The sociological literature on Asian communities during the 1980s moved away from such essentialized cultural accounts to acknowledge the historical contexts of communities. The 1990s literature focused more on Asian subgroups. Within contemporary Asian studies literature, there now exists emerging feminist writing, including religious translations, that draws on feminist viewpoints (see Bakhtiar, 2011) and critical interpretations on the meaning of 'choice' and agency for Muslim south Asian women (Afshar, 2008; Martino & Rezai-Rashti, 2009; Haw, 2010; Mirza, 2013). It is important to understand the word *patriarchy* as not relating exclusively to south Asian groups of women since it operates across the lives of all women but to different degrees of intensity (Beechey, 1979).

Since 1947, while south Asian populations have most certainly been established and become embedded in the UK, it is also the case that they have retained much of their socio-cultural identities and cultural distinctiveness including religion, customs and language. For instance, the south Asian Muslim (Urdu), Hindu (Hindi) and Sikh (Punjabi) communities are seen to have developed and recognized in very different ways. So, for example, there is considerable acculturation taking place in, say, the wearing of Western clothes and in the availability and sharing of cuisine and foodstuffs, while there is also increased mistrust and a sense of alienation after the events of Twin Towers 9/11 bombing in New York and 7/7 bombings by young Muslim British men in London. Moreover, some Bangladeshi and Pakistani communities in the UK experience housing difficulties, low employment prospects and low economic activity while, simultaneously, Hindu and Sikh housing is seen to be of better quality and located in areas of healthier economies (Peach, 2006). Furthermore, the differences mentioned by Archer and colleagues (2013) highlight the lower socio-economic distribution of the dominant British south Asians (Bangladesh, India and Pakistan). The UK's census 2011, for example, reports that White British, White Irish and other White ethnic groups are least likely to live in the most income-deprived neighbourhoods. In comparison, Bangladeshi and Pakistani are three times more likely to live in deprived neighbourhoods and twice likely to live in income-deprived neighbourhoods. Simultaneously, Indians were reported to be least likely of all ethnic groups to be living in the most deprived – and most employment-deprived – of neighbourhoods. Some reasons for ethnic and social class inequalities include the alignment of immigration with downward social mobility (Platt, 2005), parental social networking among and within working-class employment sectors (Patacchini & Zenou, 2012) and limited financial support to fund higher education resources (Flap & Völker, 2008; Zuccotti, 2015). Therefore, working-class (Bangladeshi and Pakistani) pupils are disadvantaged well before entering university (Archer, 2018), that is, display poor academic qualifications, underachievement and low aspirations for successes in science, while others (Indian pupils) aim high towards vibrant entrepreneurship and traditional professional occupations (Aspires 1, 2013; Aspires 2, 2020). However, this provides only a part of the picture – for example, it is reported that the UK's ethnic non-White students are most likely to obtain a university qualification compared to UK's ethnic majority White population of students (Crawford & Greaves, 2015). Moreover, parental education within the ethnic minority communities is not a reliable indicator for their children attending higher education and so their children's identity development (Department of Business Innovation and Skills (BIS), 2015). These points certainly complicate the story and so we rely on the lived stories more than generalized indication of low aspirations for successes in science.

South Asian families in the UK

Some of the recent discourse surrounding south Asian girls and women has tended to be ambivalent and regressive, where Asian girls are viewed by some, for example, teachers/lecturers, as 'ideal' students because of their quiet, passive and studious natures (Shain, 2003; Mirza, Meetoo & Litster, 2011). Such double-edged stereotypes have been documented as far back as the Bullock Report (DES, 1975) and Swann Report (DES, 1985), where *tightly knit* British south Asian community and families were seen to create a supportive, educational environment, yet at times, the same families engendered too great a level of stress in girls. In addition, while some south Asian parents have been noted for valuing education for their daughters, their concerns have been discussed in relation to the effects of 'Westernization', particularly if daughters contemplate leaving home to study at university (Ijaz & Abbas, 2010). Muhammad Anwar (1998) has noted the 'need to be modest', exploring parental reasons for restricting daughters' socialization principally within like-minded religious and cultural groups. A variation on these views comes from Fauzia Ahmad's (2001) qualitative fieldwork undertaken with mainly working-class, London-based undergraduate, British Muslim women. She used semi-structured interviews with fifteen students aged between nineteen to thirty years. Despite low levels of parental education across her sample, these respondents' parents strongly valued and promoted education for their daughters, where higher education was viewed as necessary to maintain social prestige and respect, rather than just economic capital. Parents spoke of educational success as a useful backup plan that assured a certain degree of security against worst-case scenarios – for example, marriage failures. Suitable future husbands were perceived to appreciate a potential wife's mental acumen and career, and therefore they would be less patriarchal in their behaviour. Educated daughters signalled *liberalism* for the family, positioning parents as *modern* and socially astute.

In a similar vein, other empirical research incorporates a dynamic view of girls' identities (Shain, 2010; Tyrer & Ahmed, 2006; Hussain & Bagguley, 2007). Religion has been discussed as a useful life structure in these studies, Abbas (2004) notes that for Muslim women, Islam has presented particular tensions. The young women in his study wanted to discover a *proper Islam*, rather than the outdated religio-cultural practices of their parents (discussed also through Bakhtiar, 2011; Mirza, 2013). Abbas's research also revealed that *being a good Muslim* was seen to be more demanding than *being a good Sikh* or *good Hindu*.

Elisabet Weedon, Sheila Riddell, Gillean McCluskey and Kristina Konstantoni (2013) published a detailed report on the experiences of Muslim families in Scotland and England, emphasizing that there is no one 'homogenous' Muslim parent or pupil group. Rather parental aspirations for their children are shaped by their own self-perceived experiences with education, society, social class, culture, national and geographical context. Overall, Pakistani pupils in Scotland perform better in exams (Hopkins, 2017) compared to Pakistani pupils in England, which Weedon et al. believe could be because the majority of Scottish Pakistanis have lived and integrated in Scotland for a more extended period compared to their counterparts in England. This report has pointed to various interesting data – though emphasizing parental viewpoints rather more than their children. For example, like any parent, White or non-White, Muslim parents want their children to be educated in good schools and universities. Moreover, religion was a prominent indicator in both England and Scotland. Parents want their children to be 'brought up with a set of values based on Islamic principles, but many felt these values were not particular to Islam but were shared by other religions' (Weedon et al., 2013, p. 65). In addition, parents believe that it is the family's rather than the school's responsibility to provide religious information/education – religion is seen to be sacred and separate from school. Science and religion, too, are seen to be quite separate (Avraamidou, 2020a, b).

Although Weedon et al.'s report is very useful, it does not specifically comment on the intersection of gender, social class or religious beliefs on science achievement. Some indications are evident within the case studies, for example, where parents support freedom to educational and professional choices by not pushing children to become doctors or dentists. The year following Weedon et al.'s work, a Wellcome Trust report (2014) introduced aspects of socio-economic status to the debate, noting low levels of engagement of lower socio-economic disadvantaged students (aged nine to nineteen) from Glasgow, in comparison to three England-based cities. This Wellcome report does not explicitly mark differences between the four cities, although the geographical, historical, political and educational systems in England and Scotland are quite different. Nevertheless, the results match the decade-long science education-specific England-based ASPIRES programme. So, the most recent 2020 'ASPIRES 2' report on students' aspirations (aged ten to nineteen) indicates that south Asian boys and girls – not specifically Muslims – are more likely to aspire to become scientists, but feelings of *being sciencey* are most prominent among high-achieving middle-class boys. South Asian students portraying high *science capital* (e.g. having a family member in a science profession) are very well represented in science careers, though science self-concept decreases over time among south Asian students even from advantaged backgrounds. This extensive report does not comment on religion having (or not) any impact on such career choices. Though their outcome resembles to Weedon et al. (2013) take on religion that Muslim parents having advantaged socio-economic status and social mobility were much better in supporting their children's academic and professional achievements than parents living in socially disadvantaged demographics. However, the aspect of science self-concept mentioned in ASPIRES 2 is not covered in Weedon et al.'s report (more discussion on families in Chapter 3).

South Asian women and science identity

Focusing on Sci-ID development, Veena Meetoo (2016) indicated that 'conceptualising a single south Asian diaspora is problematic given the variety in experiences and migration histories amongst this group' (p. 14). In general, the 'diaspora identity' phenomenon suggests that the UK-based south Asian women are simultaneously living and yet moving between the UK and south Asian self-identities (Dasgupta, Gupta & Teaiwa, 2007). This diaspora identity also determines ethnic communities' accumulative patterns of living and consumption, their sense of belonging to different nations and adopted/adapted lifestyles (Cappellinim & Yen, 2016), and generates a mode of producing hybrid cultural expressions with a view of cultural identity as fluid, which can form and be transformed (Hussain, 2017). The transnational women of Britain, though, bring with them individualized 'postcolonial histories, ethnicities, cultures, and nation states, are each positioned within the dominant and intersecting modalities of race, class and gender in very different ways' (Mirza, 2013, p. 6).

In this book, we make a point of avoiding *a single south Asian story* and, instead, explore and discuss the UK-based south Asian women not just as one community but also as individuals who voice personal experiences. We critique the two-culture dichotomy as there is no one fixed south Asian culture or a single science culture with which south Asian women interact to develop their Sci-ID. Instead, we see the science culture embedded in the everyday culture, that is, *Science in Culture*, including the varied forms of south Asian cultures perceived by the individual south Asian person. So, south Asian women's formation of Sci-ID emerges at a personalized level.

Intersectionality and Successes in Science

Various dedicated organizations focus on inspiring women (including south Asian) from primary school age and there are policies in place to support equality, diversity and inclusion agendas in line with United Nation's 2030 Sustainable Development Goals (SDG) 4 and 5. These organizational activities and policies have, potentially, supported a rise in south Asian students opting for sciences at advanced school level (A-levels) with aspirations to pursue science careers (WISE, 2015). Further, there is also an increase in the number of STEM academics from minority backgrounds (Campaign for Science and Engineering (CaSE), 2014). So, there are success stories out there, but we see that the literature on British south Asian women is generally very limited. One reasons for this limited data is because in Britain, ethnic minority groups are broadly coupled under the umbrella of 'BAME' (Black, Asian and Minority Ethnic). For example, in the 2011 census, Asians are aggregated under one category. It is reported that despite some successes by the BAME women in the field of science, only 20 per cent identify as BAME in the NHS, and the top UK's technology firms exhibit a minimal representation of BAME members at the senior management teams. BAME women make up approximately 2 per cent of boards and senior executive teams (The Lancet Digital Health, 2020) – but there is no clear indication of the percentage of south Asian women lying within the 20 per cent or 2 per cent mentioned earlier. Moreover, as we have noted, the 'A' in the BAME is quite contested as it could include people from south Asia, east Asia and south-east Asian living in the UK.

Having said that, a few science educators have specifically studied intersections of ethnicity and gender, that is, south Asian women and their Sci-ID formations as attitudes and aspirations. They have highlighted principally that south Asian women do experience discrimination, do not recognize themselves as *sciencey*, lack parents with scientific backgrounds and do not have access to resources, for example, provided by their families and communities. These are not studies that celebrate south Asian women's successes (small/large) in science. For instance, Archer and colleagues (2018, 2017a) used a Sci-ID framework to classify injustices seen among working-class British pupils (boys and girls). Their work revealed that working-class British girls of Pakistani and Bangladeshi heritage are most likely to recognize themselves as *science refusers*, in contrast to boys from high-income families (mainly Chinese and Indian) who are most likely to choose science after the compulsory age of science education (Archer, 2018; Wells, Gill & McDonald, 2015). Moreover, it is noted that Bangladeshi and Pakistani heritage A-level science students (young men and women) feel restricted to the study of physics and chemistry at the degree level – mainly because of their family influences to pursue family-adopted professions such as medicine and pharmacy (WISE, 2015). The imbalance in south Asian women and girls' choices of science degrees and professions is also noted by some science educators (e.g. Mujtaba & Reiss, 2014; Wong, 2015). That said, a rapid increase is evident in the proportion of BAME (including south Asian) women working in STEM occupations compared to White women (Business in the Community/Diversity, 2011) – but this increase is seldom discussed in current science education literature. So, we believe there is much more to explore and celebrate in the relationships between south Asian women and science.

Along with Archer and colleagues, Billy Wong (2012) explored identity constructions by zooming into the science aspirations of one thirteen-year-old Bangladeshi girl (Fay) from a working-class background. Wong's study noted that, despite being a high achiever and having a science-supportive mother, Fay had no aspirations towards a profession in science. Wong believed that Fay's lack of aspiration stemmed from her lack of social capital (science-based family and peer networking) and 'her heavy hetero-feminine investments as well her aspirations in popular culture, may suggest that the maintenance of a "high-achieving and popular" identity are complicated by ethnicity' (p. 59). We see Wong's work to be similar to ours in that we also see self-perceptions of gender to impact on Sci-ID formation. However, we also believe that Sci-ID does not conflict with the perceptions of gender or femininity and perceptions of gender identity need not necessarily decline with a young woman's movement into science. In Wong's work, we see Fay as displaying strong persistence in becoming a show business person. Even if she possessed the kind of *science capital*, she might have wanted to enter an entertainment-based profession.

Prominent science education studies such as Wong's and Archer's mentioned earlier have not, in our view, paid sufficient attention to including the intersection of religion in their studies. As mentioned earlier, within the south Asian communities, the religious difference is one of the prominent features that exhibit educational and professional differences among south Asian communities in the UK. Similarly, Abbas (2004) advocates the importance of religion as one of the contributing factors to Sci-ID, along with social class and gender (Avraamidou, 2020a). The career destinations of south Asian women are also difficult to divine in any easy fashion. Literature on Muslims and Islam shows that Islam is a highly misunderstood religion (Fadel, 2018) and that Muslims in the West are a minority community who are poorly understood (Environics

Institute, 2016). Unrelated to science, several other studies (e.g. Haw, 2010; Wagner et al., 2012) have explored the continuing oppression, inequality and transformation among Pakistani and Bangladeshi girls in Britain – inequalities, for instance, in attaining better jobs for well-educated Muslim women (Social Mobility Commission, 2016). According to Mirza and Meetoo (2018), Pakistani and Bangladeshi women interchange between Western and Eastern cultures. They move between the two, negotiate and/or shift their identities, values and lifestyles on a day-to-day basis. Some previous Britain-based studies support Meeto's (2018, 2019) viewpoint, for example, in such matters as Muslim women's veiling (Afshar, 2008) and active negotiations in acceding (or not) to south Asian parental expectations (Bhopal, 2011).

Our standpoint in the book is that there are differences between and within the south Asian families' socio-economic status, religious influences, perceptions about gender and associated educational/professional choices and so on. Such differences can be due to families, communities and/or individuals self-perceived cultural norms, values and ethos. So, these differences reflect on personalized science lives at the same time there are *personalized stories of successes in science* – which we aim to celebrate in this book.

Why stories? Narrative inquiry

People tell stories as an integral part of their lives. They gather together the various threads of the day to make a composite whole or the various strands of their lives to make a comprehensible life story. There are both formal and informal ways in which this happens so that, at a job interview for example, it is important to give a *potted version* of one's life and professional experiences in the form of a coherent project so that the interviewers have a good sense of how that fits with their expectations for the role on offer. Informally, people tell each other about their lives as they make meaningful sense of the many diverse elements in their daily adventures.

Our approach to understanding, and self-understanding, then, is grounded in narrative. This is our preferred approach to conducting qualitative research, and we outline this further in the chapters to come. When people tell a story they give *narrative form* to experience. We naturally talk about ourselves, our lives and *journey of becoming* in a storied way and much can be learned about lives from stories (Clandinin & Connelly, 2000). Our belief is that we learn a great deal about ourselves through the stories that we tell about ourselves and through the stories that we hear echoed back from others. Eventually, these stories coalesce into a life story. A life story, then, is a dynamic, moveable, collection of self-defining memories in narrative form that can be organized to represent major events and periods over a lifetime (see Conway, Singer & Tagini, 2004). This means that there is no single defining life story for any one individual. Rather, we organize and reorganize the versions of our stories throughout our lives; we select different events to include in those versions depending on our audience and our current perspectives (McAdams et al., 2006). Such *subjective perspectives* on events are an essential component of narrative theories of identity. Clarifying one's perspective on events is a means of establishing a self. From this position, autobiographical memory theorists contend that personal narratives are linked to self-understanding throughout a person's continuing development over time (Bird & Reese, 2008).

The narrative data we draw upon for this book has been generated over the course of the last two years or so, since the publication of our first book together (Salehjee & Watts, 2020). The interviews that prompted the current stories have varied in length and were generally conducted in as informal a manner as we could manage. Our aim was to create dialogues with girls and women who were relaxed and eager to talk about themselves, about their lives, their professional concerns, their histories, families, preoccupations about science and – of course – about success. We encouraged their explanations and meaning-making, self-questioning, observations, views, opinions, recollections and forward projections. Our aim was not just to set out markers for what constituted their science identities, the ways in which they saw themselves in relationship to science, but also the ways in which they constructed success.

Meanwhile, it is important to note that narrative inquiry, as a methodology, is not just about collecting stories or telling them; the narrative approach is an overarching principle where data, analysis and representation are all narrative in form (Conle, 2000). As a methodological approach, it is particularly congruent with the purposes of educational research because '[e]ducators are interested in life. Life, to borrow John Dewey's metaphor, is education' (Clandinin & Connelly, 2000, p. xxii). The use of narrative allows for a focus in two main directions: (1) the realm of *lived experience*, where people lay out how they experience certain events and confer their subjective meaning onto these experiences; and (2) the *narrative means* (or devices) they use. These are the skills and techniques they adopt in order to make sense of it all – it is *how they tell the story*. We are interested in both so that we are keen to follow the content of what is being said while also being conscious of the shape the story takes – after all, we need to make sense of the story ourselves in order to relay it on.

How narrative researchers recount the stories of their participants is not unproblematic. Researchers commonly discuss themes and make connective links that embellish and contextualize the stories they work with – putting someone's story into context is the very purpose of the analysis in the first place. Carl Rhodes (2000) offers the metaphor of 'ghostwritting', wherein the researchers are as much a part of the story as the participants. This process of re-storying inevitably produces a new story, so, in the end, exactly whose story is it? Our approach is one of participant verification or more technically called respondent validation. Jo Anne Ollerenshaw and John Creswell (2002) argue that authenticity is maintained when the participants have opportunities to reassess what they have said and then to agree a final version. This notion of authenticity is, however, problematic because it implies that there exists a single true representation. We consider this in greater detail later in the discussion.

The difference between biography and autobiography is the person writing the story: autobiography a first-person account, biography a second-person account. As Ken Plummer (2001) maintains, autobiography is comprised of three elements, *autos* (what do I mean by the self?), *bios* (what do I mean by life?) and *graphe* (what do I presume in the act of writing?). We might adapt this in our own work as *autobionarrative* – what do I presume in the act of talking – storytelling – about myself? There are many other questions that arise from the act of *storying* one's life: What is my life? How do we tell stories about a life? What is the link between a life lived and a life told? How does a life's telling connect to my culture and its – and my – history? How does the telling of my life connect to someone else's telling of my life? Are all lives to be told equally or are some better to tell than others? We see *autobionarratives* to be enormously useful in shedding light not only on the shifts and movements in individual lives but also on the importance of culture and heritage in their lives, in tracing these orientations to their source and understanding how they have – and are being – developed. To this extent, we see our participants as 'transformative intellectuals' (Giroux, 1988b) who shape their own lives while at the same time as finding meaning in the greater swell of things. The Spanish poet Jose´ Antonio Machado once wrote: 'Walker, there is no road; you make the road by walking.'

Identity is not a new construct, and it has been discussed and debated by some of the giants of psychology and some of the titans, too, of science education. Although we see identity as shifting, morphing, developing along the course of these women's lives, we have worked to retain a fairly concise set of ideas surrounding identity throughout the chapters of the book. We have reached into these women's lives through their identity stories, their positionality and their life trajectories. So, our position is that the self is open to change, and that one means for helping that change along is through the use of narrative (Illouz, 2008). Our participants are certainly women who are walking the road. It is an old story that the happiest human beings are the idiots. The Ancient Greeks called *idiotes* those who, being too concerned with their own lives, failed to understand what was going on around them did not become involved in politics and allowed others to decide their fate for them (Savater, 1997). There is a sense in which we all sideline public affairs at times in favour of dealing with our lives, our many daily personal matters – 'I have enough to do in my own life without having to sort out other people's.' It is certainly the case, though, that none of our participants in this book are idiots – certainly not in the current meaning of the word as being stupid or foolish. Nor are the women who fail to take account of the world around them – the converse is most certainly the case: they are acutely aware of the politics of life, the cultural and historical contexts through which they live. They trade *idiotic happiness* for sanguine and measured worldliness, they make clear connections between past and distant events, formative experiences and their current dispositions.

We need to say something about *our own positions*. We began the book by declaring ourselves as science educators. We are, though, also educational researchers and it is clear that, while we sometimes inhabit those two worlds separately, there are also times when these interlock. So, we try to conduct research with as much structure, openness, ethics and integrity as possible, allowing our participants to tell their own stories in as clean and analytical a mode as possible. However, when we are working with young women, school students, for example, we also know we are sometimes having both science and educational concerns, and that these may surface either tacitly or explicitly during the course of our conversations. We are not, though, counsellors or psychologists and our interests are generally ethnographic in nature: we are science educators who have taken an ethnographic turn rather than anything else. We do not see our tasks as necessarily enabling change, although we are often aware that some of the women to whom we talk do see things differently as a consequence of our encounters – they might, for example, use expressions such as 'Well, I suppose when I say it that way, then it does sound as if'; 'I don't think I have thought of it that way before'; 'it's odd, hearing myself saying that'; and so on. In some cases, stories are well rehearsed and seem to be relatively stable so that they are used as illustration or exemplification of a point being made. On other occasions, stories are very reflective and open to reinterpretation; they are instances of 'hearing myself say what I think'.

In the book, we do move away from the notion of *counter-narratives*. Back in 1995, Richard Delgado described a counter-story as a 'counter-reality that is experienced by subordinate groups, as opposed to those experiences of those in power' (p. 194). In 2020, Richard Miller, Katrina liu and Ametha Ball reviewed these (and many more) discussions, developed ideas further and arguing that, within a framework of Critical Race Theory, *counter-narratives* have emerged as powerful data sources to present the voices of marginalized communities. We understand the direction taken by these authors but also bow to the view presented by most of the women whose stories we have collected. They simply saw their stories as their own experiences and not as *counter-stories*. These are *their stories* and not necessarily accounts of resistance to, rejection of or a bending away from some more powerful, overriding account, some kind of dominant *master* narrative. They generally baulked at seeing their stories, their lives as being sensationalized in any way, theirs were projected as fairly normal stories. If a dominant narrative does exist for these women, one against which they are rebelling, it might well be the clichéd view of the scientist as a socially awkward geeky White male. They are women of colour achieving success in the *world of science on their own terms*. None of our participants actually mentioned this stereotypical image and so the hackneyed view of the *white-coated physicist nerd* may not be the storyline that inhibits women from entering science.

A pedagogy for success

In the latter parts of the book, we introduce and describe our pedagogic approach. We call this a pedagogy for success (PfS). Given what we have said so far it is clear that we do not have a single definition of success and so our pedagogy cannot be represented by any kind of simple straight line: 'do this, this and this and you will most definitely achieve success.' There are many books and magazines on the market that offer 'nine steps to success' or 'essential ways to a happy life' or even 'route maps to heaven'. This is not our way. We do not see pedagogy as a form of instructional science that gives the teacher, the educator, a foolproof recipe for generating success in learners. No such instructional science exists. We do though work at ways of organizing an environment, of building expectations, of engendering inspiration, of creating interest and excitement. We have no single mechanism but a wide range of encouraging prods, celebratory nudges, positive triggers, progressive pressure points, uplifting transformative actions. All of this in the pursuit of personal engagement, critical being and purposive change.

Chapter summary

In introducing the book and setting the scene, we have touched on many of the major themes that preoccupy us and which we develop throughout the following chapters. As we have just noted, for example, our discussion of Sci-ID earlier is short and is simply a foretaste of the much longer elaborations to come. We hope to have set the scene so that our next chapters can shape the discussion and debate much more thoroughly.

Although not specifically directed at science education, we use Heidi Mirza's approach to intersectionality and identity (Mirza & Meetoo, 2018) for a number of reasons. First, our intention is to *voice the UK-based south Asian cultures* to reveal some south Asian women's (science-oriented) experiences of privilege, negotiation, barriers and resistance towards or against the predetermined structural forces of gender, ethnicity, race, migration, class and religion. Throughout the book, though, we keep our focus on the intersection of science culture with other everyday cultures, specifically UK and south Asian cultures. Second, we mirror Mirza's approach by capturing the *embodied lived experiences* of women in order to explore the tension between the demands of globalization and *labelled traditionalism* for ethnic minority women. We accomplish this by ensuring that these lived experiences correspond to the UK-based south Asian women's science lives. Third, we see identity formation and transformation as an ongoing process of *becoming to being* and so use intersectional analysis to illuminate not only the macro social forces of inequality and perceived oppression by the society but also agentic interpretations, embodied practices and personal choices of the south Asian women to reject or 'resist and rename the regularity effects of discourses of education [and professions] inequality and subjugation' (Mirza, 2009, p. 4) in their science lives. Fourth, we introduce the idea of pedagogy for success for full discussion at a later stage.

2

Intersectionality and Science Identity

Intersectionality IS personal

'I am a Stroke Consultant and a mother of two . . . born in Pakistan. I'm not a special person, just an ordinary person – serving the national health service (NHS).'

Amna

'I see myself as a mother, a daughter, a sister, a Scottish Pakistani Muslim female, an engineer, an educator, an activist, a sponsor.'

Yumna

Amna and Yumna are both scientists, both British south Asian Muslim women of similar age – their position statements above portray both their shared connections of cultures (south Asian family, UK and science) and their personal differences. Even in that sentence, the multiplicity of social categories (or cultural facets) is clear – country of birth, nationality, ethnicity, family and associated passions. And, in addition, the mention of their science life, those aspects of science in their construction of identity all adds to their diversity. For example, although educated in Pakistan and having taken a career break to support her doctor husband and children, Amna has kept working and progressing as a medical practitioner with minimal day-to-day support from her family. Yumna, despite having strong family support, left the engineering industry after ten years to join a public sector organization which encourages young Scottish women into STEM studies and professions. In our view, this illustrates the fact that Amna and Yumna, even though grouped as the UK-based south Asian Muslim women, cannot be labelled simply within one overarching category. Instead, the exploration of the construction of their identity needs to be viewed as complex, multiple, ongoing and personal. So, 'what do we mean by intersectional diversity and multiplicity?' 'How can intersectionality be personal?' And, important in the context of this book, 'what has that to do with science identity (Sci-ID)?' We understand these questions to be multifaceted, so we look to answer them with the support of recent literature developing the discussion on intersectionality and Sci-ID. Moreover, we supplement this with more details of the science lives of Amna, Yumna and other south Asian women, some of whom we introduced briefly in Chapter 1.

Table 2 Six more participants

	Place of Birth	Self-Designation
Aasiya	Kashmir	Science student (GCSE)
Ayesha	Bangladesh	Science student (GCSE)
Hanya	The Netherlands	Science student (GCSE)
Leah	Scotland	Chemical engineer and science teacher
Kriti	India	Skin specialist
Yumna	Scotland	Engineer and women activist

We now present brief pen portraits of four women mentioned in Table 2. All four pen portraits showcase personal *intersectional stories*.

Ayesha, aged sixteen, is the eldest child of the family. Born in Bangladesh, her family moved to India, and then, at the age of three, she moved to Portugal before arriving in England at the age of nine. Ayesha's father is a market trader, and her mother stays at home. Her parents did attend school but remember little of it and were 'never into sciences'. Despite this, Ayesha's passion for becoming a scientist was evident from age five or six as, unlike other girls, she said, 'who play with dolls and are fascinated by fairies'. She used to think about why some vehicles move faster than others, why her pencil colours appear slightly different on different types of paper and so on. Over time she is more inclined to enter the physics discipline at the university level and now more towards quantum physics.

Hanya is the second child in the family, aged sixteen, when we met her for the second time in 2019. Born in the Netherlands, she moved to Britain at the age of five. Her parents were born and lived in Pakistan for twenty-five years before moving to the Netherlands and then to England. Her mother did not attend college and studied very little science at school – she currently stays at home. Her father studied science and maths to the age of eighteen and then worked in his father's mechanics shop in Pakistan. He is now a businessman and runs an automobile company in London. At age eleven,

Hanya was very anti-science, but her perceptions changed over the following years. This transformation was, in part, due to several school science-based activities, such as 'girly kinds of stories', writing poetry linked to science and attending a STEM course at a London university. A pivotal point came at the age of twelve after watching the film Inside Out. She has focused on achieving good examination grades and choosing science subjects for A-level study from that time onwards. She had also expressed a strong inclination towards studying English and law, inclinations that have also been present over the four years. However, what has changed is her current emphasis on biology and chemistry for A-level study.

Leah, a thirty-two-year-old woman, identifies herself as mixed race – her mother is British south Asian (born in Kashmir) and her father is White (born in England). Leah identifies herself to be more south Asian than White as she has spent all her life with her mother rather than her father. Leah is fair-skinned and does not share her religious sentiments with colleagues and friends. She has 'never felt discriminated against based on my ethnicity or religion as it's private'. At age sixteen, Leah needed to choose subjects to further her science education (or not). At that time, Leah was looking forward to becoming an ophthalmologist – so she went to the career counsellor and pastoral tutors for advice. Their advice to opt for all non-science subjects was discouraging for her as it was based on her best predicted and actual exam results. Still, Leah was determined and didn't listen to the counsellor and pastoral tutor's advice and carried out applying for science subjects. Eventually, she got into the 'Access Programme', which Leah thinks changed her life. The issue of poor grades versus interest troubled her since, and Leah took it as a challenge to prove this wrong and did PhD in chemical engineering and worked in the industry for several years. However, she left the chemical industry job because of the unwelcoming environment for her, especially during her pregnancy and post-childbirth.

Yumna was born in Scotland as the only child of her Pakistani immigrant parents. Yumna's father followed his brother at the age of fourteen in the 1950s for better education and profession. Yumna clearly adopted her uncle as one of her role models. She portrays herself confidently as a Muslim and British south Asian woman and would like to carry on his great work for the Muslim community, work that he started just after the Indo-Pak partition in 1947. Her feeling of being a science person was confirmed during her work experience in a multinational engineering company – then aged nineteen – but she has been 'into sciences' even from secondary school *age. For example, during her school life, she chose physics and continued with this despite being the only female student in her higher physics class. What makes her keep going? 'It was the unfaltering support from the physics teacher' that helped her to stay in this all-boys classroom environment. Yumna is a proud mother and feels successful because she has not entirely left the field of engineering and is still working to support BAME individuals as a 'women activist'. She is committed to serving the public through her commitment as a STEM consultant and non-executive board member for a student award agency.*

More about intersectionality

Brittney Cooper (2015) describes intersectionality as the 'key analytic framework through which feminist scholars in various fields talk about the structural identities of race, class, gender, and sexuality' (p. 1). The term intersectionality has certainly initiated a swathe of work that has established multidimensional modes of analysis of Black women's life experiences and seeks to differentiate their experiences from White women and Black men (Crenshaw, 1989). This contrasts with a 'single-axis framework' that considers and proposes interventions seen narrowly through a single lens. Such unidimensional tunnel focus 'erases Black women in the conceptualisation, identification and remediation of race and sex discrimination by limiting inquiry to the experiences of otherwise-privileged members of the group' (Crenshaw, 1989, p. 140). Intersectionality, then, challenges such a simple categorization of all women of colour (Dhamoon, 2011). Instead, it thrives on a conglomeration of diverse social categorizations and contexts as demonstrated by the personal quotes above from Amna and Yumna. While the term intersectionality originated with Black feminists in the United States, we have appropriated it here to explore the diverse experiences of south Asian women in the context of the UK.

As we noted in Chapter 1, this personalized approach runs counter to those who argue that intersectional analysis is essentially sociologically broad and thematic, inappropriate for *zooming in* to the level of the personal. Patricia Collins and Sirma Bilge (2016), for example, posit intersectionality as a thematic tool of critical analysis, themes that concern: (1) power, (2) relationality, (3) social context, (4) social justice, (5) complexity and (6) social inequality. At this level, the focus tends towards ideas and ideologies; on unveiling hidden discourses on poverty, racial oppression, gender discrimination – on how intersectionality's analytical perspectives have been adopted by scholars to discuss a wide array of overarching social contexts (Knapp, 2005). From this perspective, intersectional analysis reflects the ways that power struggles appear in multiple domains to create asymmetric politicized positions that disrupt and confirm institutional and organizational inequalities (Ruiz Castro & Holvino, 2016). We argue that all this is true, but that while macro (social) structures form part of the *master narratives* of identity – in our case of Sci-ID – that such struggles and also successes can be identified and felt right down to a personal micro level. In doing so, we align our drive down of intersectionality with Sung Tae Jang's (2018, p. 1275) four core premises, and these help to shape our theoretical foundations of intersectionality at this personal, individual micro level.

1. *Simultaneity – the influence of diverse social categorizations on the lives of people cannot be separated.*

This first point raises the issue of *misrecognition*. There is considerable literature to show that women, especially women of colour from lower socio-economic backgrounds, see science careers as less *thinkable* for themselves or, in many cases, as wholly unthinkable. They are not recognized by society, nor do they recognize themselves, as – even possibly – *people of science*. Men are seen to dominate the sciences – more precisely, White middle-class men dominate the field of science and science education. Such male dominance means that society misrecognizes women as non-science people (Archer et al., 2013; Archer, DeWitt & Osborne, 2015). This broad misrecognition leads to *mis-self-recognition*, thereby impacting on people's individual Sci-ID development (Taylor, 1992). In the canons of academic literature in this field, it is families (e.g. Archer et al., 2013; 2016), teachers (e.g. Archer, 2017b; Shimwell et al., 2021), peers (e.g. Breakwell & Beardsell, 1992; Park, Behrman & Choi, 2012) and work colleagues (e.g. Ong, Smith & Ko, 2018; Rainey et al., 2018) who might fail to recognize women as having a contribution to make to science. While we follow this broad trend for misrecognition, we do believe that there has been an over-reliance on focusing on social macro and meso forces and much less attention given to the micro forces of self-recognition. For example, Heidi Carlone, Angela Johnson and Catherine Scott (2015) have mapped the school science lives of thirteen nine-year-old racially minoritized girls over four years and concluded that

> larger social structures such as race, class, gender, and sexuality and classroom structures . . . constrain individuals' agency to engage in untroubled and sustained science identity work. (p. 474)

This quote highlights the simultaneity of diverse social (macro) categories impacting on Sci-ID development but, even so, it fails in our view to capture the agentic dynamism that can exist among and between young women of colour. Our view is that most science education literature undermines the key concept of individual agency (micro forces) and aspects of success that serves to make (science) identity unique, unpredictable, complex and multiple for every individual. In one of their other studies, this time of mature women scientists, Carlone and Johnson (2007) rightly observed that women's agency is heavily reliant on the structural (macro) forces within society. While they felt able to classify their participants in the study into three categories: as 'research', 'altruistic' or 'disruptive' scientists – and do so in order to capture the individual drive and dynamism of the women – they nevertheless added the coda that 'women-scientists-of-color [are] *not* free to develop any kind of science identity' (Carlone & Johnson, 2007, p. 1192) [our emphasis].

2. *Multiplicity – the relationships among diverse social categorizations are multiplicative.*

The relationships among diverse social categorizations, of gender, ethnicity, heritage, nationality, social class, religion, provide a strong platform for understanding identity development. These relationships form the basis of an intersectionality framework that captures individual perceptions, decisions, viewpoints and, therefore, a comprehensive picture of their identity development. Many science educators have explored these relationships. For example, Ong, Smith and Ko (2018), exploring the lived experiences of thirty-nine university-based women of colour (Black, Asian American, Latina, Mixed, Native American) from different STEM disciplines, revealed that women of colour in STEM are designated as 'double blind', 'double disadvantage' and in 'double jeopardy' (Malcom, Hall & Brown, 1976; O'Brien, Scheibling & Krumhansl, 2015). Such Black women are additionally viewed as inferior to White women because they do not mirror the conventional societal identification of ethnicity and gender within STEM, so society tends to exclude them from STEM education and career pursuits (also acknowledged by Charleston et al., 2014; Ireland et al., 2018; Ong et al., 2011). Lucy Avraamidou's (2020a) work, in the context of university education, extends Ong's 'doubles' into 'multiple' disadvantages by highlighting the multiplicity of power relations in the Sci-ID development of Amina, a Muslim and Kurdish-Turkish woman from a working-class background. The biography of Amina's life presents various stereotypes and the feelings of being 'other' and an 'out-grouper' during both her student and working life as a physicist. Avraamidou describes Amina's intersectional power relations of 'social class, religion, gender performance, and ethnic status' (p. 311) in various contexts that she, as a Muslim Turkish women physicist, felt as social barriers. Amina's story highlights the ways in which women try to become 'insiders' by fitting into masculine STEM cultures, although Amina went against the grain by seeing herself as a *forever outsider* in scientific contexts.

Nevertheless, we see that these double or multiple disadvantages undermine the agency of and success stories of individuals, as women of colour's relationship with social categorizations are different from one individual to another. For example, our participant Amna never perceived herself to be *double disadvantaged* and *not at all oppressed* in her medical life due to her diverse identity makeup. During our interview, Yumna, on the other hand, recounted that she felt disadvantaged due to the multiple combination of her gender, ethnicity and religion. She initially tried to mask these at the workplace but eventually discarded this mask as she found her own voice:

> Yumna: My life has actually been not as challenging as other [Muslim women from Pakistani heritage] simply because somewhere along the way I found my voice and, when I found my voice, I wasn't silenced thereafter, because I just didn't allow anyone to silence me.

In this respect, we follow Zahra Hazari, Philip Sadler and Gerhard Sonnert (2013) as they challenge the 'universalism and essentialisation' of women by pointing out that Sci-ID formation is a personal expedition:

> The experience of a women-of-color is not necessarily the combined experience of being a woman and being of color – it can be unique in and of itself. (p. 84)

3. *Power relations – diverse social categorizations constitute interlocking, mutually constructing or intersecting systems of power.*

We have made the point that people from a certain group, in our case the UK-based south Asian women, cannot be classified under a singular social category. Issues of inequalities, oppression, discrimination and marginalization depend on each individual's experiences, their relationships with social categories (of gender, ethnicity, nationality and social class) and, importantly, their self-interpretation and self-recognition of their experiences:

> The multiplicity of intersectionality arise[s] from the mutually constructing or interlocking systems of power depending on south Asian women's self-perceived unique positionality from multiple social categorizations. (Jang, 2018, p. 1277)

For instance, Yumna's statement earlier in the test, of being 'silenced' in a scientific (engineering) culture dominated by White male engineers but then finding her 'voice', portrays a mutual construction of power relations. She interprets her viewpoints by saying:

> Yumna: I've also found myself walking into situations where, my goodness, as soon as I walk in you could hear a pin drop . . . the feeling of isolation [as being a scientist women-of-colour] was apparent, but now I don't care anymore about the opinions of other people.

We see Yumna asserting her own purposive relations here in situations where people's opinions can be dismissed, the group power of her engineering colleagues. Similarly, Louise Archer, Merryn Hutchings and Alistair Ross (2003) assert that power systems, for example of social class (re)production, play a vital role in education through 'either the reproduction of (middle-class) privileges, or (working-class) disadvantages' (p. 5). The importance they attach to social class in education derives from Pierre Bourdieu's idea of unequal relationships between dominant and dominated cultures (referred to as ethnic minority and majority cultures in Chapter 5). 'Working-class femininity' is a term that Archer (2018) used in one of her recent chapters to represent the multilayered oppressions in the science lives of working-class boys and girls. Archer's work involved eight secondary science classrooms (with students aged eleven to sixteen) from five co-educational schools. These classes were observed over the course of an academic year by research teams in London and Newcastle, and discussion groups were conducted with a total of fifty-nine students. The author notes several observational events that identify the basis of working-class femininity – of 'shy', 'hetero-femininity' and of being a *nonscience person*:

> Unlike their male peers, these [working-class] girls were more likely to assert themselves through performances of working-class femininity that resisted notions of passivity and the dominant behavioural norms of the classroom. Notably, these girls tended *not* to try to possibilise themselves specifically as *science* students. For instance, girls' 'louder', more assertive and publicly visible contributions tended to be 'off task' (e.g., 'talking back', challenging boys' sexist 'banter', chatting with friends or making jokey comments), rather than making bids for scientific legitimacy. (pp. 164–5)

Louise Archer points directly to the dilemma for these girls, between the *intersectional exclusion* of working-class femininity versus the middle-class dominance of being clever. Working-class girls seldom have the privilege of 'talking science through muscular intellect' (p. 165). As she says, despite being in a non-welcoming scientific culture, not all working-class girls have demonstrated working-class performativity in being shy and passive in that some were bold and active. However, such assertive performances were unacceptable to the White colonial mindset of teachers and peers although (mostly) acceptable for some working-class boys from Indian backgrounds. Archer's findings are important in articulating notions of self-recognition and self-perception within the societal recognition of science as the territory of naturally clever, elite (White, male and middle-class) pupils.

Archer's explanations of the unequal distribution of power, of diverse 'funds of knowledge' and the different agentic performances between working-class girls and boys in the science classrooms are well put. The drawback here, however, is that Archer tends to describe ethnicity in just two broad categories: White and non-White – despite the presence of a variety of ethnic and some religious differences within the selected sample (one of the sample schools had predominantly Muslim students). Our drive is to broaden the discussion so that, we look deeper to explore the intersectionality of religion as well.

4.   *Social context – intersecting power relations vary across different social contexts.*

The simultaneous influences, multiplicative relationships and power relations of social categories acting in the lives of people vary across multiple social locations/ contexts, including educational and professional institutions. But not just in formal educational institutions, they vary too in other educational situations such as libraries, study centres, planetariums and even noneducational spaces such as parks, home, clubs, pubs and so on. We have already discussed some contexts within school science; here we focus on Emily Dawson et al.'s (2020) work in museums. Their findings resemble Jang's suggestion of *intersectional inequality* and Ong's descriptions of 'double blinds'. Dawson et al. explored the museum visits of three science classes from two inner-city, state-run, co-educational London schools, groups comprising sixty-one pupils. They highlighted the science performances of twenty-five girls aged twelve to thirteen and some involvement of their male peers, teachers (five), teaching assistants (two) and museum facilitators (six). Two (of the four) broad categories analysed by the authors focused on gender associations with ethnicity. Under the first category – 'Trying to learn science through performances of masculinity and race/ethnicity' (p. 670), the authors portrayed two racial minority girls' masculine attitudes – which we see as their way to intersect power relations of gender, ethnicity and scientific culture in a museum setting. This *masculine presentation* was adopted by these two girls to present themselves – and be recognized by others (teachers and peers) – as being *science people*. The school staff, however, saw such presentation as 'showing off' and irrelevant:

> Even when girls' [e.g., Black girl talking-with-attitude and Turkish working-class tomboy] performances appeared to be in line with successful science student positions (through confident displays of scientific expertise or assertively using certain interactive exhibits), *it seemed impossible for them to be recognised as such*. (Dawson et al., 2020, p. 672)

Dawson et al.'s second category included 'cool girls', enabling racially marginalized girls to move away from science by going with the well-established norms of the everyday culture corresponding with the power of established scientific culture. The 'cool girls' resisted science learning in the museum, which failed to represent 'people like them' (p. 675), so they protected their agency and self-invested non-scientific identities:

> The girls had little power to change how people like them were represented in the museum and even their selfies reproduced narrow, sexist stereotypes about how women and girls are valued based on (hetero)sexual attractiveness. (p. 675)

Our own research on Sci-ID in a London school-based study with eleven- to fourteen-year-old thirty Muslim young women (Salehjee, 2017; Salehjee & Watts, 2020), though, is distinctive from Dawson et al.'s work – in three distinct ways. First, in our study, the young south Asian women's gender, ethnicity and intersections of other social categories were not necessarily the reason they resisted entry to scientific fields. There were other reasons for abandoning science after the compulsory age of science education – not least for the simple reason that our participants were far more interested in other subjects and professions. These must be entirely acceptable reasons. We took the opportunity nevertheless to introduce some *science opportunities* in various contexts along the way, opportunities that corresponded to their main interests, such as problem-solving activities, stories and poetry writing using ideas in science, designing for example the school's sewing room, lunchtime chats about charging mobile phones with scientific gadgets and visiting the local park's riverside, planetariums and university laboratories. We engaged women scientists to talk about science education and careers. So, while they were making choices away from careers in science, we were keen on (and content with) enriching their *successful science lives*:

> Aasiya: I really enjoyed science in school and the different activities we did outside the school with my class, but it doesn't make me a science person. I want to be a narrator and journalist.

Second, we have also interviewed some who have retained their gender, ethnic and religious identities in scientific contexts and without any obvious struggles. These include 'wearing a headscarf' while working in a biochemical laboratory (Arshi), 'wearing shalwar kameez' (Eastern dress) at university (Pari) and talking in an Indian accent, 'I don't artificially change my Indian accent when talking to my patients in the clinic' (Kriti) and 'I never hid my Kashmiri heritage in school and industry even though I am mixed race and look White' (Leah). Third, some of our participants did talk about scientific contexts as challenges, and we have met south Asian women who resemble Dawson et al.'s analysis. For instance, we have seen the presence of 'laddish' culture at construction sites (Anchal), the non-feasibility for mothers to work engineering industries (Leah and Yumna), where south Asian mothers are seen to be more involved in raising their children rather than working in hospitals (Amna). Still, Amna, Anchal, Leah and Yumna all successfully maintained and intersected their gender, ethnic and parental identities with scientific culture.

Our third point resembles Avraamidou (2020a)'s story of Amina. In her accounts, Amina mentions various contexts and associated barriers, such as her working-class background, lack of provision and *scaffolding at home*, religious barriers that she experienced. Amina attending a non-Muslim school in a Muslim country – Turkey – where science studies were not seen as appropriate. When she moved to the United States, however, she did not see herself as discriminated against, mainly because she was living within a Muslim community. She did, though, see herself as *undesirable* because

> Anti-migrant islamophobia is on the rise and, in a city where there is not a large Muslim community, Amina perceives her religion [such as wearing hijab] as serving as the major barrier to her recognition by both her academic [scientific] as well as social community. (Avraamidou, 2020a, p. 335)

Amina, much like our participants Amna, Anchal, Leah and Yumna, self-recognized herself as a *science person* despite being misrecognized by people in her immediate surroundings. She is determined to proceed as a physicist while simultaneously rejecting the stereotypical identification of physics to be the territory of a White middle-class man.

More about science identity

Using Jang's four premises described earlier we emphasize our intention to use intersectionality to study individuals' Sci-ID at a micro level. This study, for us, emboldens our commitment to developing a commentary on the nuances of lived experience in terms of a multiplicity of identities, the ways that intersectionality is made personal. Our particular interest lies in how south Asian women approach study and/or careers in sciences, how to understand the relationships among their social identities – and how they come to perceive these relationships – and we use this as a vehicle to explore micro level *personal intersectionality*. This interest calls for a reconceptualization of Sci-ID in conjunction, and not in isolation, with other social identities, to examine how these intersect with each other and either support or hinder the process of 'becoming a science person' (Avraamidou, 2020a,b). Such conceptualization provides space for multiplicity, diversity, subjectivity, heterogeneity and hybridity to exist and, essentially, to acknowledge that there exist an enormous variety of ways of becoming a science person.

For example, Elizabeth Opara (2017) has voiced her own Black woman scientist identity, one which she believed 'profoundly affected my identity and thus my journey as a Black woman scientist' (p. 125). Opara storied her micro level explorations in a way similar to Mirza's 'embodied lived experiences' by using Carlone and Johnson's three types of scientists (research, altruistic and disruptive), in order to discuss her ongoing identity formation and transformational journey. She began by recognizing herself as a *research scientist* during her student and early years of academic life, then became a *disruptive scientist* by encompassing discrimination and perception of gender and Blackness imposed by the dominant others (predominantly White members of staff) as a hindrance. She succeeded this disruptive scientist identity due to her commitment to science and experiences gained from outside her university life. Later, Opara noted that she felt her agentic force was rooted as her need to stay with science and resulted in her transformation from being disruptive to being an altruistic scientist.

Our above discussion on theoretical positioning lays the foundation for understanding intersectionality to explore Sci-ID formations and transformations at the micro level. In the next section we present the embodied science lives of Amna, Ayesha, Hanya, Saarya and Yumna. First, though, a discussion of the methodology and methods we have used to collect science life stories of our participants.

More about our research

We have already indicated many of the ways in which our research takes place, but here we become a little more specific. First, we have, of course, scoured library resources for relevant literature in the field. This is an enormous task and is a constant battle between being rigidly systematic and following intuitive leads. There has been a large volume of work produced on each of the major themes we deal with in the book – for example, intersectionality, science-as-culture, Sci-ID, Asian lived experiences, narrative approaches and so on. We admit it here, we have not been exhaustive, we have numerous colleagues and critics who have always been willing to point us towards those books and articles we have failed to mention in the text. Our approach has been to work solidly through the most contemporary materials we could find, the latest in the field – except where there are *classic texts* from past years that still bear relevance to what we want to say. We have tried to avoid being either capricious or tunnelled visioned. On occasions where we do follow interesting leads and readings there is always the danger of disappearing down a *rabbit hole* and, while this can produce fascinating thoughts and ideas, we do have to reign ourselves in to focus more clearly on the task at hand.

Similarly, we have in parts taken recourse in official policy documents and statistical reports. This, too, is a mammoth undertaking because there are not just, for example, migration and immigration statistics for the UK but also the UK census, percentages of uptake in various school and university subject studies, employment levels in companies and businesses, mobility of social class and much more. Reliance on official statistics has been heavily criticized (e.g. by Cicourel, 1964, and Douglas, 1967) not least because such data is socially constructed and ought not – cannot – be read simply as objective factual true records of events. As an instance, the crime statistics that are produced at regular intervals depend heavily on crime reported to the police, the ways in which they are then categorized and how they are subsequently reported. This is not to say that numbers are deliberately, manipulated only that, at each stage along the way, different peoples' perceptions and actions determine which cases make it on to the next stage – perceptions and actions that depend on various interests and values. The reporting of such statistics, then, should always be treated with a degree of caution.

Third, we make use of personal observations and personal documents. This is certainly the case where we have worked in schools and asked students for use of their classroom materials and so forth. These are, in a sense, *first-person accounts* of what they have been doing. We fully appreciate that, as with stories and narratives, anecdotes of themselves do not necessarily constitute *hard evidence*. Nevertheless, our approach is to help generate – and welcome – all such data as often providing rich and detailed insights in women's lifeworlds and so are more than adequate data at the level of meaning.

We describe our narrative data gathering and analysis approach, mentioned in Chapter 1, as a series of *conversational autobiographical interviews*, similar in vein to Elaine Reese, Chen Yan, Fiona Jack and Harlene Hayne's (2010) *Emerging Life Story Interviews* (ELSI). We have sought interpretative commonalities in our conversations with our women participants as they narrate personal events in their social and cultural worlds. In general, we have used semi-structured interviews to gather data, using probes and spontaneous questioning to deepen our understanding. For example, after a suitable preamble, our usual first question has been: How do you identify yourself? And, if the response was 'as a Sri Lankan immigrant and a woman science technician' (Saarya), then our further questions probed their perceptions of the multiplicity of immigration and nationality as these intersects with their science lives. Our inclusion criteria have been fairly broad, our definitions of *south Asian* have been reasonable inclusive. We assured the participants of full confidentiality, and they were happy with the pseudonyms we have assigned to them. They were interviewed individually, discussions lasting from around forty to seventy minutes concerning educational choices and career decisions. Many interview conversations took place online (on Zoom) or face to face in quiet, private areas, at times convenient to the women participants.

Each interview interaction was 'situated and accomplished with audience in mind' (Riessman, 2008, p. 106). As mentioned earlier, we have aimed for an in-depth understanding of the simultaneity in intersectionality, multiplicity and power relationships within diverse social categories including scientific culture shaping Sci-ID of south Asian women at a personal level. Our *study of cases* approach supports 'in-depth studies of [complexity within] a single group, culture or site and have long been associated with . . . qualitative studies' (McCall, 2005, p. 57). It is similar to McCall's understanding of 'intra-categorical complexity' in favouring explorations of intersectionality among a single group of people, such as Crenshaw's (1989) focus on Black women. In aligning with intra-categorical complexity, we begin by choosing categories to start the study and have resisted any fixed choices to the possible combinations of intersections (Christensen & Jensen, 2012). There are groups we have not investigated, such as White British middle-class men, but have retained these social groupings as reference points by means of background literature. Our choice of categories has been gender, ethnicity, religion and heritage and are based on our prior 2014–15 studies, indicating that these categories had the potential to intersect and impact on the science lives and Sci-ID of British south Asian Muslim women. During our data analysis we have actively noted how other categories intersect with our choices (Salehjee & Watts, 2022).

Adapting a narrative stance, Amanda Keddie (2009) has highlighted questions that need to be asked about research with young people, such as: Who benefits from the research? What (and whose) purpose does the research serve? Academic research concerning young people should not simply be an 'exclusive conversation' between 'us' as researchers, about 'them' as participants (Cahill, 2004, p. 282); a greater degree of sharing and ownership is required. Vanessa May (2001), too, discusses the philosophical ethics of narrative researchers and ways in which they ask deeper questions, rather than accepting matters at face value. In taking our present route, we recognize that recalled experience is influenced and altered by memory and may not reflect the exact nature and sequence of events that took place (Powney & Watts, 2018) – the mere act of participating in a conversational interview is an interactional event that can shape ideas and opinions, evoke emotions, alter the recall of experiences (e.g. Roth & Middleton, 2006).

Moreover, in narrative theories of identity (Bird & Reese, 2008; Nelson & Fivush, 2004), subjective perspectives on life experiences are an essential component of a person's self-concept. Clarifying one's perspective on events is a means of establishing self. In a manner similar to Lucy Avraamidou (2020a, b) and Jonathan Osborne (2009), our science (and non-science) narratives provide the context within which intelligible action is taken. Roger Schank (1990) sees such storytelling as a form of intelligence: 'People remember what happens to them, and they tell other people what they remember. People learn from what happens to them, and they guide their future actions accordingly ... Intelligence is about understanding what has happened well enough to be able to predict when it might happen again' (p. 1).

One limitation to such a research approach lies in our positionality as researchers. We introduced ourselves at the start of the book: Saima is currently a university lecturer in Scotland. She is south Asian female and Muslim. Mike is a British White non-Muslim male, dedicated to extending and enriching the science education of his south Asian Muslim students and colleagues. So, we acknowledge that there can be – and will be – bias imposed by us on our work. Therefore, the data transcription, analysis and presentation of the data was undertaken by Saima and Mike individually and separately and then cross-checked between them. We then asked Asian female colleagues to be *critical friends* and to evaluate/critique our analysis of the data. Where possible, we also engaged in respondent validation with our participating women.

A second limitation concerns the trustworthiness of intersectional data involving the distinctive nature of each of the major strands (Squires, 2007), particularly where different intersections are mutually constructed at the level of personal agency (Phoenix, 2011). For example, when asking Ayesha about her career choices, as we show later, she highlighted both ethnicity and gender by discussing the privileges experienced by south Asian boys over south Asian girls. There were many such intersecting interactions, for example, explications of south Asian families' expectations of *obedience* from daughters; matters of age and respect; the distribution of domestic and non-domestic *responsibilities*; facility with English and the *language barriers* of Bangladeshi parents; the weight of *family history* – Hanya's father's small mechanics shop, for example, in Kashmir. These personal details are interwoven with broader intersectional categories – not least of which is 'being multi-national Muslim daughters' (Salehjee & Watts, 2020). To mitigate our biases, we sent the full-individual transcripts, the short pen portraits (such as those presented in this chapter and Chapter 1) and our themes to our willing participants for member checking – and their thoughtful comments and amendments were then incorporated accordingly.

Some outcomes

Here we present just some of the headline outcomes of our work. This is, in part, a flavour of things to come. We showcase five stories here of Amna, Ayesha, Hanya, Saarya and Yumna under six progressive themes. As can be seen, these themes are progressive in that they increase in complexity and multiplicity from one to six. These are:

1. Being multinational
2. Being multinational religious women
3. Being multinational religious daughters
4. Being working-class or middle-class multinational religious daughters
5. Being successful working-class or middle-class multinational young science students
6. Being successful working-class or middle-class multinational women in science.

We discuss these in order as follows:

1. *Being multinational*

All five of our multiaged south Asian women – Amna, Ayesha, Hanya, Saarya and Yumna – are confident that being a UK citizen has had a positive impact on their education and professional choices. For instance, Ayesha (aged sixteen) identifies herself as British because she has lived in the UK for quite some time:

> Ayesha: On the whole, I believe I have opportunities as a British citizen to study what I like – much more than my parents did when they grew up in Bangladesh.

She also mentioned that being south Asian and working class could influence her future university life simultaneously, as both a privilege and a challenge:

> Ayesha: I don't think that my south Asian identification will hinder me from going to university because in universities there are lots of Asians and there are lots of Pakistani and Bangladeshi transfer students. Their parents are rich, though, and this is the reason they're able to study in the UK. I believe I will be an outcast [among these students]. But then I will be all right with them because they will be Asians.

Hanya, current age sixteen, did not mention her immigrant status during our conversations, possibly because she came to England even before attending preschool. In one conversation she talked about visiting Pakistan during her summer holidays and gave evidence of her multiplicity when talking about her nationality in (both) a Pakistani and British context – she mentioned that her cousins in Pakistan see her as 'very different' – which Hanya attributes to her fluency in English, and 'posh accent – and nothing else'.

> Hanya: I have British identification in terms of a passport. I see myself as a student who studies in Britain. So, it won't bother me because I have a

British passport and all the rights as any other British girl. However, as I said before, some [people in Britain] might see me as an outsider – maybe my appearance worries some.

Hanya was conscious of her appearance because she wears a hijab, the headscarf worn by Muslim women in public – therefore intersecting heritage with religion.

Amna, currently in her forties, came to England in her mid-twenties as the spouse of a NHS doctor, making her the oldest immigrant woman we describe here. She talked about her education and family life experiences in Pakistan and her continuation with education and profession as a doctor in England. As an immigrant, during her initial medical training days, she felt the need to do 'more than what is required of me so that I can keep on getting the training posts' – compared to other UK-born junior doctors. She recalled that

> Amna: . . . when I was the house officer . . . on a gastro-rotation, a
> gastroenterology consultant, in a bit of a discriminatory tone, asked me a
> question 'what sort of murmur do you get in this heart condition?' I gave
> the answer . . . he then looked at me in an insulting way – and asked the
> same question from a UK-born Indian doctor who gave the wrong answer –
> but the consultant said 'Yes, thank you!' I didn't say anything, though I knew
> I was right because when I learned those concepts, my memory of them was
> very clear . . . I stayed quiet, feeling that I could be wrong because of [my
> initial education in Pakistan] and five-year gap. So, I didn't discuss it further
> then – mainly because of respecting the consultant [as a junior doctor] – as
> in Pakistan, especially in the army, there is a strong hierarchical concept . . .
> it took me some time to get frank with a consultant straight away.

Saarya, currently in her late thirties, like Ayesha and Hanya, immigrated with her mother 'as a kid' from Italy. Both her parents were born and educated in Sri Lanka. She views herself as British more profoundly than Sri Lankan, because

> Saarya: I honestly don't follow the south Asian culture because I disagree with a
> lot of them. I rarely speak with them as I don't think they should know what's
> happening in my life. So, you need to learn how to be independent, just
> make your own decision and go with it . . . as I live in a British culture . . .
> [which] supports individuals . . . [and their] personal choices.

Later Saarya mentioned that sometimes it is like surviving in two different cultures:

> Saarya: . . . because our way of thinking in Britain is different to the way of
> thinking in Sri Lanka. Sometimes there have been clashes with my parents,

clashes with my husband . . . So, I think maybe if I knew a bit more about
Sri Lankan culture – then perhaps I would have understood them, BUT
then comes my arrogance, my stubbornness, I don't want to know a lot, only
[want to know] the good things. I want to know is what is right, if I think it
is wrong, I am going to question and challenge it.

Despite the clashes with her parents and her recent immigrant husband, Saarya
doesn't want to move from one culture to another. Instead, she finds the middle
ground of following fundamental humanitarian values of being trustworthy and
open in thinking and talking with others.

Yumna, unlike our other four respondents, was born in Scotland. Her father
followed the footsteps of his elder brother and immigrated to Scotland at the
age of fourteen in the 1950s in the pursuit of better education and professions.
She is proud to be the niece of the first Muslim south Asian Scottish man who
established a Muslim south Asian community in Scotland and served various
public sector institutions, including police, judicial and charity originations.
Despite her family being settled in Scotland for such a long time, she felt that her
work colleagues behaved towards her in a way that was different to White female
staff in the department. For example, because of being a south Asian woman, she
was viewed by her colleagues to have been:

Yumna: Coerced into a forced marriage. And I thought, dear God, you
    don't know me at all! I became aware very early on that the stereotype that it
    suited them to believe meant that – at some point – I would be forced to
    wear a headscarf [and] at some point I would be forced into marriage. They
    seem to think there is a lot of coercing and forcing going on in my life!

In addition, Yumna felt isolated while working in the engineering industry as
being the only south Asian female and the only Muslim on the premises. She
believes that there was a 'chronic lack of awareness' – twenty years back – among
the colleagues and little support offered by the senior management team at the
American-based engineering industry:

Yumna: It became very clear to me that there's a chronic lack of cultural
awareness as compared to today – they just had no concept of diversity at all,
diversity with respect to how you can ensure that our workplaces are more
inclusive. For an American organisation to have those work practices, well, I
put it down to the fact that it's very much the behaviours that have been adopted
within this site within these premises. You can have beautifully worded global
policies that relate to equity and inclusion in them – mind you, perhaps at the
time they didn't even have those policies. But actually, it's the people in charge

that matter . . . any impact on workplace behaviours depends on whether they [senior managers] choose to address inappropriate workplace behaviours or whether they choose to turn a blind eye.

2.   *Being multinational religious women*

Ayesha's determination to study science and Amna's working life as a consultant transcended any religious barriers – they would quietly and safely observe their religion regardless of any counter opinions from the society. As Ayesha mentioned:

> Ayesha: Obviously, I'm very religious because I go to a religious institute. So, as a Muslim, I think I'm okay. I have a lot of determination towards science-based future studies . . . I know who I am and so I know what is good for me – or I will certainly find a way!

Moreover, Amna views herself as a religious person and makes efforts to practice all the religious rituals despite being a busy consultant and a mother of two children. She said:

> Amna: So, I'm a religious person. I may not look like a religious person [as I don't wear a headscarf], but I'm a very religious person . . . though I wouldn't say to an extreme level. I do my Namaz [and other compulsory rituals] . . . and ensure not to miss the first ten days of Majlis [during the month of Muharam]. I am actually the driving force for the whole family – because the kids will not want to go, like any kid . . . and my husband was not that motivated before . . . though now he is.

Next, Amna, intersecting gender and religion, believes that Islam is not 'anti-working' for women:

> Amna: I feel that most of the people leading Muslim religion are men, like the Molvees and Alahmas [Religious leaders] . . . [so] I think there is some bias in spreading our religion because they have used the religion to keep the females inside the house . . . it's silly, and it's not in our religion at all. There is equality in gaining knowledge, including religious knowledge.

Like Amna, Ayesha intersected gender, religion and nationality categories while describing her perceptions about religion and society. But they differ in terms of elements of societal misrecognition. As mentioned earlier, Amna talked about the misinterpretations by Islamic scholars, while Ayesha mentioned that she would be seen as a Muslim girl wearing a hijab, possibly (in the eyes of others) putting herself at a subordinate level compared to Muslim boys, and being discriminated against by others:

> Ayesha: I have British values and morals, but some people don't see that. So, it could be possible that people won't accept me as a British girl. I would need to be modest and show them that I'm not what they think I am, and the stereotypes are wrong. In today's society, we have to continuously prove ourselves to be worthy of something because we are seen as outsiders to some people. And I think because of what is happening in the news and society, and we Muslims especially Muslim girls, are discriminated against because Muslim south Asian men might be seen as a Christian, Hindu or Sikh – you cannot [instantly] see differences in them. But Muslim girls wear headscarves and, because of that, people can easily identify them as Muslims.

In comparison, Hanya and Yumna seemed more determined to present themselves as Muslim women (of colour) within social spaces and as science students or science professionals. Hanya's experience and interpretation of being in an informal science space intersected with her religious and visible characteristics:

> Hanya: I especially liked the university course we did. At first, I was not going, but my teacher persuaded me. The good part of it is, when I went there, I really enjoyed it – we were the only two Muslim girls there – and I feel that I actually have to put myself forward to grasp these opportunities. It felt good to represent us as Muslim women doing science. There were not even other girls in the sessions. You just have to push for it; you can't just wait around for the opportunities to come out for you . . . I see myself as a Muslim girl who wears the hijab and who follows Deen [complying with Islamic law, beliefs, character and deeds], who wants to learn, seek knowledge [through the Quran] and do well so that I can make Allah satisfied with me. I think a Muslim girl gets fewer opportunities, but – like I said before – you just have to strive for these opportunities. You can't wait for them to come to you.

While Yumna was working for the American engineering company, she sometimes masked her Muslim identity. However, this all changed after 9/11 when her colleagues and friends began to talk negatively about Muslims in front of her. She began to feel that she would be 'dragged into this judgment' despite all the effort and knowledge she would put into her job as a design engineer. In addition to her religion and gender, she now ensures to present herself in multiple ways. At one instance, she said:

Yumna: I'm representing women of colour and Muslim women. When I go
into a [STEM] environment as an individual, I may be the only person of
colour and the only Muslim. I want to think that will change. And that will
only change if I actually present all the aspects of my [British, south Asian
and Muslim] identity and my personality and the strengths and the values
associated with those different identities. Otherwise, who will know what
change I brought about and how that changed was brought about? I'm now
at that point of my professional journey where I no longer have instances
or occasions where I don't bring my full identity into that environment;
whether it's a physical environment or a virtual environment, I don't feel the
need to mask anymore.

Saarya did not talk about her representation as a scientist from her Hindu
background or following religious practices like Amna, Ayesha and Hanya.
Rather religion for her is universal:

Saarya: I just pray, take the good things [from religion such as], 'don't lie', 'don't
hurt people', 'don't do unnecessary things', 'stay away from jealousy and evil
eye'. There are a lot of religious things [rituals] which I don't follow. Because
I think a lot of them [are] superstitions and I don't believe in them, I just
pray for good, take the good things – like I take 5% [from the rituals and
attending annual religious festivals and] 95% I don't follow.

Saarya's take on religion is based on humanitarian values and rights rather
than performing rituals, prayers and other practices mentioned in the religious
books.

3.   *Being multinational religious daughters*

Contemporary families may not map directly onto households; families are
often spread between different houses or maybe all live under one roof. In
transnational families, family members commonly live dispersed among
households that are, quite possibly, situated within two or more nation states.
We asked our respondents to talk about them being a daughter. Ayesha said:

Ayesha: As a daughter, I'm quite caring – and I can say that for certain because
I do a lot for my parents. I am the oldest daughter, and I have to do certain
things – my parents immigrated to England, so I have to do paperwork,
talk to solicitors, and do some local council work for them. I believe that,
because of this experience, I've grown as a person. I don't think other
girls have to do this stuff at my age, but I do it, and I'm grateful for that.
In relation to science, my parents talk like I should become a dentist or an

optician. I guess Asian parents always want their daughters to do something very professional like becoming a doctor and their sons to be engineers or businessmen. Obviously, my parents are quite strict because they are Asians – and they do want me to get into dentistry. But I will have my own say on that!

Similarly, Archer et al. (2013) point to the discrimination among parents in seeing some sciences as inherently masculine. Ayesha is an obedient and caring daughter and is only mildly critical of her parents; she realizes that, compared to *elite White parents*, they are unaware of the depth and breadth of other sciences. She says:

> Ayesha: My parents want me to become a dentist like my cousin Saira. But my role model is someone like Einstein or any other physicist. Which is kind-of sad because I know that for a British White girl, if their parents are doctors or engineers, then their children can become scientists or whatever they like to become. But in my family, my parents are not in the field of science, so I don't have someone to talk to about quantum physics.

Like Ayesha, Hanya portrays herself as an obedient daughter but at the same time has strong agentic control in becoming a surgeon, rather than what her father's choice of career is for her:

> Hanya: I see myself as a responsible child in the family, and I also see myself as someone who can make my family happy through helping my siblings. My Abba [father] talks about engines at home and about his work [at an automobile company], but it never interests me. When we are sitting down, he talks about how he learned about motors through his experiences working in his father's small mechanics shop in Kashmir. Sometimes, he talks about university options in [mechanical] engineering. My brother gets involved in this because he is interested, but I get bored very quickly. If I get very good grades in physics – which I don't think I will – and if my father says that I should do physics at A-level, I will consider this. But I don't think I will carry on with it later [at university]. Instead, I will . . . work towards becoming a surgeon. This would not be exactly following where my father's interest is, but . . .

In this respect, and compared to Ayesha's parents, Hanya's father offers more space for her to choose her education and profession. With Einstein as her role model, Ayesha might 'go against the grain' and challenge her parental professional preferences, but, at this moment, that rebellion seems to be limited. The intersectional dimension for Ayesha, of having south Asian parents unfamiliar with science, is evidently a barrier. Hanya, on the other hand, seems more determined to challenge her father's ideas. Thus, we see some family powers and the provision of differences in parental ideologies, although in the same context of the home.

Our science professionals, Amna, Saarya and Yumna, like Ayesha and Hanya, also mentioned that they were (and still are) obedient daughters. They understand this obedience as caring and respectful towards their parents rather than always saying 'Yes to their [parental] orders. It is nothing like that' (Saarya). Amna, for instance, belongs from a family of doctors and is highly supported by her parents; even though some family members suggested her parents and to Amna of becoming a dentist rather than a doctor mainly because it is a 'shorter route' and 'easy life', but

> Amna: I thought – that's so boring, to look into just the mouth of a person and
> I'll feel very uncomfortable that I don't know the whole person. And so, I
> need to help people and get rid of their illnesses, but I need to know the
> person as a whole- rather just a single part of the body.

Later we asked Amna, would her parents be as supportive as they were when she decided to do medicine if she had wanted to choose a non-science profession instead? Amna said, 'Yes, 100 per cent – they always wanted me to be happy and be successful.'

Saarya and Yumna's parents did not have a science background, nor did they attend university like Ayesha's and Hanya's parent. But, unlike Ayesha, neither found their lack of parental education to be a barrier. Instead, their parents motivated and supported their daughters against the broad backdrop of south Asian cultural and religious norms:

> Saarya: I did science through my mom's motivation, and against the
> community expectations. My mom was always like a really 'can do' person,
> she's always kind of drilled this down to me, you need to be positive, don't
> be negative, be positive.

> Yumna: Most of my friends applied for subjects like business and accounting,
> and I was the only one who applied for computer information systems . . .
> my parents, at no point, objected to me applying to computer information
> systems, even though they knew nothing about it. There was complete
> support – unfaltering support [from them]. Even when I turned down
> a Russell group university to then attend a modern university, there was
> no level of criticism that you might expect. Yet, even today, from many
> BAME parents, [who] would prefer the more traditional universities and
> traditional subjects because of prestige and the elitism associated with them.

4. *Being working-class or middle-class multinational religious daughters*

At this point, Ayesha's religious values intersect with her working-class family life. While she needs money to go to university, she is adamantly against taking a bank loan and paying interest. Again, her determination to go to university makes her think of other possible ways to achieve this. She recognizes the dilemma – the extra hard work she might have – including paying bank interest contrary to her religious values. We asked: 'How does being from a working-class family impact on your future science education and career plans?'

> Ayesha: Because my parents earn a certain [low] wage, I may or may not be able to go to university, because of the fees. Obviously, because I'm Muslim, I have my own principles of not paying bank interest – but then I might have to because my parents can't afford it. Or I have to struggle with my parent's money and do some extra work shifts to go to university – so that I don't take interest to pay my university fees. I will be really struggling to get the knowledge that I want!

Hanya, on the other hand, takes her working-class identity as a positive trigger to repay her parent's sacrifices to give her numerous opportunities in life. She clearly intersects religion and family elements with her class identification – intersecting, too, with her Sci-ID – in a positive way:

> Hanya: [Being from a working-class family] motivates me because, if you think ten years ago, my parents were still in Pakistan and didn't have opportunities [as] I do. My mum didn't get to go to college and my father had to work very hard in this country [England]. They have expectations of me like all parents of immigrants have when they come here, and their children must study hard and get good jobs like any other British person. They have done so much for me, it not only motivates me, but I also understand I have so many opportunities over here. Obviously, I don't want to let them down and want to prove that I can be productive – as a Muslim Pakistani woman.

The three professionals see themselves as having middle-class backgrounds. Saarya, currently a professional earning a reasonable salary and 'living a very comfortable London life', was raised to be an independent south Asian woman by her working-class, open-minded and hardworking parents:

> Saarya: my parents raised me to be very independent as a south Asian female – you make your own choices, know what you want – let not the external catalysts [other people] get involved, and if they do, I tell them 'it's my life

I get to decide what I want.' I even I say that to my husband; he sometimes tries to influence my career decisions – I'm like 'No, I want to do it'. Or not – because, in the end, it is my career, my choice . . . I need to be happy, which is important.

Amna and Yumna's parents had a middle-class status in society regarding their education and/or professional stability and standards of living. Both these professionals were provided with all the facilities that 'most families cannot provide to their children' (Yumna). Despite this difference in comparison to Hanya and Saarya, as mentioned earlier, their parents provided the basic principles of independence in decision-making and full support.

5.   *Being successful middle-class multinational young science students*

Both Amna and Yumna were confident about their science ability, of seeing themselves as a *science person*. Similarly, in answering the question 'Do you see yourself as a science person?', Ayesha said:

Ayesha: Well, I see myself as a sciencey person. Science has always been part of me because I love science a lot. I think science is the only subject that I get excited about. But I sometimes feel that my classmates ruin it – I remember once I was talking about quantum physics and a few of them got frustrated with me and saying, 'you always talking about it all the time'. It is not that they don't want to do science, they just don't want to get so much into science in the way I do, like I want to go deeper in science, but they don't.

Ayesha is a confident and able science student of her class; she prefers doing what she wants to do – make meaning of her life through the lens of science, especially physics (Archer et al., 2017b) – despite her classmates. Hanya, on the other hand, is pleased that her peers view her as a 'crazy' (determined) science person. Hanya mentioned:

Hanya: Yes, I do feel sciencey myself, I am comfortable with it; as I am comfortable talking about general scientific issues with my school friends, and that automatically makes them see me as a sciencey person.

From these descriptions, they both (Ayesha and Hanya) exhibit considerable agentic control of their aspirations. While some reports describe young Pakistani and Bangladeshi women as having high aspirations but low achievements (Department for Children, Schools and Families, 2008). In the initial interviews in 2014, both girls believed that being south Asian would not hinder their future science education and/or professional choices because of the multi-heritage city (London) in which they live. Lately, though, they do recognize some of the challenges they might encounter at university (Ayesha – finance; Hanya – being seen as an outsider). Despite this, both seemed *agentically* determined to become scientists.

6.   *Being successful working-class or middle-class multinational women in science*

Amna, Saarya and Yumna's also answered our questions – 'Do you see yourself as a science person?' with a 'Yes'. However, their reasons and explanations were different. Amna's explanation of being a successful science person included becoming a consultant in the UK, despite having her initial medical education from Pakistan. She maintained the view that she established herself as a science person very early in her life:

> Amna: My father was a doctor, and my uncle and many of my cousins are
> doctors, so we are recognised as a family of doctors. When I was young,
> people used to say you are very intelligent, so you will-definitely-become a
> doctor like your father.

Second, Amna's father worked as an army doctor, so as a child she moved from place to place with the purpose of serving the army and, in turn, serving the public – so her ambition to serve people became deeply rooted in childhood. Third, she enjoyed learning sciences (except physics) much more than humanity-based subjects; she was so good in sciences that the school science teachers always used to say that she would be a successful science person.

For Saarya, success entails her being 'a very hardworking, very motivated, ambitious [person]'. Alongside these characteristics, she first saw herself as a science person with the introduction of practical work in her school life during the two years of applied science of A-level studies.

> Saarya: The two years of applied science were the best time of my life. The
> teaching involving full-on practical work and recognition of a million
> careers [in science] because you know science offers a wider range of career
> opportunities. Yeah – practical offerings at A-levels knocked me – like
> strengthened my passion for science – definitely . . . and I got stuck into
> biomedical science [so] progressed in it.

Currently, she sees herself as a science person, not with respect to her current work as a science technician but rather in her ability to ask and find answers to questions related to her life. As she mentioned:

> Saarya: My journey in getting pregnant was tough – I had to go through
> fertility treatment because I was diagnosed with polycystic ovaries. When

I tell doctors that I've done a biomedical science degree, they're very fascinated about it, and they'll go through all the science behind fertility and stuff. Now I am pregnant – still, I ask questions – a lot of questions. I never leave them [doctors and midwives] quickly, especially after the scans because I studied scanning at A-level – we did a bit of radiography, so I'm always fascinated. So recently, I questioned them about vaccines. Because at the time, prior to April, the government said that pregnant women can't take the [COVID-19] vaccine. But now, they said, you can take it, but before I took my first dose, I asked my hospital GP, then my midwife. The hospital GP told me about the coagulation of blood clotting and everything. So, she explained to me about it, what impact it might have.

Yumna always knew that she could do science and could be successful in science. For example, during her school life, she chose physics and continued with it despite being the only female student in her higher physics class. But, like Saarya, she understood herself to be a science person later during her work experience in a multinational engineering company – then aged nineteen. Yumna challenged the *status quo* further by moving away from home as a Muslim south Asian female for one year – a possibility that was not acceptable to her community thirty-five years ago. All of her determination to go against community norms and to achieve what she wanted was supported by the freedom and trust given to her by her parents. This work experience had an enormous impact on her science life because it was during this time she actually felt like an engineer and confirmed her intention to apply for an engineering post after graduation. She said:

Yumna: I went away for the year and worked in a multinational organisation [South England], and I have to say, it was one of the *best experiences I've ever had*. My manager was a BAME male. He was incredibly supportive; he had an incredible amount of empathy because he knew how hard it was for my parents. So, yes, in the first instance, he very much looked out for me because he knew that was the first time I was living on my own. And the diversity, the ethnic diversity in that organisation was very encouraging. It was the first time I'd walked into a professional environment, a technology environment, and there were people from different racial and professional backgrounds, socio-economic backgrounds and religious backgrounds. It was great. And my mentor was also a BAME female, and she remains a dear friend, even to this day, decades later.

Yumna currently feels successful because she has not entirely left the engineering field. And she is still working to support BAME individuals as a 'women's activist' by serving the public through her commitments as a STEM consultant and non-executive board member (a student award agency of her country).

Intersectional science identity

Giordano (2017) calls for an 'expansion of access to a kind of [science] knowledge that is traditionally kept out of the hands of marginalized groups' (p. 18). In this chapter, we have taken an intersectionality approach to Sci-ID highlighting mainly three cultures (science, south Asian and UK), using it as a framework to explore the science lives – as embodied lived experiences of Amna, Ayesha, Hanya, Saarya and Yumna. We have sought to shed light on the multiplicity of their power relationships with (mis)recognition and (in)equality within different social (formal and informal) settings and how this shape their science identities.

Our starter questions when talking to women participants were designed to discuss simultaneity in intersectionality – including the aspects of misrecognition, inclusion or exclusion, intersections of power relations and corresponding social categories and contexts. The south Asian women responded by discussing how social categories (gender, ethnicity, religion and social class) influenced (or not) their lives – not least in how these interact and intertwine to form the basis of their personalized Sci-ID development.

We see identity making, then, as a dynamic, contextual and relational process (Sluss & Ashforth, 2007; Sang, Al-Dajani & Ozbilgin, 2013). In revisiting Jang's (2018) points from earlier, we have made a point of discussing the simultaneous influences of diverse social categorizations on our five respondents' lives as talented middle- or working-class multinational south Asian women in the context of science education within the UK. We see (as they do) their relationships among such diverse social categorizations as multiplicative. It is simply impossible to pull a single thread of their lives for discussion separate from all the others. Diverse social categorizations constitute interlocking, mutually constructing and intersecting systems of power in their lives – being south Asian immigrant women and/or daughters of immigrant parents, school students, scientists, religious adherents and middle- or working-class UK citizens all bring the impact of associated social systems.

Moreover, it is certainly the case that intersecting power relations vary across different social contexts and respondent south Asian women recognize, for example, the particularities of studying within UK schools, universities, workplaces, being UK citizens and immersed in science cultures. In this way, our findings resemble Crenshaw's (1989) ideas of multiple grounds of identity formation, as:

(i)   While all the five respondents see themselves as UK citizens, they understand the possibilities of being viewed as *outsiders* because of being immigrants (Ayesha, Saarya and Yumna), their working-class status (Hanya) and being Muslim girls - through wearing hijabs (Ayesha and Hanya). In some case they saw these issues as *cultural differences* rather than *power differences*, they felt different but not oppressed and subordinate.

(ii) Ayesha, Hanya, Saarya and Yumna seemed intent on re-paying the struggles endured by their parents' migration to the UK. However, Amna did not mention her parents' struggle as they live in Pakistan; instead discussed the motivation and privilege she received from her doctor father in helping Pakistani army and civilians.

(iii) Ayesha and Hanya were willing to counter their south Asian parental wishes about professional choices. However, other respondents' parents were very supportive of their choices and decisions and these women did not have to challenge their parents.

(iv) For all, except Amna, being multinational immigrants or the daughters of immigrant parents has provided opportunities to achieve better science-based education and careers than was available to their parents. Amna said she did not find Professional and Linguistic Assessments Board (PLAB) 1 and 2 medical exams to be additional burdens on overseas doctors because the 'NHS is one of the best in the world', so these exams were needed.

(v)   Ayesha and Hanya will seek ways to meet the financial struggles of university studies, despite Islamic prohibitions on bank interest (Ayesha) and any overt discrimination through wearing a hijab. Such issues were not raised by Saarya, who, like Ayesha and Hanya, was raised by working-class parents. However, Saarya received her education for free; instead, Ayesha and Hanya had to take the student loan to pay the university fees.

(vi) Amna is very religious and Saarya not so religious – but in a way, they were both critical of some scholars in terms of proscribing gender (Amna) and rituals intersecting with self-beliefs (Saarya) – which both women thought were unnecessary as essential practices in their lives.

These outcomes allowed us to voice women's agentic inclination of Sci-ID (trans) formation on an ongoing process – the process of becoming scientists for Ayesha and Hanya and the process of being a scientist for Amna, Saarya and Yumna. All this while remaining within their religion and belonging to immigrant south Asian communities and appreciating parental sacrifices. None of them saw themselves as Avraamidou's (2020a) 'forever outsider' even while also negotiating the intersecting social categorizations impacting their sense of personal agency. Needless to say, each role and relationship illustrate additional complexities that rely upon context, responsibilities, expectations, obstacles, opportunities, balancing cultures (Chapter 3) and successes in developing a Sci-ID.

In presenting these stories, we acknowledge that *intersectional approaches to the development of Sci-ID* in these women are unique but not singular. They are quite similar in many ways and yet also really quite different. South Asian Muslim women from a middle- or working-class and immigrant backgrounds tend to take these social obstacles as opportunities, successes and challenges rather than see them as double or multiple jeopardies; they shape circumstances according to their intentional agency. That said, their responses to *intersectional powers differ* in how they negotiate their intersections with these powers as they develop their Sci-ID.

Chapter summary

In her article 'Women in Science: Why So Few?', Alice Rossi questioned the shortage of female scientists in academic careers (1965, p. 1196). Nearly fifty years later, the same question continues to reappear. The kind of research we describe here invites educators and education policymakers to invest time and funding in equipping parents, teachers, schools and students from diverse backgrounds to acknowledge and strengthen the agentic control of women towards education and careers 'from' and 'in' science categories (Wong, 2015). This articulation of identity development is not the end but rather an invitation for further development. As Carbado et al. (2013) maintain, theory, including intersectionality, 'is never done, nor exhausted by its prior articulations or movements; it is always already an analysis-in-progress' (p. 304). In taking this approach, we believe that of viewing intersectionality from the eyes of the south Asian women and challenging universalism and essentialism, science education will benefit from such a theoretical framework. It raises awareness of respondents' unique positionality and the issues and insights of neglected groups of women, acknowledging and highlighting their science lives. That is, *intersectionality made personal*.

3

Families and Family Culture

This chapter examines the varied and complex forms of parental influence that shape young women's decisions to begin – and continue – studying science subjects in school and beyond. In the two previous chapters, we have discussed some of the major, macro (social) forces that come into play in discussions of science identity (Sci-ID). We have noted, too, some of the micro (personal) forces, such as interest, engagement, preference, choice, agency, resilience and persistence. In this chapter we consider mid-range meso forces. In general, we mean by this is the influence and impact of real people both near and far. These can be teachers, colleagues, peers, youth workers, counsellors, role models, community members, employers, religious leaders and so on. We have considered some of these elsewhere (Salehjee & Watts, 2020), and in this chapter we focus on just one form of influence close to home – from parents and families.

There are numerous studies that identify parental involvement as an important means of promoting academic success, but the nature of parental influence often remains vague, usually seen as a general form of influence rather than specific to the study of science. In our own work (Salehjee & Watts, 2015), we noted that, while such influences may be present, individual students seldom report this quite as important as might be supposed. Susan Whiston and Briana Keller (2004) have noted numerous studies that report young people's perceptions of parental influence on their career choices, though only about 21 per cent of young people claim that their career choices are made collaboratively with their parents, and only about 2 per cent then state that their parents were the main drivers behind their actual decisions. Similarly, Nadya Fouad and John Bynner (2008) concluded from their three-year study that it is the self-confidence instilled by parents that is important for school learning, rather than directing a young person's scholastic interest. This chapter looks specifically at south Asian families and the specific influences on sisters and daughters in these situations.

Gender norms and gender stereotypes are formed and internalized at a very early stage in life, and it would be very surprising if family upbringing, circumstances and perspectives had no influence whatsoever on the directions taken by young women in the family. So, the emphasis in this chapter is on the shape and mechanisms involved in that influence. Our narrative approach to research lies in understanding women's experiences in relation to their educational and occupational choices and the successes they experience in both of these. As we have discussed in earlier chapters, all of our data have been collected through interviews with south Asian women, often using purposive and snowball sampling as convenient opportunities have arisen to talk to as wide a constituency of south Asian women as possible, some indicated in the table later in the text as they appear in this chapter, along with some pen portraits of our participants.

Table 3 More participants

	Place of Birth	**Self-Designation**
Fawzziya	England	Trainee science teacher
Hajira	Indonesia	University engineering student
Ifrah	Pakistan	University chemistry student
Ramia	England	University biology student

Here we add four more pen portraits of some of our women participants (Table 3).

Fawzziya is twenty-three and fully immersed in a one-year university teacher training course. She has always, she says, wanted to be a teacher and this conviction has grown with time. Fawzziya gives a lot of credit to her south Asian parents for raising her with their cultural and religious ethics, morals and values, which she wants to share with others by being an excellent primary school teacher. As part of her degree programme, she was required to undertake work placements to gather professional experience, and she chose to do this in primary schools in her locality. After her degree and before embarking on a postgraduate course, she spent a year as an unqualified teaching assistant. This year solidified her ambitions and she applied to train fully as a teacher. She really enjoys science very much and has recognized that primary schools need science specialists to help inspire and guide teachers and teaching across the school. It is a recognition that feeds her motivation; she has a strong feeling of wanting to 'give back' to her community in one form or another. Being a teacher, improving science education within her school is one way she sees of doing this.

Hajira is thirty-eight, born into a large family in a rural part of Indonesia, worked extremely hard at school and eventually, after graduation, took a position in the Ministry of Education in Jakarta. She moved to the UK with her husband and took the UK nationality. She decided that, once her children were old enough, she would enrol for a master's degree with a specialism in STEM education. She has no particular goal in mind beyond the degree, preferring to see 'what life throws up' – for the moment she is captivated by being back in an academic sphere and enjoying the intellectual demands of the course. Why STEM? In Jakarta, she had worked with a unit that oversaw the education of gifted and talented students across the country and she had been astonished at the high quality of work these youngsters could achieve. These young people had developed projects in 'saving the environment' and had generated technical engineering and social solutions to some of Indonesia's environmental issues. This in turn had inspired Hajira's growing interest in science. She video calls her family regularly back in Indonesia, and they are hugely impressed by her life in the UK, so very different from their own rural lives.

Ifrah was born in Pakistan into a non-science family; her parents are working-class merchants and traders. They immigrated to the UK when Ifrah was five and so her acclimatization and acculturalization happened throughout her school years. She was studious at school and is the first of her family to enter university; she has become the pride and joy of her extended family. That adds to the pressure, she says, because there are high expectations that she will do well, achieve a high degree, find a big job, be the leading light of the family. Her younger brothers and sisters have been curious and have occasionally accompanied her to the university campus 'to see what she does every day'; she knows that she is trailblazing as far as they are concerned. When her fourteen-year-old brother announced he wanted to be a car mechanic, her father was delighted until Ifrah said, 'Why just fix other people's cars when you can go to university and design the next generation of new ones?' She took him to visit the university's automotive engineering department and his future was sealed there and then. Her own degree in chemistry will take her into industry, she hopes.

Ramia is twenty and in the second year of a biology degree. Why biology? She grinned, 'It had to be science but certainly not physics or chemistry, my maths is simply not good enough!' Biology because she went on several school visits to the Natural History Museum in central London, 'You see the skeletons and you get this huge buzz about evolution of species, the way that evolution happens, it is incredible. Richard Dawkins is my favourite author, he writes so well, I wish I could write like that. He makes evolution so clear and reasonable.' Biology because she liked the biology teacher at her local London comprehensive school, 'She had this way of dealing with the stupid boys in the class, you know, when anything about sex was mentioned. They would giggle and pinch the girls, but Miss Morris was aware of it all and could really put them down. I remember that all of us girls were being kind of, well, really sophisticated and superior [laughs] and knew everything about bodies and stuff. And we snubbed the stupid boys and became the swots, got the good grades and went on to do A-level biology.' Still biology? 'I think I am actually heading towards science communication. I want to do a master's in journalism and then get a job writing about science.' Your family? 'Oh, they support me in anything and everything I want to do.'

We see family involvement as the extent to which the parents or other family members are involved in the career plans of the female children. Stephen Gorard, Gareth Rees and Ralph Fevre (1999) note the strong family effect on all transitions and educational trajectories in a family and Joan Payne (2003) comments that parents are 'probably the most important source of advice and help when decisions about post-16 routes have to be taken' (p. 2). Parental decisions about their children's education are based on their beliefs, life contexts as well as their own desires for their children's educational paths. These studies suggest that parents are generally ready to invest a great amount of emotional, social and economic resources to support their children over the course of their education. In this sense, then, they 'have a pervasive influence in shaping young people's attitudes to education over a long period of time, so that the broad direction of what they will do at 16 is simply taken for granted' (p. 30). This framework of (unspoken) expectations rarely stops at age seventeen, and families continue to exert an influence on degree subject choice and affairs much later in life (Liu, McMahon & Watson, 2015; Rosenblatt, 2015).

At one level, this is through parents and others giving or providing (recommending) information to their children on the type of school and university subject choices and employment they want to pursue. It includes the extent to which the parents are responsive in giving encouragement, approval and financial support in matters concerned with the study and career plans of sons and daughters – although it is clearly the daughters who are of interest to us here. At a second level, there exists a *weight of expectation* that women experience. For example, an American study (Leong, 1993) reported that Asian American women may not choose a career based on their own interests or intentions but on *whole family* decisions. The younger generation is seen to owe a duty to carry on the family tradition and accomplish the wishes of the older generation (Tang, Fouad & Smith, 1999). A similar case has been made for families in many other countries, for example, Thailand (Pimpa, 2005). While these three studies are some two decades old, such familial attitudes can still be seen in many of the responses of young British Asian women today as they have narrated their stories to us.

It is important here to begin by separating parents from other members of the family. Many studies in this area (e.g. Mazzarol & Soutar, 2002) focus on parental influences and do so in terms of what might be called *recommendation* and *financial support*. As we note above, recommendation entails making suggestions, providing information, giving advice, counselling. Financial support, too, comes in many forms, from continuing to live within the family home while studying to direct financial transactions through the *bank of Mum and Dad*. It is clear, though, that family influence does not begin and end with just these two aspects of life. Various family members impact on one another's choices and actions in many ways. The family is a reference group that has significant influence upon individuals' evaluations, aspirations and decision-making process, and family members have the ability to shape behaviour and lifestyle, influence self-concept and contribute to the formation of values and attitudes. For example, by self-comparison, if one family member sees another as having a higher education or workplace status, greater achievement or success, then she may feel dissatisfied with her own achievements and strive to do at least as well as her brother or sister – if not better. This element of sibling rivalry and competition is not something developed widely in this field of literature but does emerge at times in the stories we have collected. Nor need this simply be by self-comparison, in that members of the extended family may well comment on how well one sibling is doing with either the indirect or direct comparison being made with others. Nor need rivalry remain within the family at all because, clearly, competition between peers and friendship patterns can also be powerfully influential. However, we focus here on just the family (Olmos-Gomez et al., 2021).

There are gender-based patterns, too, described in some of the studies in this field. Thus, mothers are sometimes seen have more influence on their daughters (Paa & Mcwhirter, 2000) especially when compared to the influence that fathers have on their sons. Although sons are more influenced by their fathers, and daughters by their mothers, this rule does not deny the existence of studies where this relationship between parents and children crosses and becomes counter to this (Lease & Dahlbeck, 2009). Sandra Hanson and Emily Gilbert (2012) comment on the rise of the 'tiger moms' both in China and in some American Asian households and the mother's role in driving the success of her children. In some households they note that, despite a prevailing patriarchal presence, there also exist traditions of *virangana*, of *warrior women*, that give considerable power to women. This has been popularized from the publication of Amy Chua's (2011) *Battle Hymn of the Tiger Mother*. She argues that tiger mothers are tough on their children because this will give them the edge to be successful in a very competitive workforce and economy.

So, more important than simple recommendation and support, then, is the perceived culture expectation from parents and siblings. This weight is above and beyond the *weight of wearing culture* that we go on to discuss in Chapter 4. On many occasions and in different forms our respondents have discussed the enormous impact these expectations had – and continues to have – on their decisions on what and where to study, how and where to seek employment. This is not just about subject choices, academic courses and career destinations but has also encompassed, for example, their choice of university and even their choice of country in which to study. For some, their parents had instilled in them from an early age the idea that the UK – and US – university education is superior to any other. In some cases, their family expected them to obtain an overseas academic qualification in the United States, France or Germany, be fluent in a foreign language and to gain valuable life experiences abroad. And then to 'bring their expertise home' to benefit the family.

It is wrong, of course, to view families always as being challenging, antagonistic and conflictual. Families create spaces of great caring and intimacy. The affective and emotional relationships that give substance to a family, the *family atmosphere*, are an important means of understanding the influence and guidance provided to individuals. A secure atmosphere within the family allows a young person to develop an internal model of the self that is worthy of consideration by parents. It is part of the *ecology* of self-identity, and Sci-ID, as we set out in Salehjee and Watts (2020). Feeling special and important to parents and siblings has been found to engender learner behaviours, such as effort, persistence, as well as to stimulate positive emotions such as interest and enthusiasm (Furrer & Skinner, 2003). Viewing oneself as worthy of attention may also develop one's perception of competence in exploring the world (e.g. high self-efficacy in learning science).

We have to mention, too, that *family type* matters. There are clear differences between the influences exerted on a daughter by a small *two-point-four* nuclear family and that of a large extended family ranging across several generations and multiple households. The influences on an only child would be different from that of, say, being a twin or a middle offspring in a large family wherein she might be *lost in the crowd*. One of our respondents, Hajira, was the seventh child in a family of seven:

> Hajira: My mother always got my name mixed up with my sisters. She'd be busy cooking and she'd sort of run through them all saying, 'Fiza . . . Nada . . . Rasheeen . . .' 'Mum, its Hajira.' 'Oh yes, Hajira, please go put the knives and forks on the table.' She was always amazingly kind, my dad too, but by the time they got to me I think they were tired, and they'd had enough. I was allowed pretty much to go my own way. I think they forgot I was even there, sometimes.

Similarly, women who come from traditional families are more likely to accommodate to familial influences, while those from non-traditional or less traditional families are more likely to be supported in making their decisions. As we have already discussed, cultural factors, too, for example, values, work ethos and attitude towards religion, will have important influences on young women's career choices. At this point it is difficult to continue an analysis of families without a discussion of Pierre Bourdieu's theory of social capital and, although we have mentioned and discussed this in other places in the book, we consider and critique this here in terms of the family.

Bourdieu and capital

Capitals, field and habitus are the 'conceptual cornerstones' of Bourdieu's social theories (Bennett & Silva, 2011, p. 429). Bourdieu's argument is that these economic and non-economic criteria work together to maintain social status and social hierarchies (Bourdieu, 1986). At one level they give society considerable stability in that social and economic conditions are broadly reproduced and remain the same generation after generation. That said, Bourdieu recognizes that the social world is more complex than simply being based upon economic wealth; rather, he maintains that certain forms of *capital* work to support not just wealth but also act to maintain hierarchies of power. According to Bourdieu (1986, p. 241), capital takes time to accumulate and contains a tendency to persist in its being, and it is a social force that means that – for some people – not everything is equally possible. In this view, meritocracy simply does not exist.

For example, 'cultural capital' is largely bestowed via family membership much in the ways we have described earlier, through various embodied, institutionalized states within families, whereas his idea of social capital refers to networks of social connections that are held by people, *who they know*, and the entitlements and opportunities these connections provide. These networks produce or reproduce inequality and are largely reproductive, ultimately legitimizing the positioning of the powerful and dominant classes. Cultural capital is understood as access to characteristics, knowledge, skills and forms of expression that are culturally valued (Bourdieu, 1986). Cultural capital can be described as existing in three forms, comprising embodied cultural capital, institutional cultural capital and objectified cultural capital. Institutional forms are regarded as formal certificates, such as academic degrees and diplomas (Bourdieu, 1986). Objectified forms are manifested in the form of cultural resources, such as books, instruments or works of arts. Embodied cultural capital is seen in the form of long-lasting dispositions of the mind and body (Bourdieu & Passeron, 1977). Cultural and social capitals are not distributed equally; those in higher-status groups are argued to have greater access to the valuable forms of capitals compared to those who are identified as being in the lower strata of society. Both cultural and social capitals are maintained by *symbolic exchanges* and retain a certain level of taken-for-grantedness or invisibility within society.

Another tenet of Bourdieu's social theorizing relates to 'habitus', which he regarded as the ways in which people act, react and behave based upon social connections and cultural beliefs. Habitus then refers to the norms and practices of social groups or classes (Bourdieu & Passeron, 1977). While discussions of habitus do not deny some individual agency, Bourdieu does argue that elements of the self, such as beliefs, values, speech and dress, are framed and informed by social structural factors such as class, gender and ethnicity. An individual's habitus is not fixed or bounded but is instead characterized by unpredictability and arbitrariness. This is summed up by Diane Reay (1998) who describes habitus as

> primarily a dynamic concept, a rich interlacing of past and present, individual and collective interiorized and permeating both body and psyche (p. 521)... Hence, habitus can be regarded as a 'transforming machine' that while reproducing the dominant social conditions does this in a 'relatively unpredictable way'. (Bourdieu, 1990, p. 87)

Bourdieu (1986) argued that individuals enter the education system with various capitals and habituses, each contributing to levels of academic success. Lucia

Tramonte and Douglas Willms (2010) highlight how families from lower socio-economic backgrounds are generally perceived as having lower levels of cultural capital to draw upon, which in turn limits the educational success of the learners in the family. These authors explain that

> low income parents fail to support their children in succeeding in school not because they see too low a payoff to such action, but because they lack the skills, habits, and knowledge needed to effectively assist them. (Tramonte & Willms, 2010, p. 201)

While Tramonte and Willms (2010) are largely concerned with school education, this conceptualization of different forms of cultural capital can equally be applied to higher education as, just like schools, higher education institutions are also 'places where codes from higher socio-economic status groups are recognized and where the possession of cultural capital is rewarded' (Tramonte & Willms, 2010, p. 202). Equally, a student's habitus may impact upon her or his skill in understanding and translating the implicit *rules of the game* confronted within university (Aschaffenburg & Maas, 1997, p. 573). As such, there is recognition that students do not necessarily arrive with lack of knowledge but rather that the knowledge or cultural capital that is favoured within their own social situation may not be valued within the higher education environment in which they find themselves, or they may not have knowledge of the *institutional habitus*. The latter term has emerged to refer to 'the impact of a cultural group or social class on an individual's behaviour as it is mediated through an organisation' (Reay, David & Ball, 2001, para 1.3).

In Bourdieu's view (1986, p. 241), the educational system makes a contribution to the reproduction of the social structure by sanctioning the hereditary transmission of cultural capital. For middle-class families the decision-making is relatively straightforward and reinforced in the round by the immediate and the extended family. There are many more dilemmas within a working-class family because of forms of self-exclusion, confusion as to possible destinations, financial constraints and simple lack of knowledge and experience.

Our critique of Bourdieu

At one level we appreciate what Bourdieu and his adherents are driving at. There are *macro (social) forces* at work in society that act to sponsor and support those who are within elite groups and inhibit those people who would want to move upward into such elite social groupings. It is seen to be hard work for working-class people to become middle class, for middle-class people to become upper-middle class or, from then on, for aspiring people to join the aristocracy. Our more focused critique is with the idea of habitus.

For Bourdieu, one's habits, routines, unthinking actions are largely unconscious and they reproduce the essentials of our dominant culture. That is, social forces *get inside us*, we internalize these and we then unconsciously reproduce them in what we do and say, and how we behave and act. He views a habit as an unconscious principle of action, a deeply internalized set of dispositions, schemas and ways of knowing (Swartz, 2002) which locate habits in a cultural, economic or social field. Habitus is a product of history, which in turn produces more history (Bourdieu, 1990). In our opinion, the main problem with this analysis is that it largely accounts for human action being reproductive of an existing field, rather than being transformative. Bourdieu's habitus blocks human freedom with *social bonds*, because actions are seen to emerge directly from the internationalization of social norms and practice. It limits an individual to reproducing only what they know. There is very little emphasis in his work of critical questioning or of transformation of an existing status quo and any role for human self-determination in generating actions that can interrupt and interrogate the field. So, for example, Nick Crossley (2001) makes the point that Bourdieu provides no theoretical means of connecting 'embodied dispositions' to personal acts of thinking and reflecting, of agency, and 'offers us relatively little in the way of an analytic toolbox for opening up and exploring the subjective side of the social world' (p. 98). Campbell Webb et al. (2002) defined agency as 'the idea that individuals are equipped with the ability to understand and control their own actions, regardless of the circumstances of their lives' (p. ix). Our stories of success are built on the premise of agency and of the possibilities of transformation, as we discuss in further chapters.

A second issue arises with the ideas involved in social mobility, the idea that – to succeed – one must acquire and accumulate both the economic and cultural capital required to move up through the hierarchy and social order. There are very few studies to examine what happens to social or cultural capital when mobility is downward. That is, what exactly happens to that accumulation of capital, the knowledge, skills, expressions, the social connections and networks and so on when – through certain circumstances – a family or a person ends up at the bottom of the hierarchy? One instance of this might be where families move countries, particularly when middle-class families become working-class in their new country of adoption. What exactly happens to the capital then? It is a stubborn mathematical fact that the top fifth of the income distribution in the UK can accommodate only 20 per cent of the population. If we want more poor young people and families to climb the ladder of relative mobility, we need more rich people sliding down the chutes. The question, though, is what happens to their store of capital when this happens? Does it simply evaporate?

Immigrants to a country, especially one that is more industrialized and more developed, means that they are more likely to work in low-skilled occupations, and in many cases, they have lower employment rates and experience higher unemployment than other sectors of the population. Their downward mobility is largely attributed to four factors: language barriers, differences in educational attainment, difficulties obtaining recognition for credentials and experience gained abroad and problems accessing opportunities through social networks and other recruitment channels (Papademetriou, Sumption & Somerville, 2009). The extent to which they remain confined to these jobs at the *bottom of the ladder* matters. It affects social cohesion, since integration and assimilation are difficult when immigrants are marginalized in the labour market. In many cases, some of which we document here, it is the second generation, their children, who take advantage of the opportunities provided by immigration. In general, the second generation is more economically successful than the first generation, and in some countries, such as the United States and Canada, second-generation workers currently outperform their non-immigrant peers in terms of education and earnings.

Balancing cultures

It is worth another comment here on the ways in which our women participants have balanced their cultures. At the individual level, the process of acculturation refers to the socialization processes that take place by which individuals blend the values, customs, norms, cultural attitudes and behaviours of their heritage with those of the majority culture. As we mentioned in Chapter 1, in our case such a blend is, to a large extent, determined by a three-way interplay of the individual's traditional home culture, the culture of the UK and the culture of science. And science was seen as important. A dominant theme in our participants' responses to our questions was that an academic career would be the best path through which to realize their scientific interests and goals, fulfil the promise of their training and become a leader in science. Directly or indirectly, the female students in this study expressed a desire *to have it all*, an amazing scientific career and a rich family life. In this sense, as we illustrated in Chapter 2, Sci-ID is a multiperspective, multimodal, complex, personal and social endeavour. Ours is not a stand-alone position in that we relate solely to a south Asian context. Sci-ID embraces social aspects and personal perspectives incorporating multi-level cultural dimensions, becoming an important part of learning science that complements formal education.

We also noted in Chapter 1 that not all of our participants saw their lives in terms of *power barriers*. In several of their comments, they did not necessarily feel the overt exercise of social power in their lives. They tended to attribute any perceived difficulties as cultural differences rather than stemming from uneven power relations and of them being in subordinate or marginalized positions in society. In this sense, culturalization is a process where given situations, problems or differences are interpreted and explained on the basis of generalized cultural interpretations, rather than structural and institutional mechanisms related to individual and social positions (Rugkåsa, Ylvisaker & Eide, 2018). This leads us to our actor-centred perspective, whereby concepts like identity and belonging – rather than subordination and marginalization – are viewed as central to our analysis. We have already used this quote from Ayesha, but it is worth repeating her in a slightly different context:

> Ayesha: I moved from Bangladesh to India, then to Portugal and then I came here. So as a British girl I say that I have lived in England enough to know what British values are, and I have incorporated them into my life, you know, like I will show tolerance to people because obviously I want the same thing back from them.

Incorporation, for Ayesha, means adopting local values as much as she can so that she becomes as British as possible and expect that she is treated as such. Fawziyya, a university undergraduate, sought a different combination:

> Fawziyya: I like so many things of my own culture, my parents' attitudes, the food, the clothes – the jewellery! I know it sounds so . . . well, superficial . . . but I simply love jewellery. In another life I would be a jeweller and make it all myself. And it's nice to stand out in a group, you know, in a crowd, in beautiful colourful clothes. I think English people dress so drab. It's odd, isn't it? – I want to blend in yet I want to stand out at the same time!

She captures the tension between being confident and assertive within her parental heritage, wanting to showcase this in certain circumstances and yet appreciating that *standing out* may also be antithetical to *blending in*.

Ifrah is a science undergraduate:

> Ifrah: A white lab coat is wonderful. It's THE science uniform, isn't it? It covers
> over everything else you are wearing, protects your clothing from all the
> spills and stains but it also makes everyone look just the same. If I wear a lab
> hat, too, with safety glasses then I am no different to anyone else. They can't
> tell where I come from. So, then we are just doing science, it is the science
> that matters then, not the people.

In our view, this is an expression of *wanting it all* – indeed, in *having it all*. Ifrah
enjoys the anonymity that arises through the uniformity of laboratory clothing
that allows her to be indistinguishable from her peers working in the same
laboratory space, and it enables her to focus simply on the task at hand without
being distracted by other issues. We discuss *wearing the culture of science* in
the next chapters though we herald it here where Ifrah quite literally wears the
clothing culture of science. She is able to be a scientist above all else; she can be
both herself and a scientist at the same time.

Sonia's parents are both working people, her father a local council
administrator, her mother works in a small gift shop. They are enormously
proud and supportive of her being at university, as is all the extended family
– she is the first in the family to take up a university place. We have explored
some of the issues surrounding *first-generation* university students elsewhere
(Wainwright & Watts, 2019), and we see Sonia as being very similar to past
student participants in this respect. She is working at balancing several cultures
all at once:

> Sonia: I didn't know what to expect when I came to university . . . a load of rich
> kids, I think! But they're not, there's a lot just like me and my family. Oh,
> there are some snotty one's OK, but there's enough of my kind to allow me
> to fit in. It's really funny. It is a very different place to what I was expecting –
> I don't actually know what I was expecting! – and the lecturers are great.
> And there are lots of others who have to work part time like me. But the
> whole place is strange at the same time. The campus is strange, it took me a
> while to find my way around. The labs are strange places, there are doctoral
> students around and they can be tough on you, I have to get used to where I
> can do my prayers. So, I have to work hard to keep it all together!!

Sonia is a practising Muslim and made several references to her need to observe
her religious practices while within a secular university context. She knew of
the Meeting House where she could pray within comfortable surroundings, but
her lecture schedule did not always allow her time to do this as appropriate.

She mentioned that, on occasions, she would find a secluded stairwell where she could pray without being disturbed. She found the central student services very helpful in advising on how best to manage, to *juggle*, her studies with her new-found hobbies and the expectations she drew from her family culture. Like Ramia described later in this chapter, she was not a woman who saw particular power differentials in her life (besides officious postgraduates in the lab); she saw cultural differences rather than social barriers.

> Ramia: I'm a bit like my Mum, I'm a bossy woman. I pity my poor Dad, {laughs} we both get at him! Mum and I won't take anything for anyone, we both have big opinions, and we aren't afraid to say them out loud. Maybe I'm even worse than she is, with my siblings and my friends. I am the eldest and so I have a right to boss them around! I think they're really glad when I'm at uni. I say a lot in class, I say a lot out of class. I don't want to let anything get in my way, I want a good degree, a good job, a good marriage. I may be different to other people, but I want the same things . . . a good life, I guess.

Finally, we present some more of the conversation with Fawzziya. She already has a science degree and is now training to be a science teacher in order, she says, to give back to her local neighbourhood:

> Fawzziya: I want to give something back, you know, to my community. I think I can do that by being a good teacher. Give other kids what I got from my parents. I got a lot, my values, my religion, my ideas, my education. And education is vital and so I want to make sure other kids get some of what I got. Especially science. There are so few science teachers in primary schools, I want to make a difference.

This is a recurring theme within stories of success and appears in many of the conversations with these women – there is a strong altruistic streak in many of their accounts. This altruism takes the shape, as here, of working within a community, of being a nurse or doctor, using one's achievements in science to benefit society at large or closer to home. We explore this again in later chapters.

Chapter summary

Before we leave this discussion of the family influences on women in science, a word about achievement motivation. This is the desire to accomplish a difficult task, overcome obstacles and attain a high standard. There is some evidence that high-achievement motivation coupled to a low fear of failure is a recipe for success in reaching goals (Tseng & Carter, 1970). These authors show that achievement motivation is essential for – and is related to – female students' decision to go into mathematics, science and technology-related occupations. It is expected that the higher the achievement motivation of the female students the more likely they will choose science, mathematics and technology occupations. That the students' achievement motivation significantly predicts their career choices brings the need to encourage the female students and develop in them high-achievement motivation so that they can overcome any barriers or obstacles of occupational stereotyping – both in Asian society and society more generally. With this, more female students will be able to go into wider range of careers and occupations according to their interests and abilities. Given the stories from our participants, it is certainly the case that parents and families are instrumental in urging daughters and sisters to be confident, to see failures as lessons, to look to achieve as much as possible.

4

Engagement with the Culture of Science

In Chapter 1 we introduced key ingredients to our understanding of intersectionality as a theory, bringing together ideas on *intersectionality as personal, culture of science* and *the nature of success*. In this chapter, we discuss further the culture of science, its interaction with other cultures, its role in our formulation of intersectionality and ways in which these play into ideas of *science literacy*.

The first point to note about the culture of science is that, like any other culture, it is really not homogenous, firmly fixed or fully organized. Instead, it is heterogeneous, fluid and dispersed in and across both the disciplines of science in themselves and in people's lives. In addition, the culture of science is not a separate entity; rather, it is part of, and embedded within, our wider *everyday culture*. We refer to the latter as everyday culture and include in this *everydayness* the issues of gender, ethnicity, nationality, race, religion, social class and so on. Our second point is that these everyday cultural engagement with science is not something general – there is no exact sameness or singularity within certain group of people even though they may exhibit sameness in other respects. For example, while people may share the same visible characteristics – for example, being female or male, dark or light skin colour, wearing headscarf, bindi, baseball caps or hoodies – this does not automatically mean that they also share the same invisible characteristics (personalized values, ambitions, traditions or sentiments). More important, as in previous chapters, we emphasize that the interaction of science with culture cannot be singular. Instead, the engagements of science overlap with varying cultures at different levels – some cultures have a greater propensity for scientific and technological development than do others. There have been some interesting studies, for example, on the varied use of smartphone technologies in Brazil, Italy and Ireland (Garvey & Miller, 2021). These three very different cultures respond quite distinctively to a global phenomenon, the ubiquitous smartphone. In Ireland, for example, the availability of this technology looked to be increasing the capacity of the extended family rather than decreasing it, reversing the trend of many decades. That is, it enabled relationships between generations and multiple strands of the family tree that had previously shrunk to nuclear family size. The important element here is that accommodation to a powerful worldwide system lies in the hands of the individual as they craft their own lives. These two points allow us to ground our theory of science identity (Sci-ID) and to study people's science lives at the micro (personal) level.

In Figure 3, we pull together facets of everyday culture and Sci-ID following on from the metaphor of diffusion we presented in Chapter 1. To illustrate fluidity and dispersion at a personal level, we use dotted lines to represent permeability among family cultures, UK cultures and the culture of science. This overlapping of permeable cultures is also influenced by intersection of large-scale social categories (ethnicity, gender, nationality, race, religion, social class, etc.).

As we began in other chapters, we now introduce some more of our participants – in particular those who are highlighted in this and the upcoming chapters (Table 4).

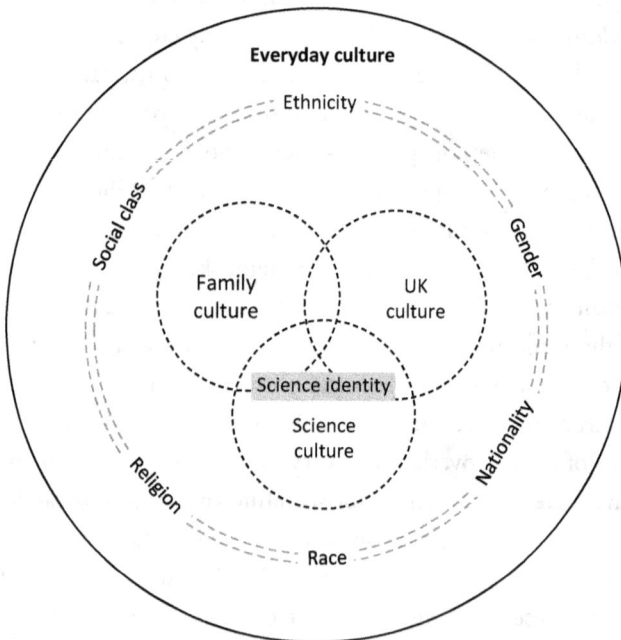

Figure 3 Everyday culture.

Table 4 Five more participants

	Place of Birth	Self-Designation
Amal	India	Science student (A-level)
Fiza	Spain	Yr11 GCSE student
Iman	England	Science student (A-level)
Lubna	Scotland	Pharmacist and student teacher
Zaynab	Pakistan	Scientist mother

Of the five south Asian women mentioned earlier, pen portraits of four are as follows:

Amal was born in India and came to England as a two-year-old child. At the time of writing, she is an eighteen-year-old A-level student. Amal views herself as a high-achieving student from primary school age. She was (and is) interested in learning science, loved school science, consistently achieved high marks in science and maths exams and her parents wanted her to get into medical school. Still, she did not pursue science at A-levels, not because she hates science but rather because her passion is to become an Islamic scholar/teacher (Alima). So, the last time we met her, she is studying A-level Islamic studies, English and history. Despite her non-science-oriented educational and career directions, Amal's engagement with the science culture intermingles with the culture of religion very strongly. She self-willingly studies the biological parts of science and is always passionate about connecting science with Islam teaching, that is, connecting the disciplinary and interdisciplinary science. As Amal believes that the 'Quran and Hadith can answer all the scientific queries and support human's scientific explorations for living and leading a successful life'.

Fiza is a seventeen-year-old final-year GCSE student. She was born in Spain and moved to England at seven. She portrays a strong English literature/ language predilection, overshadowing other subjects she studies at school. Initially, she hated science and did not appreciate the importance of science in her life. But over time, she entered the science culture with the help of school science teaching and learning activities. This change is (somewhat) influenced by the compulsory nature of science to be learned and examined at the GCSE level. Fiza mentions that her family does not dictate her educational decisions. Still, she views herself as an active part of her English-literature-loving family. Moreover, like Amal, the necessity of scientific teachings and discoveries is less vital in her life than Islamic teachings and revelations; still she does not deny (anymore) that science is an integral feature of her life.

Iman was born in England and she recalls that, even from age six, she has been immersed in science learning and always saw herself as studying and working within the disciplines of science. Iman sees herself as a religious and obedient daughter of her Pakistani-born parents. Regardless, according to Iman, her parents and community do not influence her interest and decisions towards becoming a heart surgeon. From thirteen to date (seventeen), Iman has been determined to become a heart surgeon. However, there was a slight dip in her immersion in science at age fourteen when she achieved relatively poor exam grades in sciences. After a period of self-reflection, she worked extremely hard to gain better grades in GCSE science. This hard work paid off, as she continued with A-level sciences, including biology and chemistry.

Zaynab is in her early forties and a mother of two children. Neither of her parents studied science after school, and she is the first person in her immediate and extended family to study science at university. Her fascination was always to become a doctor, but her parents could not afford to send her to a medical school. She could have left studying due to financial issues, but she continued studying science subjects with financial support from the college and university. She completed her MSc in chemistry in Pakistan and worked as an A-level chemistry teacher in a British private school, then left teaching after getting married to a medical doctor before residing in England. Currently, most of her time is spent looking after her young children and household. She stays in touch with science by reading about new research in the medical field and psychiatry studies. Nowadays, Zaynab is interested in exploring the science behind gardening, and she confidently intersects her south Asian and UK cultures with the culture of science.

Everyday science

In this chapter, we first make a distinction between the formal disciplines of science and *everyday science*. Formal science can be seen as the construction of reliable knowledge that has evolved through a system of disciplines. 'Smaller' disciplines such as statistics or computer science can be defined as 'enablers' (Wilson, 2022) in relation to the 'big' disciplines of – for example – mathematics, philosophy, the physical or biological sciences, the socio-economic or the environmental sciences. It is even possible, then, to add professional disciplines such as medicine and law. These disciplinary areas subdivide and then subdivide further, usually through a number of increasingly specialized layers. On the other hand, everyday science is inherently interdisciplinary so that conversations, discussions, explanations, debates, arguments, understandings of phenomena in the world around us draw upon a wide range of background knowledge from a wide range of sources. So, for instance, a discussion of air quality in an area around a local primary school might incorporate measurements and monitoring of air pollution at different time of the day, week, month, year; the nature and chemistry of particles; issues of respiratory health and susceptibility; the nature of disease; formulations of risk; matters of traffic management and control; local politics; and so forth.

The study of disciplinary science is most commonly arrived at through formal systems of education – schools, colleges, universities, commercial companies, science organizations and such like. Science literacy, though, is constructed much less formally and is usually drawn from reading, TV programmes, leaflets, discussions with specialists, internet searches, visits to museums and galleries and so on. The diagram later in the text from the work of Yujuan Luo (2022) illustrates this (Figure 4).

While purposive, formal learning of science most commonly arises through formal institutional settings, there are many other informal means and situations through which learning science takes place at both an individual and group level.

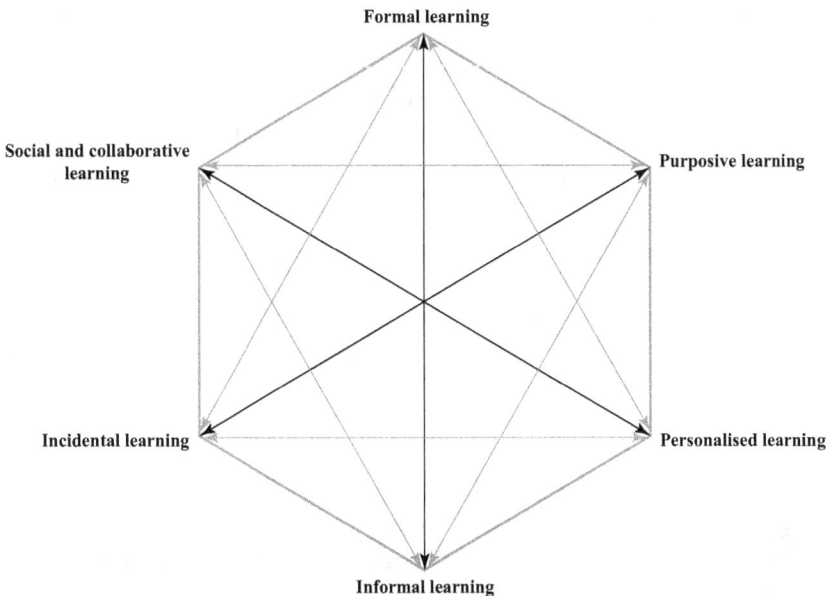

Figure 4 Intersecting formal and informal science. *Source*: Luo (2022)

A further point needs to be made: being a specialist scientist does not mean being a *specialist in all and every part of science*. We made this point earlier. Specialist scientists in cosmology, gene biology, chemical engineering, agronomy or earth science may in actuality have relatively poor knowledge outside of their specialist field and, therefore, relatively poor science literacy. So, in our view, specialist formal science is a subset of the broader, wider culture of science. We positioned our *missions* as science educators in Chapter 1 and in later chapters we discuss more fully how our work relates both to the study of specialisms within science and the more general issues of developing strong science literacy and science success more generally.

Our professional participants, for example, Leah as a chemical engineer in industry and Najma as a doctor in a health centre, are already successful in their own branch of science, be that as a chemical engineer, medical consultant, science educator or whatever. They also live in everyday culture – with its infusion of science – and their specialist knowledge may give them some insights into other disciplines and fields of science – or may not. That is, while they may probably have some success in the wider sense of science literacy, this is not a given.

Our discussion in this chapter explores our participants' engagement with, and immersion within, their science specialist and the everyday science in their lives. We support this discussion with many more stories, highlighting the intersection of their immediate lives (including their perception of ethnicity, gender, race, religion, social class) with their perceptions of science. We then make use of Anne Phillips's metaphor, the *wearing of a culture*, to deepen our understanding of these intersections of everyday life with science. Phillips makes the case that a culture can be *worn heavily*, *moderately* or *lightly* by people, and we look to explore what this means through our participants' stories. First, though, we challenge the idea of science as a separate culture.

A criticism of *discrete cultures*

As we have argued, science, its practices and institutions are a very particular subset of – and embedded within – everyday culture as a whole (Gieryn, 1999; Bly, 2010). So far, we have envisaged this simply as two intersecting circles, science intersecting with everyday society or, as described earlier, as one circle (science) lying inside the other (everyday life). As Psillos (2018) points out, this could be reasonably straightforward if we knew exactly what scientific knowledge is and what comprises everyday (non-scientific) life. However, both are infinitely hazy and ill-defined. A similar two-circle diagram could be constructed for *science* and arts, given that they are often seen as separate and at odds with each other. Thus, for example, the Arts and Humanities Research Council (AHRC, 2021), a major UK government funding agency, initiates regular annual calls for funding bids on 'Science in Culture' to develop the 'reciprocal relationship between the sciences on the one hand and arts and humanities on the other' (np, online). This suggests that these two areas of knowledge belong by default to different cultural research paradigms – a throwback, perhaps, to C. P. Snow's 'two cultures' being still alive and well in the West.

Given our opening chapters, it will come as no surprise that this is not how we picture science, arts or everyday life. Ours is a *diffusion model* wherein science, arts, humanities, cultures, life and all else intermingle in shifting combinations and constellations. We have already mentioned Pauline Garvey and Daniel Miller's (2021) description of the advent of smartphones in the lives of older generations of people in Ireland and the accompanying volumes about smartphone use in Italy, Brazil and the UK. There is a general wisdom that old people are traditionally clumsy and inept where new ideas and new technologies are concerned; they are not the *digital natives* of modern society and so lack the adroit facilities that the young seem to enjoy in abundance. But what is the reality? How accomplished are older people with the ideas of touchscreen technology, apps, multimedia presentations, voice activation, search engines, predictive text and much, much more? The answer is that this technological device, with all of its associated scientific wizardry, has been very successfully subsumed into everyday life, whether this entails organizing group activities through WhatsApp, Googling for health information, Facetime with children and grandchildren, checking destinations through online maps, making travel arrangements and so on. The important point here is not whether a smartphone is actually science or technology, but the ways in which it is absorbed within, that is diffused throughout, everyday culture. Our argument is that, like smartphones, science itself becomes an integral and embedded part of everyday culture in myriad ways. So, for instance, we are urged to have five a day helpings of fruit and vegetables, be wary of glutens, understand viruses, appreciate the role of insulin in late-onset diabetes, value the efficiency of inoculations, understand issues surrounding global warming and climate change, electric cars, know what fracking for oil entails, avoid obesity, engage with ash dieback disease, grasp the implications of breast cancer or hip replacement surgery and much, much more. This diffusion of science throughout culture, then, means that science is not confined to professional scientists, that is, anyone can enter, reside and grow in the culture of science. So, science is not the authority of a particular elite group of people. Therefore, our participants' stories of engagement with science and their immersion in the wider everyday culture are *personal, agentic, heterogenous and ongoing.*

As in the earlier chapters, we have used the theory of intersectionality as an important way to explore the lived experiences of people. There is no sense that intersections of gender, ethnicity, social class and religion present a *single story* of oppression, discrimination and challenges. Nor do they present a single story of success, privilege or advantage for specific ethnic majority groups. Two decades ago, Gerd Baumann (1996) condemned the use of ethnic identity, or *Asianness*, interchangeably with the 'culture of their [Asian] community'. In his view, this universal view of Asianness means that

> All agency seemed to be absent and culture an imprisoning cocoon or a determining force. Even their children, born, raised and educated in Britain, appeared in print as 'second generation immigrants' or 'second generation Asians' . . . suspended 'between two cultures'. (p. 1)

In our view, Bauman is highlighting a case of *ethnic reductionism*, where Asian communities are reduced to a single stereotypical view. It is a reductionism that denies the complexity of personal agency of (south) Asian people. As our many participants here attest, south Asian culture cannot be reduced to a single insulated entity because it not only houses a range of significantly diverse cultures within itself, but it also overlaps with at least two other cultures (UK and science). So, we believe that there is enormous variety and diversity in practices, viewpoints and attachments of people in everyday life, as well as in and around science. This occurs at a community, family and personal level – and allows us to tie back to our concept of *intersectionality as personal.*

This returns us to our need to rebalance the discussion of the social versus the personal. Our sense is that Baumann's ethnic reductionism is determined largely by analyses of the macro forces acting at national (and international) levels towards what it means to be (south) Asian. This analysis, in turn, informs the possibilities of inclusion and exclusion of individuals in their engagement in the culture of science. This is not the direction we follow. Cultural paradigms that promote a singular categorization of specific groups within – or outside of – science commonly result in divisions between the majority (men, White and elite) and the minority (women, non-White and non-elite) groups. Instead, Bauman's (1996) view entails a greater sense of agency, similar in many ways to our own description (Salehjee & Watts, 2018, 2020). So, aligning ourselves with Karine Chemla and Evelyn Fox Keller (2017) and Phillips (2010), we bring ourselves in line with Max Maddock (1981), who wrote,

> science and science education are cultural enterprises which form a part of the wider cultural matrix of society and that educational considerations concerning science must be made in the light of this wider perspective. (p. 1)

Maddock's *wider perspective* is one not confined to two or three fixed cultures, for example, between science culture, family culture and the UK culture; rather, as Stephen Jay Gould says,

> science is an integral part of [all everyday] culture. It's not this foreign thing, done by an arcane priesthood. It's one of the glories of the human intellectual tradition. (Gould & King, 1998, p. 1)

In the next section, we present the ways in which the culture of science intermingles with other cultures while simultaneously operating in a wider everyday culture exhibiting scientific literacy attributes. We do this through presenting the story of Zaynab. Zaynab's engagement with, and immersion in, the *science of gardening* features her intersections with science culture as well that of her family and British cultures.

Everyday science: Action at a personal level

We have already drawn attention to the fact that science itself is not a homogenous entity; it is not a singular self-contained body of knowledge. Numerous concerns and criticisms to be found in science education books and articles make the same point: they illustrate the similarities and dissimilarities, for example, between science knowledge and the practices of different scientists – even within the same scientific disciplines and contexts. For example, the knowledge and practices of physicists would commonly be seen to differ from those of a microbiologist; the physicists of Western countries would differ in their practices from non-Western countries physicists, or an acoustic physicist's knowledge and procedures would vary from the physicist working as an astronomer (Chelma & Keller, 2017). We are ourselves guilty at times of reductionism when we refer simply to *science* rather, say, than *the sciences*. However, our overarching aim is to capture the intersections of personalized principles, self-beliefs and expectations, actions, decisions and attitudes of people, of south Asian women, towards science in general (as much as there is such a thing). Therefore, given our discussions so far, we feel exonerated in those times when we make simplified references to science.

The south Asian women participants in this chapter range from British young school-aged women, to university students, and to professionals working as chemists, biochemists, medical doctors, nurses, engineers, educators, school science teachers, scientific mothers and so on. This broad range of participants allows us to confirm our previously mentioned declarations:

- First, that the culture of science is not confined to professional scientists, that is, anyone can enter, reside and grow in this culture. So, as Maddock said earlier, science is not the authority of a particular elite group of people, and
- Second, the stories of engagement with the science culture and its immersion into the wider everyday culture are personal, agentic, heterogenous and ongoing.

We have already discussed the first, the culture of science, and so our aim here is to further detail the second declaration by elaborating on our view of everyday culture. Heterogeneity in the second declaration does not imply there is no resemblance at all between south Asian traditions, values and practices. Within particular groups, these traditions, values and practices can become unique due to the ways in which people perceive and engage with them in their lives. Moreover, stories of engagement of different kinds are strewn throughout our data. For example, Lubna attends almost all the extended family gatherings and takes these as opportunities to act as a 'community pharmacist'. She regularly talks with her community about medicine, south Asian diets, eating habits and associated side effects. She likes to think she is having an impact even though she is aware that not all her community members are prepared to take her advice. In contrast, Leah and Saarya both stay distanced from their Kashmiri and Sri Lankan communities; they seldom share their scientific knowledge, enthusiasm and practices – not least because their respective communities have been markedly anti-science in the past. Both women have faced criticism for their so-called *unusual choices* of science education and science careers, and this criticism has been seen as an unwelcome intervention in their private lives.

Chemla and Keller (2017) in their book *Cultures without Culturalism: The Making of Scientific Knowledge* use three main assertions in tune with our second point described earlier. However, unlike the wide range of our south Asian women participants, Chemla and Keller's work is focused on professional scientists only.

Nevertheless, their assertions usefully supplement our understandings. Their three assertions are that the culture of science is

- forged by actors in relation to the questions they address, the goals they address themselves, and the resources [e.g. scientific knowledge and skills] they have available and which they recycle
- in constant interaction with other cultures [e.g. family, UK culture] and the external environment [i.e. social forces including gender, ethnicity, social class, religion] and for that very reason
- more open rather than it is closed. (p. 22)

The expressions Chemla and Keller use, 'forged by actors', mirrors our own inclination towards everyday science where people construct explanations in response to – implicit or explicit – questions and do so as 'active, self-directed, and constructive learner[s]' (Salehjee & Watts, 2020, p. 53). Moreover, people read, write, talk and make meaning of the science-related questions of which they are curious and for which they *feel the need to know*.

Chemla and Keller also use the terms 'address' and 'recycle', maintaining that over time people use or even extend their existing scientific knowledge and skills. The questioning, reading/writing/talking, meaning-making, addressing and recycling scientific knowledge practices are not stagnant; instead, they grow over time, even in a disorganized manner (Watts, 2015).

Figure 5 summarizes this section focusing on the ways individuals conceptualize everyday science, work as a scientific literate person, so to develop Sci-ID.

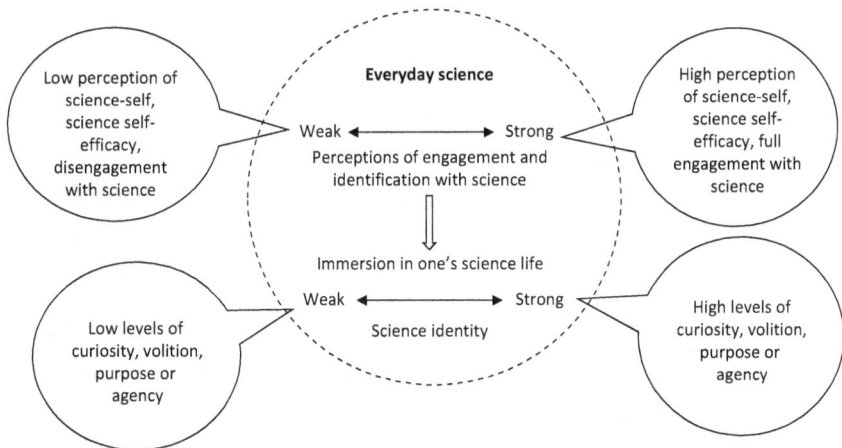

Figure 5 Everyday science.

Figure 5 broadly indicates two key steps leading to Sci-ID:

1. An individual's perceptions of her own engagement and identification with science, that is, how she sees herself in terms of science. This self-perception of science engagement and identification lies on a spectrum ranging from weak to strong. On the weak side of the spectrum lie low perceptions of science-self, science self-efficacy and non-engagement or disengagement with science. The other end signifies strong features like high perception of science-self, science self-efficacy and full engagement with science.

2. This weak or strong engagement and identification with science in turn also determines their immersion in science, that is, intentional engagement with science and having a strong science life with an appreciation of scientific literacy in life and so a strong Sci-ID. The strong side of the spectrum corresponds to an individual's deeper immersion in everyday science, exhibiting a high level of curiosity, volition, purpose and agency towards engagement with science and/or appreciation of the impact of science in their lives. On the other hand, the weak side of the spectrum exhibits individuals' *surface immersion* in science, portraying low levels of curiosity, volition, purpose and agency towards engagement with science and/or appreciation in their lives.

Sci-ID, then, is a composite notion of perception, preference, individual's personhood, self-identification, self-narrated stories and agency as people engage, identify and live a science life (Salehjee & Watts, 2018, 2020). Having said that, we acknowledge there are individuals who can be perceived as having *no* Sci-ID, which could (or not) intersect with their perceptions and practices of the varying cultural facets mentioned earlier. For example, 'I have nothing to do with science . . . I even don't do gardening because it will mess up with my painted fingernails' (Danielle) (Salehjee & Watts, 2015). However, we argue that people like Danielle do not always give a true indication of their immersion in science culture – because people do not live in a science-free vacuum. Rather they are engaged and immersed in everyday science in various ways. For example:

*   'We argue about acrylic nails or about camera sensors in their phones' (Arshi).
*   'There's big self-interest in the science of bicycles, motorbikes and cars' (Saarya).
*   'An inclination for numbers and patterns by predicting the probability of deaths within a month while standing at the graveyard' (Salma).

- 'Count the amount and types of the different species of butterflies in their local park and reporting it to the "Big Butterfly Count" UK-based survey' (Hanya).

Everyday science: Zaynab's story

Zaynab is a scientist mum. Her family recently moved to a new house in the south side of London where she is a tenant with a 'small but a very demanding garden'. During our initial conversations, Zaynab mentioned that she is a first-time gardener and has no previous interest in gardening. However, she felt the need to maintain the garden properly because

> There is a clause in the tenancy contract that the garden, especially the rose plants, apple and pear trees, need to be well maintained; otherwise, it will be a breach of contract. So, it is enforced on us – not our choice.

Over the next three months, we had three extensive conversations (once each month) with Zaynab about settling in the new house; in all these conversations, gardening always took a great portion of our time.

Zooming in to the first part of Figure 5, we see Zaynab's *self-perceptions, engagement and science identification* (step 1) growing towards the strong side of the spectrum. This strong side corresponds to her increasing self-interest and self-efficacy in science through gardening. Zaynab expressed her growing identification of being a science person in various accounts:

> Yes, I believe I was once a science person working in chemistry labs – I am still a science person, I guess, but not much as I was before. This gardening activity reminded me of the herbarium that I made during my BSc course – it's all coming back to me!

We gradually see a transformation in Zaynab's hesitation towards gardening as she enters the second step towards a *deep immersion in science* in her life. She begins to exhibit high levels of curiosity, volition and purpose with the science of gardening as this family activity grew over time. For example, in all of her conversations, we see her paying special attention to *scientific terms and expressions*, such as,

> Using the 'Identify plant' App – I found the name of the Hydrangea shrubs from Google because I wanted to find out how to look after them and found a lot of information, [such as] it is a perineal plant.

Moreover, Zaynab scientific *curiosity* to know more about gardening, led her to view the Royal Horticultural Society (RHS) website and several YouTube videos on *gardening for beginners*. She consumed these online resources sometimes on her own but more commonly with her eleven-year-old daughter and husband.

In addition to the name of the plants and caring instructions of Hydrangea shrubs, Zaynab said in our third conversation:

> I am so glad that I found the rose plants' tags (care cards) [that were not identified by the App]. These rose plants are grown around the rear side of the fence – only the names on the tags were readable, and all the caring instructions have faded. Still, it's very useful as then I found out more about them on YouTube.

In some of our early conversations, she told us about fake brands:

> So many videos were saying that XYZ brand of weed killer is great, five star-ed on Amazon, very popular among Brits, easy to use, and there is no particular need for the gardener to remove the weed manually. We bought this five-star rated weedkiller – and it was rubbish. Nothing happened!

She then demonstrated her *sense of causality* along with various *logical explanations* and *argumentation*. For example, she argued that the brand of weedkiller was useless because she did all the right things, mixed the correct proportions of liquids etc.:

> I was a chemist, so I know how to measure and mix stuff. Of course, even my eleven-year-old can do that.

She then mentioned that the environment was appropriate:

> The high temperature was suitable for the herbicide as mentioned on the box, so it was 30 degrees that day, no rain, and it was not windy for a few days too – still it didn't work.

So, they removed the weeds using the hand tools, though they used the short-handed weeding tool 'as the plants are packed in the small space, requiring more effort.'

Zaynab's engagement with science exhibits agency and an ongoing process, which was not confined to the boundaries of science culture. Rather, her energies permeated the things she was doing, crossed disciplines and intermingled with other cultures. For example, during the conversations on rose plants, she began to recall her father and her birth city, Karachi:

> My father loved roses; after he was back home from the office, he used to sit outside with us and used to talk about them [roses] for hours – we were not

allowed to pluck them as he used to say if you do that, the fragrance in the garden will fade away. My garden's fragrance is not the same as my father's garden. Here [London], there is gardening through different seasons, but back there [Karachi], we had the same roses, Motia [Arabian Jasmine] and Raat ki Rani [Night blooming Jasmine] all year around.

She further talked about plants and their fragrances by intersecting these with her south Asian family culture, for example:

people fill their houses with [mainly] red flowers on the Milad day (Birthday of Prophet Mohammed), during weddings and petals on graves, so the fragrance diffuses all around.

Moreover, she talked about the benefits of rose water as an anti-inflammatory agent for skin and how her grandmother used to decorate rice pudding with rose petals. Moreover, while Zaynab was talking about weeds, she mentioned that she felt she ought not to remove them – because she remembered a particular plant as Morning Glory in Pakistan, rather than it being a weed, and said, 'flora and fauna of Britain are quite different from Pakistan.'

Zaynab's engagement with and immersion in science highlights the cultural facets of ethnicity, nationality and religion, such as in our last conversation, she mentioned that she had

ordered a Mehdi plant – it has a beautiful fragrance – and growing it [a Mehdi plant] will be an experiment! It's [fragrance] has an Islamic tradition too.

She added that the alternative to flowers during religious gatherings is Agarbatti (Oud incense) or Oudh in Arabic traditions.

Overall, Zaynab's narrative about gardening moved along a chain from botanical names to fragrances to weedkillers to chemical compositions – each link accumulating her past and current experiences with plants. We see Zaynab as developing a stronger Sci-ID over time. She is a science-literate person, and her science intermingles with other (family and UK) cultures within the wider everyday culture.

The *wearing* of science culture and science identity

Earlier in the chapter, we used expressions such as 'cultural essentialism', 'erasure of heterogeneity' and 'cultural inability'. We took these from Chemla and Keller (2017) and Bhikhu Parekh (2001), and these terms are associated with the ways people experience the weights of culture as a burden – and sometimes even as a penalty, especially when going against cultural norms. In essence, though, this is contrary to Zaynab's story, where – although tending the garden might initially have been a chore – she grew to enjoy plant biology as she worked the soil.

As we talked to our participants, we sought to gauge just how they felt about the weight of their own culture and the weight of science in their lives. We viewed the impact of this weight on their Sci-ID development – especially those of our participants studying or working in different science-related fields. We discuss this further using Phillips's cultural framework, then present our own adaptations and implementations in our empirical research.

Phillips (2010) set out the idea of a woman 'wearing her culture'. Culture is worn in a weighted fashion: worn 'heavily' by 'those who are deeply embedded in their cultures' or worn 'more lightly' (p. 8), perhaps, by those seeking to move more easily between prevailing (everyday) cultures. In her work, Phillips draws attention to the extent to which a person actually chooses to immerse herself in her own *native* culture. Much of the debate about *cultural immersion* concerns the extent to which an outsider might look to become an insider – might want to share (adopt, appropriate) a culture other than their own. In using this idea, Phillips is also tapping into an age-old debate on the interactions between broad culture and individual personhood – what, two decades ago, Anthony Giddens (1991) termed the duality of agency (micro) and structure (macro). It is evident in the lives of south Asian women that culture weighs differently across individuals and groups (Brah, 1996; Phillips, 2010). While Phillips acknowledges the 'cultural and other pressures' across women's lives, she does assert that women should not be presented as 'captives of culture' or their bodies as a 'passive recipient of cultural meanings' (p. 1):

> everyone has agency, even though some clearly have more options than others. We should, in other words, recognise the agency of women even under conditions of severe oppression and exploitation, and not ignore the choices they make. (p. 11)

Here, Phillips is trading on Giddens's (1991) 'reflexive proposition' that, as much as society has a strong influence on people, each person has the capacity, the personal agency, to shape their lives and, in some small ways, to influence society. Giddens believes that there exists 'ontological security' that gives an individual a 'sense of continuity and order in events' – the *self* is not simply a passive entity, determined solely by external forces.

Moreover, Phillips's wearing can be seen as a measure of Dwight Atkinson's 'surface' 'deep', 'immersion' and 'embeddedness', within cultural heritage concept. Atkinson and Jija Sohn (2013) favouring a 'bottom-up' approach to view culture, in a way, distinguishing between surface and deep immersion in one's culture, where the first is the *visible culture*, understood to be easily observable elements such as language, food, tourist places, geographical sites, national symbols and famous people. Deep (invisible) culture, on the other hand, embodies complex meanings related to socio-cultural norms, lifestyles, beliefs, symbolic and intangible aspects of identity, assumptions and values (Hinkel, 2001; Trujillo Sáenz, 2002). These deeper meanings extend to concern for sensitive topics, for instance, collective and individual attitudes towards dating, honesty, religion, sex roles, independence, interdependence, money, education, justice and injustice.

Phillips's notion of wearing culture, connected to Giddens's duality and reflexive propositioning, along with Atkinson's surface and deep immersion concepts, serves our understanding of *wearing a science* culture, which we set in three broad categories of people, who:

1. *Wear their science culture 'heavily'.* In these individuals' lives, the culture of science is deeply embedded in their everyday culture. Science dominates over their engagement with other cultures and corresponding social categories, such as ethnicity, gender, race, religion and social class. Therefore, an individual's everyday culture is heavily occupied by, or deeply immersed within, scientific values, beliefs, expectations, codes, conventional actions and attitudes.

2. *Wear their science culture 'moderately'.* In the lives of these individuals, the culture of science is moderately embedded in and engaged with their immediate prevailing culture. This category resembles Phillips's wearing of culture as a flexible matter as the individuals show suppleness in moving among the more comprehensive cultural environments. We include this category in addition to those by Phillips.

3. *Wear their science culture 'lightly',* where the intersections of social categories, such as ethnicity, gender, religion, social class, are deeply embedded in and engaged with other cultures (such as, family, UK) embedded within their immediate everyday culture, and the impact of

science culture in their lives is thought to be minimal. The term 'lightly' is adopted from Phillips.

Adhering to the literal concept of wearing science culture, we present five stories of multiaged south Asian women as they wear the science culture heavily, moderately and lightly, but first we will present the data gathering methods, presentation and modes of analysis used in this study.

Our respondents and data

This section of our research involves a study of cases, in two age bands and across two institutions. The sample comprises seven schoolgirls from a secondary school, for whom one of us was their science teacher for two years (2014–16) and so the data collected from them was when they were age thirteen- or fourteen-years-old. The second set of data was collected in 2019, and by this time the girls were aged sixteen or seventeen. In addition, the sample comprises four of our student teachers studying at university (2018–19), who are now newly qualified teachers, all of whom have previously worked in the science industries as scientists. Our respondents are all UK citizens, south Asian, Muslim women and have their early education in the UK.

As with our other participants, these twelve multiaged women have been part of a broad series of parallel sister studies, using a narrative approach and intersectional analysis procedures. We have discussed these approaches earlier in the book. Each interview was one of several with the same respondent; they were not single one-off encounters. They occurred over a period of time, primarily while they were studying with us, but some interviews occurred beyond that point. Each respondent was interviewed at least twice, conversations lasting between forty and seventy minutes. As we have discussed in earlier chapters, all of our participants were assured of full confidentiality, and they were happy with the pseudonyms we have assigned them throughout the writing of this book. In addition, interview conversations with the schoolgirls took place within their school and with student teachers/newly qualified teachers via the Zoom platform, in quiet, private areas, at times convenient to the respondents. Five women of these twelve have been identified here for the clear articulation of their stories and for the issues involved – and their cases are intended, therefore, as illustrative rather than an exhaustive analysis of all the responses we gathered.

The five women are characterized in Table 5.

Table 5 Introduction to the five participant women

Respondent	Age When First Met	Age When Last Met	Profession When First Met	Profession When Last Met
Amal	Fourteen	Eighteen	Year 9 student	A-level student
Fiza	Thirteen	Seventeen	Year 8 Student	A-level student
Iman	Thirteen	Seventeen	Year 8 Student	A-level student
Leah	Twenty-eight	Thirty	Student teacher	Newly qualified teacher
Lubna	Twenty-six	Twenty-seven	Student teacher	Newly qualified teacher

The stories

We present our analysis by showing how these women see themselves in wearing the weight of science culture – heavy, moderate or light – in relation to their surface or deep engagement, identification and immersion into the culture of science.

1. *Wearing their science culture 'heavily'*

Iman

When she was a thirteen-year-old (Year 8) student, Iman was reserved and shy with a high proclivity towards science despite being (by her own and school measures) a rather indifferent science student. On one occasion, Iman mentioned that she wears a headscarf because her mother and sisters wear one. She portrays herself – then and now – as an obedient daughter on different occasions. However, when it comes to science education and career choices, family members have not been influential because none of her parents or older siblings was (and is) interested in science.

In conversation, she mentioned one significant occasion at the age of six, when she was taught at school about human body mechanisms using a human dummy – this led her to self-study about the organs and hormones. This, and related activities in her primary school, inspired her towards becoming a doctor and, more specifically, a heart surgeon. Things, though, started to change with age, Iman's science teacher has become less influential, and her interest in the school science curriculum also waned. During this time (age fourteen), Iman mentioned experiences that might have moved her away from science, for example, when she received poor science examination grades. That said, these poor grades seem to have galvanized her and have had the effect of making her think more critically about her science abilities and her subject choice preferences. This reflection supported her to push back the actions that could have resulted in her not achieving her passion, so she worked 'day and night' to succeed in science exams and tests.

Iman, now aged seventeen, is undertaking A-levels in biology, chemistry and psychology. She regularly watches documentaries on 'any kind of surgery', started to visit medical schools' websites and has online talked to two education counsellors to fulfil her ambition of becoming a (heart) surgeon.

In this first story, we see Iman wearing her science culture heavily through her engagement and identification with the sciences, for example, gaining scientific knowledge not only from school science but also through self-study – expressing a degree of *agentic conformity* towards the culture of science. However, the deep cultural immersion in science, that is, towards becoming a heart surgeon, derived primarily from herself and the school and not from family – in all her conversations, she focused principally on herself and her science lessons, science teachers and science examinations. Thus, we see the minimal interconnection between her passion for becoming a heart surgeon and its engagement with the surrounding family culture and associated practices of her religion.

Lubna

At the time of writing, Lubna is in her late twenties and started to work as a newly qualified teacher of science in a secondary school. The passion for science as the entry into the science culture started early on for Lubna. The earliest memory that she could recall was age eight when her uncle gave her a 'science encyclopaedia' from his study. She passionately read everything about 'atoms and particle physics, genes, RNA, DNA and universe'. The pictures and illustrations mesmerized her attention entirely and, even after twenty years, she has the same encyclopaedia on her bookshelf. During secondary school, she was never doubtful whether she wanted to continue (or not) with the study of science, not least because she used to excel in all her science exams and tests, but also Lubna had a motto:

> There weren't many role models for us [south Asian females], and we, [south Asian female friends] as a group, decided, why can't we be successful in sciences, go into science.

This passion for entering into science and becoming a role model for others sparked in school. Still, during this time, Lubna didn't feel like a *science person* until she joined the university because 'everybody was doing it [school science], so nothing special, and it was just basic science'.

Once Lubna joined the university, she 'loved each and everything about my university life, liked all her lecturers, and class fellows and friends at the university were incredible'. After graduating in pharmacy with first class, Lubna quickly found a job in the community pharmacy services as a locum – the managers there were very supportive and offered her to continue. Still, she didn't like the same day-to-day routine. So, she then worked in a hospital hoping that the job would bring some learning challenges – it did to some extent, and her seniors appreciated her work to the extent that they encouraged her 'to go up the [promotion] band'. Still, her aim of becoming a role model for other south Asian girls was not prospering while working in the hospital. So, while working as a pharmacist, she joined an organization affiliated with the Scottish Parliament which supports the minority groups – especially girls and women – to get into better education and professions. This opportunity started to facilitate her passion for showcasing herself as an ambitious south Asian role model, as a first-in-the-family scientist, to the schoolgirls and boys from low socio-economic south Asian backgrounds. Through this work, her feeling of 'empowering [school-going] girls' and seeing herself putting across her passion grew further. This resulted in a career change – from being a pharmacist to a school science teacher. Currently, she enjoys working as a school science teacher and volunteers at the local council's diversity and inclusion hub.

Lubna, like Iman, wears science culture heavily and shows a substantial *agentic conformity* and her deep immersion into the culture of science through showing a *can-do attitude* towards science aligning firmly with the self-efficacy attribute of science literacy. In addition, to Iman, her vision and self-expectation to become a role model for other south Asian girls from low socio-economic backgrounds to inculcate can-do attitude in other girls like her highlight the intermingling of science and the south Asian cultures influenced mainly by gender, ethnicity, nationality and social class.

2. *Wear their science culture 'moderately'*

Amal

At the age of fourteen, Amal saw herself as a bright and confident Year 9 student – her parents want her to become a doctor. But, Amal never wanted to take up any science subjects at A-level (pre-university) or beyond. In this respect, Amal did not exhibit the image of an *obedient* south Asian girl in pleasing parents who continuously urged her to pursue science-related education and a future career in science, not least because of her impressive science examination grades. Unlike Iman, Amal in school was considered a *top-set student* in science and mathematics. However, her disinterest in science was not because she 'hate[d] science' instead because her inclination was (and is) towards non-science subjects. In addition to excellent exam and test results, Amal also enjoyed science lessons in school science classroom settings because 'science activities are fun'. She liked to learn things she saw to be relevant to her daily life. She was (and is), however, disinterested in most of the science content knowledge.

While praying five times a day and reading the Quran regularly, she was/is also very interested in reading books written by Islamic scholars based on the lives of the twenty-five prophets mentioned in the Quran. She is also a very active member of the school's religious education (RE) club, where her main responsibility is to organize assemblies and update RE assigned display boards. On a few occasions, Amal indicated that her father supported her passion for becoming an Alima (Islamic scholar/teacher). For example, her father asked her what she had 'read about Prophets Adam or Abraham' during family dinner-time conversations, helped her register with online Alima courses and bought related books. Amal believes that Islamic teaching can answer all the scientific questions that a human can enquire about and provides explanations for leading a successful life, including various daily-life activities. For example, previously in science classrooms, we mostly saw her linking the taught topics with Islam such as 'good and bad eating habits', 'helping people [regulating] good hormones [Serotonin]', 'hygiene – and making wudu five times a day [ritual washing]' and so on.

Currently aged eighteen, Amal has taken Islamic studies, English and history at A-level and is still very persistent in exhibiting a strong drive to continue with Islamic studies in university. She sees herself as a future Alima.

We see Amal as wearing her family culture (parental expectations) lightly throughout our conversations while wearing the science culture moderately. She exhibited the ability to bring in Islamic discussions at any point in all our conversations. And she rejected her parent's expectations of becoming a doctor demonstrating *agentic non-conformity* towards her family. Still, she regularly and without any effort links science with the Islamic teachings – exhibiting a strong ability to find and discuss differences and sameness among and between her Islamic and scientific knowledge. Her ability to link Islam with science, in turn, demonstrates her appreciation of science and portrays her engagement with science through argumentation and imagination. During the conversations, we see her wearing the science culture moderately with religion heavily dictating her movement into the culture of science.

Leah

Leah is of mixed race – her mother is south Asian (Kashmiri), and her father is White (English); she identifies herself as a south Asian woman, as she has always lived with her mother. She is fair-skinned and does not share her religious sentiments with colleagues and even friends, so 'I have never felt discriminated on the basis of my ethnicity or religion as it is private'.

Like Iman, Leah's school science was not exceptional – she was not seen as a 'good student' among her science teachers. At age sixteen, when it came to her choosing subjects – at that time, Leah was looking forward to becoming an ophthalmologist – so she took advice from an external career counsellor hired by the school. The counsellor looked at her grades and suggested that she should not seek science courses at university but rather choose subjects in which she has received better grades. But Leah was not looking for this counsel, so she talked to her school's science teacher, who happens to be her pastoral care tutor as well. The pastoral care tutor discouraged her from doing science – even more harshly than the career counsellor. She recalled the conversation in the following way:

> I said to my pastoral care teacher [at school] that I'm interested in science – how do I become a scientist. My pastoral care teacher was just like: 'unless you follow what, you've got good exam results in [Drama and Business Studies] – you're not going to get anywhere. [On the other hand], if you continue with science, I wouldn't be surprised to see you just working in ASDA [a superstore]'.

Leah strongly criticized her pastoral care tutor's 'lack of care and support' towards her as she missed a lot of school during this time because of some personal issues. So rather than taking that into factor, her tutor saw her as a 'problem child' and was confident that she couldn't do well in science. Still, Leah continued talking to other student support organizations and went for interviews at colleges. During one of her interviews, she met a person who saw her passion and persistence of wanting to go into sciences but struggling to get a place because of her grades – so he helped her get into the access programme. This programme was designed for adults aged twenty-two and above, but Leah got a place even at the age of seventeen – which she thinks was 'very lucky for me . . . it made my life'. The tension of, as mentioned earlier, exam grades versus personal interest troubled Leah since, and she took it as a challenge to prove this wrong and so did PhD in crystallization (a branch of chemical engineering).

Like Lubna, Leah took the challenge to act as a role model for other girls like her. Therefore, during her undergraduate and postgraduate university studies, she joined various organizations to enthuse fifth- and sixth-year school pupils into science education. After PhD, Leah joined a university-based science outreach project and, through this project, travelled around the UK, contributing to various science festivals and 'conducting little workshops for all school-aged children'. Further, she joined a recruitment team supporting school students to pursue college or university subjects according to their (students') interests.

After a great university life, Leah joined a pharmaceutical company as a research scientist because she has spent quite some time in research, 'so I should embark into the industry'. Although she quickly realized that her family life would suffer due to the 'unhuman industrial culture', she describes favouring men and women who can work 24/7. Leah's shares her observations of the industry:

> So, all the upper management staffs were men – as expected – and only one White woman. She was a single woman with no partner and family, which gave me the perception that if you want to get on top, this is how you should behave – I actually found that for real as well after I fell pregnant.

During her second year in the industry, it came to the point that Leah was asked to leave the industry when she disclosed that she was pregnant and would like to be removed from those laboratories, which involve carcinogenic materials. Still, she fought back and stayed in the same company for some years until she felt that her managers were adding more to her workload despite seeing her struggling with her current duties. So, after some months of reflection, Leah left the profession and started looking for opportunities to work as a school science teacher.

Currently, she is working in a secondary school as a newly qualified teacher and continues to enthuse her students in the sciences. She is an active scientist mother and aunty at home as she does 'home-based experiments with my [her] daughter and niece to initiate discussions about science' which Leah thinks is important, so they are then 'not scared of science and can talk about it'. She finds it challenging to discuss everyday science with her mother, though, 'who never really went into education'. But Leah still finds ways to talk about science by generalizing the scientific concept a bit further, 'such as the pattern of rain and melting ice-caps'. In addition, she continues to be an activist in a voluntary company for women's rights where she voices her concerns about the industrial 'culture of working crazy hours and [not] understanding the personal needs of family lives of women with families'.

Leah resembles our 'wearing their science culture heavily' respondents Iman and Lubna in various ways, such as: like Iman, Leah was not bright in school science but worked hard to stay in science and acts as a role model for other girls. Moreover, her engagement with the science culture as a science-literate person is very prominent through her continuation with science education after school, practising science at university, pharmaceutical, school science classrooms and home settings.

But still, Leah's conversations portray a huge impact of family culture influenced mainly by gender (women with children) corresponding with the industrial working environment – sadly in a negative way. She said: 'So, if you want to be on top, you need to dedicate everything – there's no way you can have room for a family life.' On the other hand, Lubna (although, like Leah, is a newly qualified teacher) didn't leave the industry because of the negative experiences concerning family life but because it did not fulfil her personal desires. Therefore, we see Leah as, what she calls herself, 'a bridging the gap enthusiast' for young women. But she is wearing her science culture moderately and family culture heavily (motherhood) triggered by the unfavourable industry experiences. For instance, upon asking Leah 'how can we be more inclusive for underrepresented and minority groups in science industries', her viewpoint was 'this is probably never going to happen for women with children'.

3. *Wear their science culture 'lightly'*

Fiza

We met Fiza first when she was thirteen and a Year 8 student. She was then (and still is) serious about her studies, very organized and loves reading English literature. In the beginning, along with the study of English, she wanted to choose mathematics but slowly, throughout our conversations, the choice of mathematics faded. At first, aged thirteen, she exhibited the low influence of parents on her science subject choices at A-levels and beyond. She saw her parents be 'like friends and never have or will force her to choose science or non-science subjects'. Later (aged fourteen), she disclosed that the primary reason for choosing to continue with English is that 'it runs in the family'. Her brother and parents have a strong interest, which was the main trigger in her life that supported her inclination towards English: she wanted to 'live up to them'.

At the end of GCSE year, we asked Fiza about her science practices – she kept it restricted to her GCSE exam preparations and she is a helping hand for her sister 'with science homework and nothing much'. Moreover, she told us previously (at age around fourteen) that in future she will become an English teacher and write/author books; after three years – Fiza aged seventeen – we asked her whether her thoughts have changed, and she said:

> You know, I still believe that, but when I answered these questions before, I used to hate science literally. I never liked it at all; but now I actually enjoy coming to school and doing science, especially biology, but I will still go into English based subjects.

She vaguely started to see the relevance of science in her life, which she completely refused previously. But it was restricted to her GCSE biology textbook's contents. She mentioned:

> So probably while you are cooking – well, now I think of it like temperature, materials used for cooking, cooking handle to be insulators and not conductors – yes, some GCSE biology links with everyday life.

Still, she became increasingly disengaged with school mathematics and decided not to continue with science at A-levels as she believes that science doesn't complement English. Rather she carried out doing history and arts. Furthermore, while she previously believed that a degree in science is important, she now believes that other subjects are equally important for her (and anyone's) future career choices.

Fiza wears family culture heavily, exhibiting *agentic conformity* towards religion. The influence of her family, coupled with her own interests, translates into further study of English and a rejection of gaining and practising scientific knowledge and skills. This rejection into science was reduced over the years, but her engagement with science was limited to the GCSE biology textbook in her recent conversation. Beyond that, her motivation to make meaning of science, enquiring and being curious about science, was very limited. We believe Fiza exhibits *cultural conformity* away from science – as she disowns science culture's immersions in her immediate everyday culture – displaying *agentic non-conformity* towards the science culture – despite the enjoyment, engagement and understanding she gained in science classrooms. In her final statement at the end of our last conversation with Fiza, she stated that

> the world could survive without scientists and scientific discoveries if we properly follow Islamic teachings of living a successful life.

Table 6 Engagement between and within cultures

The Weight of Culture	Strong Science Identity				Weak Science Identity	Cultural Conformity
	Iman	Lubna	Leah	Amal	Fiza	
Heavy	Science	Science	Family		Family	Agentic conformity
Moderate			Science	Science		Agentic conformity
Light	Family	Family		Family	Science	Agentic non-conformity

Table 6 consolidates the stories and personal analyses of our respondents. Within our five case stories we see contrasting views in the weight of cultures embedded within the everyday culture with respect to the: (1) weight of culture corresponding to the immersion of cultures and (2) cultural conformity or non-conformity.

As mentioned earlier, the weight of culture and cultural conformity is linked with the perception of Sci-ID and can determine an individual's strength of Sci-ID. For instance, we see a strong perception of Sci-ID in Iman and Lubna corresponding with high engagement and deep immersion into science and wearing the science culture heavily. At the same time, although wearing the science culture moderately, Leah and Amal exhibit high engagement and deep immersion into science. Amal perceives this immersion to be less deep, and Leah perceives to be immersed into science but less as compared to her previous life – and we see this decline in immersion due to her wearing of the family culture more heavily. Still, we see, both Leah and Amal exhibit strong science engagement, identification, immersion and Sci-ID – though less strong than Iman and Lubna. In contrast, Fiza portrays weak perceptions of engagement, identification and immersion into science along with wearing the science culture lightly – ultimately weak (or no) perception of Sci-ID.

Chapter summary

This chapter has discussed various aspects of everyday culture and the complexity of this wider culture that cannot be generalized or objectified. First, as we maintained our standpoint in previous chapters, we cannot predict and assume the everyday culture embedding various cultures, say, science, family and the UK, to be crossing over identically for a specific group of people with protected characteristics. Why? Because people's lives are personal, their self-perceptions, aspirations, engagements, identifications and immersions into and away from the cultures are personal and unique. Second, we reinstated the concept of cultural facets that influence the ways everyday cultures intermingle at a personal level and used the metaphor of wearing the science culture with our focus to explore the viewpoints of some of our selected participants.

The five stories we discuss reveal many implications for science teaching in schools. For example, we see work done by schools and teachers to achieve *culturally responsive teaching* by transforming any negative attitudes and beliefs based on cultural, gender, ethnic and racial diversities they may hold (Gay, 2013). The impact of women's engagement with the culture of science and acting as role models is a vital implication (Leah and Lubna). Schools can implement schemes where girls engage with global challenges such as health, pollution or addiction in young adults. This would be of high importance for the girls like Lubna and Leah, who are keen to *do something for the women like them*.

Finally, we recommend schools, teachers and curriculum designers should incorporate a culture of science that is not distinct and separated from the other cultures. Instead merges with the other aspects of everyday cultures, such as family and the UK and their influencers, for instance, gender, ethnicity, social class, religion and so on, to which the children can relate.

5

Stories of Success(es) in Sciences

Here in 2022, we are still writing about women from minority groups being under-represented in science postgraduate programmes. Statistics presented by Advance HE (2020), for example, provide details of how ethnic minority women are under-represented in science at school (Grossman & Porche, 2014) and at university (McGee & Bentley, 2017). One of the difficulties we see in this body of work relates to the negativity we have discussed in Chapter 1, as one of our four insertions into the theory of intersectionality. In *The Troubled Success of Black Women in STEM*, Ebony McGee and Lydia Bentley (2017) object strongly to a model of the 'survival-of-the-fittest', that is, that White men predominate in STEM settings simply because they are the best fit for those roles. In this way of thinking, the 'unfit', women of colour are entirely responsible for their own under-representation through complying with commonplace 'stereotypical assumptions' (p. xx). While appreciating the academic successes and resilience of some high achieving women, McGee and Bentley have focused on the downside, their participants' experiences of exhaustion, anxiety, distress, trauma, helplessness. They labelled this 'racial battle fatigue' (Smith, Allen & Danley, 2007) as their participants' ongoing experiences of structural 'racism, sexism, and race-gender bias' in STEM settings (McGee & Bentley, 2017, p. 282). There is a similar negative sense in Wong et al. (2021) study, where he highlights three forms of discourse gained from in-depth interviews with forty-two UK-based ethnic minority undergraduate STEM students. He described these three as naïve, the bystander and the victim. Likewise, in reporting similar ethnic discourses, Jennifer Grossman and Michelle Porche (2014) noted anxiety and distress among Asian American (predominantly Chinese) high school-aged students as barriers to science success, their concerns with structural powers, societal beliefs and assumptions, alongside frequent everyday insults. Grossman and Porche's students held mixed views on whether (or not) there was progress to be seen on aggressive attitudes and the quality of support provided to them by their schools.

In 2007, Carlone and Johnson commented on the persistent inequalities and inequities experienced by – even successful – women of colour (see Chapter 2). We see that still happening today. Summer Finaly and colleagues (2021), in their chapter *From the Margins to the Mainstream* indicated that misrecognition and inequality towards non-Western practitioners and students continues to exist. These are given as examples of how south Asian women's feelings of success are seen by various educators to be affected by the social inequalities they experience in their lives. For example, there still remain firm stereotypes that make women engineers unthinkable – largely because of 'the role allocated to women in modern society as well as pre-existing prejudices that form glass ceilings while encouraging male presence in the workplace' (Dimitriadi, 2013, p. 1). There are elements in society which perceive Indian and Chinese students to be very academically successful and Bangladeshi students to be less so, even though both Indian and Bangladeshi students achieve high examination grades at age sixteen (Wong, 2012). In the context of the United States, Tahseen Shams (2020) indicated that Bangladeshi Muslim parents prefer their children to gain a STEM education – not just because this can bring success in their children's professional lives but also 'because of their feelings of insecurity in light of their stigmatized and racialized Muslim identity' (p. 660) so that STEM subjects would possibly guarantee better employment.

In this chapter we switch the emphasis. Here we highlight south Asian women's experiences and feelings of being successful in science. This returns to our discussion in Chapter 1 of science successes being our third key insertion into the theory of intersectionality and Chapter 2 where being a *science person* and having a *science life* was regarded as successes by some of our participants. It also heralds what we have to say in later chapters about *infusing life with science success*. We have already intimated that being a successful woman of colour is multifaceted and multidirectional. It differs from person to person and from one situation to another (e.g. Carlone, Johnson & Scott, 2015; Carlone & Johnson, 2007). That is, it is both intersectional and personal (Salehjee & Watts, 2022). The science lives depicted so far in the book are *personal intersectional stories* in terms of our participants' lives and their interactions with the culture of science. For example, in Chapter 2, we depicted clear progression in the study of science despite our participants having overt and visible characteristics that might ordinarily not be seen as part of the culture of science. All of the stories so far illustrate intersectional complexities based on situation, context, responsibilities, expectations, obstacles and opportunities that these south Asian women have negotiated in developing their science lives and their science identities. Our aim here is to explore how our participant, south Asian women, navigate their experiences, feelings and actions, and the extent to which they have been motivated, persistent and resilient towards science education and science professions. Moreover, we look to see how everyday culture (including science culture) contributes to both social equality and inequality as catalysts to feelings of success and failure.

Successes in science: Everyday culture prompting social (in)equalities

We see those women from minority groups who do emerge with strong science identities as having perseverance and have been very 'optimistic about overcoming such obstacles' (Grossman & Michelle, 2014, p. 698). They exhibit 'grit' (Duckworth, 2016). Our aim is to reverse the polarity in these discussions, and it is this perseverance, determination, resilience and intrinsic motivation that we feature in this chapter. We want to build on the work in science education that explores the means, strategies, remedies, tactics and approaches used by women as they learn from their own or others' experiences. Some of these strategies will be very evident in the stories we present in this chapter and in the ones to follow. So, for example, Lily Ko, Rachel Kachchaf, Apriel Hodari and Maria Ong (2014) explored the persistence and success of twenty-two women from minority groups who held undergraduate and postgraduate degrees in physics and astronomy. These women recounted their experiences of *social isolation* – but they simultaneously exhibited strong agency by *refusing to be passive* victims of their departmental cultures. Instead, they

> employed multiple forms of agency, including eight navigational strategies: seeking an environment that enabled success, circumventing unsupportive advisors, combating isolation using peer networks, consciously demonstrating abilities to counteract doubt, finding safe spaces for their whole selves, getting out to stay in STEM, remembering their passion for science, and engaging in activism. (p. 171)

This is an exciting list of skills and strategies, and we develop these further, principally through the autobionarratives to come.

Successes in science: Personal uniqueness

Let's meet more of the cast (Table 7).

Table 7 Nine more participants

	Place of Birth	Self-Designation
Anchal	Scotland	Civil engineer
Fariha	Maldives	Home scientist, digital learning consultant
Kulwant	Bangladesh	University undergraduate, microbiology
Najma	Pakistan	General physician
Nyla	England	Microbiologist, full-time mother and carer
Pari	Pakistan	Nurse, professor
Sahar	England	Science student (GCSE)
Salma	Pakistan	Science educator
Sana	Maldives	Science teacher

Four more pen portraits.

Anchal, civil engineer, was born in Mauritius and moved to Scotland when she was one-month-old. Both her parents are senior nurses. Her father moved to Scotland at the age of seventeen in the early 1960s when the National Health Services (NHS) was 'desperately looking for people to join the NHS workforce'. However, her father was interested in being trained as a footballer in the UK. Though, he found his way into the country by receiving a full scholarship to become a nurse and then just worked his way up. Despite Anchal being involved in discussions with her parents involving medicine, NHS and care homes, her recollections were that she never wanted to become a medical professional: 'there is still stereotyping of being Asian in the medical field, which I didn't want to be part of.' She views herself to be a successful engineer from a very young age, mainly in the building and constructions side of engineering, 'building forts and stuff like that, and I was always a bit more creative as well'. At the age of twenty-four, Anchal achieved a master's degree in civil engineering and worked for an onsite construction company. At the time of writing, she is working as a design consultant in a well-reputed civil engineering company. Being a climate activist, enduring everyday engagement with science, she is determined to introduce electric-powered buses all over Scotland.

At the time of writing, Fariha was in her mid-fifties. She had no mother from a young age, so all she had was her father. Her father's main focus was that she gets good education as he used to say: 'you have to get an education; that's how you're going to survive in this world. You may have money and all these things, but it's not going to work if you don't have an education.' Keeping this golden advice, Fariha took computer science at school though wanted to become an engineer, but she was discouraged in school as 'girls don't do engineering', and her father suggested that 'it is better that you become a teacher' instead of an engineer. After her bachelor's and teacher training, Fariha started to teach in the Maldives, soon got married and moved to Canada with a child and husband. Continuing with her science success ladder, she completed her postgraduate degree in computer sciences in Canada. Fariha then moved to London to do a master's followed by a PhD in education. Currently, she is a digital learning consultant at an international college. Most of her time, she reads about new technologies for learning and is involved in the 'art form of scientific activities' such as sewing clothes, bedsheets and quilts and views success as an interdisciplinary (science and arts) learning endeavour.

Nyla was born in England in a Sikh family and always liked to learn about microorganisms in the air, water, soil and animals. She attended local primary and secondary schools before entering university to study microbiology. Soon after her BSc, Nyla began working as an intern in a multinational cosmetic and pharmaceutical company. She was happy with the role and worked in the same company for five years. She became pregnant (aged twenty-six) but subsequently had a miscarriage, followed by her mother having a heart attack. So, Nyla took a six-month break from work but then resigned after that period and dedicated her time to looking after her mother. Nyla is currently forty-seven-years-old; she is a mother of a six-year-old child and has become a full-time caretaker of her elderly mother. Despite two decades of career gap, Nyla views herself as successful by being an active member of a professional microbiological research-based society and voluntarily engages with the publications and activities this microbiology society offers. Currently, she is looking for voluntary work involving science communication to enthuse teenage children into sciences through blog writings and public engagement, such as working in science centres, museums and planetariums.

Pari gained the privilege to be the first Pakistani-born British female professor in nursing, and we see her as a very successful professional and mother. She is the oldest of six siblings and views herself as self-navigating her education and career decisions. She is the oldest in the family and so has served as the role model for her younger siblings. She recalls that she was a 'very sick child' and at that time, her father was working for the Pakistan navy, so she was treated in a navy-based hospital. The one thing and probably the only thing she liked in the hospital was the nurses' elegant and monogrammed white uniforms. So, it was that time when she decided to become a nurse. Though she was never able to wear that uniform, the image of a nurse is still well and alive. After completing her basic school education, Pari completed her training in a highly reputed nursing hospital in Karachi before moving to England in 2004. She worked as a nurse in England and continued her education at a medical college. She later attained her doctorate in health services research and public health and currently works as a professor of nursing in a university and teaching hospital. Nursing is what identifies her the most as despite being a professor, she is 'proud to be identified as a nurse'.

Personal uniqueness, and the strong sense of personal agency that emerges from these biopics, plays a central role in our descriptions of women who are determined to do science and to do well at science. At one level, success for these determined women could simply be the elation at passing science examinations (Delahunty & O'Shea, 2019; Yazedjian et al., 2008), with the corresponding promise of both strong employment choices and feelings of achievement in reaching a significant position in their scientific careers (Pritchard, 2011). Our successful south Asian women participants indicated their firm self-motivation and perseverance, and these constitute what Peggy Pritchard (2011) has called their 'mental toughness'. In Success Strategies for Women in Science, Pritchard describes six elements of success, which include strength, agility, flexibility, balance, proper nutrition and endurance. These six, like Ko, Kachchaf, Hodari and Ong's eight navigational strategies, reinforce a powerful sense of personal agency: drive, belief, values, self-ability, intellectual and emotional resilience and self-affirmation. In one way or another, our participants demonstrate the robust trait of disapproving of any perception of being unwelcome within the culture of science – simply because they belong to minority groups. So, can such disapproval, such structural perceptions, norms and customs become the parameters of science success among women from minority groups? The answer is yes. As these disapprovals take on various forms, such as the determination to change people's stereotypical viewpoints, highlight their presence as women from minority groups in a science environment, self-ability to choose science education and careers, disregard what society expects them to select and pursue and work outside the comfort zone and so on (Chapters 2 and 4). We aim to extend this disapproval in this chapter by presenting real-life examples of our south Asian participants (e.g. under sections on going against the tide; supporting others as a responsibility).

Lucey, Melody and Walkerdine's (2003) 'inner resources' resemble our understanding of personal uniqueness with respect to intrinsic factors such as self-resilience, self-control, self-motivation and relying less on extrinsic factors; 'there are no structural reasons why they [working-class high achieving girls] should succeed and therefore they have to rely on their own inner resources' (p. 297). Moreover, the authors also warn us that these inner resources could drive towards self-destruction:

> These very inner resources which are necessary to success can also be self-destructive and this contradiction needs to be understood in order to assist children and adults in this transition. (p. 297)

We acknowledge the involvement of inner resources necessary for success and sometimes self-destructive as it leads to anxiety, stress and feeling inferior and hopeless because of going against the tide, that is, macro in association with meso forces. For instance, Yumna left the engineering industry (meso force) two decades ago, but still, she shared her worries that even today, are leaving the STEM industries, as Yumna mentioned:

> On some occasions, when I hear someone has moved from the STEM sector [industry], they've moved into an organisation supporting diversity in STEM. [So] I feel gosh that's somebody else that we've lost because they've moved into a non-technical role, now so we've lost that intellectual capacity from a technical role to a non-technical role again.

Moreover, Anchal very recently left the onsite engineering work due to being exposed to sexism, as one of the male colleagues would make her feel incapable and discriminated against her sex, as Anchal says:

> I don't know if this is just the fact that he's probably never seen women onsite or women in a contract office. He just needs to make it seem like, Oh he's a big man, he's in charge when the truth is it's not really like that at all, and he just want to make you feel a bit intimidated a lot of the time, . . ., which isn't a nice feeling at all and this is probably where I did report this kind of behaviour.

And Anchal, even on reporting this act, the colleague was 'just told off' and sent on an 'anger management training, and that's it'.

Still, Yumna, Anchal and other south Asian women, like them, also recorded that they learned/are learning to push away or tackle experiences and resources over time, which could lead to self-destruction, which in turn inhibits their success. And pull in and adhere to experiences and resources, which support positive thoughts and feelings about their abilities and determinations of succeeding in sciences. This pull is supported through participants' involvement with constructive dialogues with peers, critical thinking, questioning and pondering in their everyday lives (Dou et al., 2019; Salehjee & Watts, 2021). For example, Nyla likes to be appreciated by her class fellows during a combined study: 'You teach better than the science teacher.' Leah becomes vocal when she was discriminated against her being a working mother in a male-dominated workplace. Hanya self-queried, 'why do I like chemistry when my exam results are not so good, and it is not very welcoming for women?' On the other hand, Areeb ponders why she feels that mathematics is difficult despite being a top grader as she is an 'A'sian and not 'B'sian. Next, Hannah depicted herself as 'not [intellectually] perfect in whatever I do, but thinking and questioning about science makes me feel satisfied and urges to learn more about different scientific issues'. And Anchal is determined to work in the engineering sector 'to prove that women from a Mauritius background can be successful engineers too'.

Yet more about our research

In this chapter, we have selected stories from four *sister* studies between 2016 and 2020 in five different contexts (meso levels), primary school, secondary school, higher education, STEM industries and informal settings. The twenty-eight participants mentioned later in the text have all looked to take on STEM education from the school age, are studying science at school or STEM subjects at the university, are already in STEM or currently stay at home with a STEM degree. In addition, all our participants exhibit an early passion for science that they have carried throughout their lives – both formally and informally.

Employing the kinds of qualitative approaches, we have already discussed, we interviewed the participants by asking about their successes in their science lives. We probed their answers, where needed, to deepen our understanding and discussed the key objectives of successes in science in relation to the usual social categories of gender, ethnicity, class, religion and so on. We adopted an intra-categorical approach (McCall, 2005) to analyse the data. The limitations of our positionality and trustworthiness of intersectional data were minimized as we describe in Chapter 2. The interviews range from forty to seventy minutes in duration, and our interpretation and analysis focused on how these multiaged south Asian women have learned to enjoy the feelings of success and becoming successful in sciences. We generated five main themes from the data and these are listed in Table 8 alongside the main participants in the study.

The participants represented under each of these headings display some of the key features of successes in science. The data presented here are not generalizable to *all* south Asian women, and the opinions under the five themes do not reveal fixed differences based on age, level of science education, profession and position. Instead, as we highlight in the book, our view of success is personal, independent and intersecting with the everyday culture. Nevertheless, we highlight some broad trends to present the data.

Theme 1. Contentment and happiness

Nine of the twenty-eight participants described how being happy and content in sciences made them feel successful. Yumna, a STEM professional in her early fifties, mentioned that success for her is that she is happy and that the people around her are happy. In terms of her education and career, Yumna thinks that if she has done her job the best, that's success for her:

> Yumna: Umm, education-wise, I think personally is always knowing that you're doing the best you can, and that'll always be a success. If you don't do as well as you can, I think you'd feel disadvantaged or devalued because you have the potential, but you didn't avail it to its fullest. So, I think, if you know that you're doing absolutely everything to succeed, you see yourself successful.

Fariha gives credit to enjoyable experiences in being successful:

> Fariha: The first thing is to be happy in something that I want to do. I want to make my everyday job enjoyable which equals to success.

Amna, a stroke consultant, expanded what Yumna and Fariha say by expressing her own contentment relies upon her personal satisfaction, even when she was a junior doctor, registrar or consultant:

> Amna: For me, success is enjoying work and being good at your profession and having professional satisfaction. For me, satisfaction in becoming a specialist is evident, but conducting a good job even when I was a junior doctor was a success.

Similar to Amna, Leah too acknowledges that success for her is much more than money and positions, and she realizes this more as she gets older:

Table 8 The five themes and participants from the four different settings

Context: Meso Level	Primary School (age 9–10)	Secondary School (age 12–16)	Higher Education (age 21+)	STEM Industry (age 25+)	Home (age 40+)	Responses
Sample Size	5	7	3	9	4	28
Themes						
1. Contentment and happiness	Beena	Hanya	Leah Lubna	Amna Pari Yumna	Fariha Nyla	9
2. Going against the tide	Husna	Areeb Ayesha Shahrazad Zahra	Leah Lubna	Anchal Pari Saarya Yumna		11
3. Supporting others as a responsibility						
(i) Role modelling	Beena	Areeb Hanya Shahrazad	Lubna Kulwant	Anchal Yumna		7
(ii) Being mentored or mentoring	Beena		Leah Lubna	Anchal Pari Saarya Salma Sana Yumna		9
(iii) Being altruistic	Beena Faizan	Areeb Hanya		Anchal Pari Amna		7

4. Being involved in the processes	Beena	Ayesha Areeb Hanya Sahar Shahrazad Zahra	Leah	Anchal Najma Saarya Salma Yumna	Nyla	14
5. Continuing with the informal learning of science	Ayman Beena Husna Meena	Ayesha Areeb Hanya Shahrazad Zahra Khadija		Anchal Salma	Ambala Fariha Nyla Zaynab	16

Leah: Success is being happy in my career and enjoying it rather than money or titles. So, I think it's just about being happy and enjoying what I'm doing because I think that's the most important thing in a career. Because you could have all the money in the world, but if you hate your job, you're not going to be happy going home at the end of the day – it doesn't matter how much money you have.

The professional mothers mentioned here decided they were successful because they could balance their work and home lives. Leah, a scientist mother; Amna, a doctor mother; Pari, a nurse mother; and Yumna, an engineer mother all managed to keep their families secure and well, and this added to their feelings of contentment and success, for example:

Pari: Success is when I'm able to manage my outside as well as my housework. When I have been able to manage all my responsibilities effectively, it is success for me. I'm able to give time to my children. I'm available for them. My house is clean, and I cook food for the family. I am there when family needs me. I meet deadlines outside work, so in summary, when I'm able to balance my profession and motherhood, that is a big success.

Nyla, currently unemployed, believes that being happy is itself a success. She added that happiness could be gained from a satisfying job. But, unlike Amna and Leah, a satisfying job can bring happiness if it also brings in financial stability:

Nyla: Success is having the feeling of fulfilment and happiness and having good health for my child, me and my family – that is a success. Not all but a significant proportion of this happiness relies on being financially stable – [so that] is also a success.

Some participants saw contentment as a decidedly privileged position to be in, certainly compared to their immigrant parents or women living in south Asian countries. For example:

Beena, said: Mum and dad working day and night, [which is] maybe [working] much more than parents born in this country, it puts an impact on me.

In a similar vein, Hanya, aged sixteen, talks about having more opportunities as compared to her parents who were not born in England. Their struggles to succeed in the UK motivates her – she does not want 'to let them down':

Hanya: This motivates me because, if you think ten years ago, my parents were still in Pakistan and didn't have opportunities [as] I do. My mum didn't get to go to college, and my father had to work very hard in this country [England]. They have expectations of me like all parents of immigrants have when they come here, and their children must study hard and get good jobs like any other British person. They have done so much for me; it not only motivates me, but I also understand I have so many opportunities over here. Obviously, I don't want to let them [parents] down and want to prove that I can be productive and successful – as a British-Pakistani Muslim woman.

Similar to Hanya, Lubna also appreciated that she is in a much more fortunate position because she lives in Scotland and is privileged compared to other south Asian women living outside the UK. She did not mention her parents struggle explicitly but

Lubna: Living in Scotland supports my ethnic diversity. I mean, I'm in a very fortunate position even to have an education. So many girls around the world, especially south Asian girls, don't get that opportunity. So, the fact that I've got it [education] – it's a big success. So, I am very fortunate. I've had advantages because I'm Scottish. It doesn't makes me any better than anyone [people living in south Asian countries], but a hundred percent more privileged.

Theme 2. Going against the tide

Eleven of the twenty-eight participants mentioned that managing to *swim against* societal expectations is a success. Several secondary school pupils understood that *going against the tide* was a way of demonstrating self-determination over their own decisions. For example:

Areeb wants to become a surgeon: It could be possible that people won't accept me as a Muslim women and surgeon. I would then need to be modest and show them that I'm not what they think I am, and the stereotypes are wrong. In today's society it seems like that we have to continuously prove ourselves to be worthy of something because we are seen as outsiders to some people.

In similar vein, Shahrazad aspires to become a scientist and sees herself going against the tide. To sustain her determination, she watches inspirational videos:

Shahrazad: I do watch inspirational videos in which women wearing headscarf and women of colour are talking about science.

Ayesha discloses her worries about being a Muslim girl and opting for a non-traditional science education and profession. Simultaneously, though, she believes that studying quantum physics would be a success for her. Moreover, Zahra wants to prove her brothers wrong that she can succeed in physics too:

> Zahra: I have two brothers, and I don't have any sisters. I never wanted a
> sister, and I've grown up among two boys who always talk about maths
> and physics concepts and theories, play games that involve these subjects.
> They never let me be part of their conversation [Laughs] because they said
> 'What you say just can't be true and you don't even understand the basics of
> physics'. Then, subconsciously, I started to like physics and so focused more
> on physics to challenge my brothers that I could do physics too.

Like Zahra, Saarya sees success as being steadfast in her ambitions. Moreover, her success lies in resisting the influence of her family decisions. She is intent on living a happy life so that

> Saarya: I even tell that to my husband when he sometimes tries to influence my
> career decisions; I'm like 'no'. I want to be a technician because, in the end, it
> is my career, my choice. I'm going to be living if for seventy or eighty years
> and I need to be happy, that is important.

Four schoolgirls, Areeb, Ayesha, Husna and Shahrazad, worry that they will most likely be one of very few south Asian women in their future scientific workplaces. Anchal sees this not as a worry but as a success, something she has experienced quite recently. She was one of the very few female students:

> Anchal: In my uni year, when I finished, there were around seventy-seven
> students, and I think there were about just fifteen girls . . . and then
> working onsite where I was one of the two girls in a well-established civil
> engineering industry.

After some unsavoury experiences, Anchal left the industry as we have previously discussed. She is adamant that such *men-oriented STEM industries* must change by transforming the mindset of people working in these industries, particularly those who think that only men can work onsite, and that women engineers, if any, are more suitable for *desk jobs*.

Leah, though, considers that doing something out of her comfort zone itself constitutes a significant success:

> Leah: Involved in talks and science conferences and feeling entirely out of my
> comfort zone and talking to professors and doctors sitting in an audience

who are then going to question your research, well, it was all very nerve-wracking – but very fulfilling.

Lubna worked as a pharmacist. She did not see herself going against the tide because of the support provided to her by her family, friends and colleagues:

> Lubna: The people around me are constantly pushing me and showing me that I can do it. 'You're not any less than anybody else', 'you can do it', and 'you will do it', so I guess that's something that I've had in my life. I know not a lot of people have this push from the family. I know I've had that, so I'm really quite lucky.

Like Lubna, Leah mentioned her non-scientist mother acts as one of the strongest pillars of her science life, and she feels successful and proud in proving her 'mother's family wrong'. Her mother married a White man and then they divorced – but my parent's divorce 'does not mean that I cannot lead a successful life':

> Leah: My mother always motivated me. She always says that you can do more – don't let anybody else tell you what you should or not be doing and that you can do better than me. My mum says 'I don't want you to be like me in that struggle'. So, I think my mother is my motivation for me to just keep going. And I wanted to show my mom's family and everybody that just because I'm mixed-race or my mum, in their opinion, has made incorrect decisions in life, doesn't mean I'm going to be less prosperous than others. I can just be successful, just as successful as the rest and even more – [therefore] I am the only PhD in sciences in the entire family.

Success for Pari is being able to do her job effectively and, more importantly, keeping her self-identity intact. For instance, she wears – and has always worn shalwar kameez – at her workplace as a 'proud British Pakistani' and develops her research in the area of inclusion and diversity:

> Pari: . . . being able to keep your own identity and your own research identity alive, and being able to kind of, you know, perform all your activities. That's more important, so it's not so much about the positions but about respecting yourself.

We have met Yumna in earlier chapters, an early fifties engineer and women activist. She views herself as successful, as are many other women like her, through placing her self-identity at the centre of all her work. She worries that women in STEM sectors are silenced; they do not speak up for themselves or for other minority people. Rather, Yumna is very concerned that, too often, women leave their technical roles and join non-technical organizations:

Yumna: I think many of us are going against the grain in different capacities. I
see that in the engineering and STEM sector. Those [women] that are part
of the STEM sector are still very much part of the same STEM sector . . .
and tend to stay quiet. It's easier for us to speak up and challenge the status
quo and go against the grain when we're not part of that STEM industry
anymore. As an external person, it's easier to voice what's not working, than
when you're part of an institution.

Theme 3. Supporting others as a responsibility

There are three subsections to this theme, role modelling, mentoring and being
altruistic.

1.   Role modelling

Seven of the twenty-eight participants talked about their role models or, in fact,
being a role model for other south Asian women. As we mentioned earlier,
Shahrazad wants to become a Muslim scientist and watches inspirational videos
of successful Muslim women. However, not all the women she believes to be
inspirational are scientists. Still, she looks up to all of them as her role models
because they have successfully gone against the tide and managed to progress
with their ambitions. Areeb chose her science teacher and father – both Muslim
and from south Asian – to be her role models:

Areeb: So, they [teacher and father] are people like me and are successful. So,
I can see them as motivating models, such as my science teacher [born
in Pakistan and a practising Muslim]. My dad inspires me too because he
learned under challenging conditions, unlike me. But, still, he is an engineer
now, which inspires me to do [science] as well.

Anchal mentioned a successful woman, Emma Dixon, who acted as her role
model. Emma is not a British south Asian woman and so Anchal believes it is
her responsibility to set an example for her younger south Asian community.

Anchal: I would love to see more women in higher positions . . . [like] Emma
Dixon. She's probably the most high-up woman in my field. She's a technical
director at Arcadis. Funnily enough, she's a big voice out there for women
in my type of engineering. And she is currently doing her best to get as
many women into engineering as possible. But to me, it's a bit of a warning
that she's the only woman I know in such a high up position, and she is not
south Asian. [So] one day I'd like to see myself in that same kind of position,
like Emma, to inspire more girls like me into [civil] engineering.

On the other hand, some participants, including Hanya, Kulwant and Lubna, wanted to change other people's perspectives in their immediate, local, environment, including family, peers, teachers and colleagues. They want to change the mindsets of society both locally and internationally. In this respect, Kulwant, for example, talked about acting as role models themselves for other British south Asian women:

> Kulwant: It has been a hard decision to stay in STEM; I mean, I've not had many role models in the [Bangladeshi] community or even in media to show south Asian women who are successful. So, I have not had many role models; you always have to do things on your own, so yeah. All I've got is a big family – younger than me and still in school. So, I want to become a role model for them.

Similarly, Yumna highlighted the importance of south Asian women role models to give confidence to other south Asian women and change societal self-perspectives that STEM is not for women like them:

> Yumna: because they [south Asian women] are comfortable with you and they are aware of your skillsets and your personality, I would like to think that someone is saying, 'Gosh, if she can be appointed, I can be appointed too.'

While people's appreciation triggers feelings of success, it also brings added responsibility:

> Yumna: For me, success changes. It changes according to what I'm doing at that time and who's affected by it. I think that's important. I possibly didn't appreciate but, for example, I was appointed as a non-executive board member at SAS. I possibly didn't appreciate what it meant at the time until messages came in from BAME colleagues. And instantly, I think, my perception changed [that] it wasn't simply a matter of being an effective non-executive board member [in the job] . . . it was about I'm not just representing myself here; I'm representing the whole community. I may be the first, in some capacity. But, still, I can't be the last; this has to be about succession planning so that you are ensuring that your colleagues are then perceiving your transition into that role as an opportunity.

2.　Being mentored or mentoring

Nine of the twenty-eight participants mentioned success by learning from and supporting each other. Beena recalled an experience in a science laboratory where team working enabled them to complete the task with limited instructions. They were a diverse group and even went beyond the given instructions:

Bena: I felt successful, like [when performing] the fizzy drink experiment . . . when you add menthol to read how the colour changes. We learned a lot about teamwork and following certain instructions without much guidance from the teacher, so it was pushing yourself forward along with other people who might be a bit behind or ahead of what you are thinking. We went so far with the armour experiment that we were asked to do. It was a 1 metre drop but we carried on doing it for many metres to see how much stronger our armour was. And this is what we learned by doing this practical of going beyond instructions as a team.

Moreover, Lubna did not experience any difficulties in becoming a pharmacist. Rather, she found that their seniors acted as great mentors, where Lubna's mentor encouraged her to apply for a promotion. Pari, Salma and Yumna, three STEM professionals, indicated the importance of mentoring in professional settings, for example:

Salma: A solid mentor-mentee relationship with my PhD supervisor reinforced my professional development – he made me realise that societal norms and customs (heritage, nationality, gender, religion) cannot stop me making progress in my life. Out of his way, he supported my part-time school teaching job – he intended to help my ambition of providing better learning opportunities to teenage pupils from minority backgrounds. Moreover, he dedicated additional time to talk about the barriers and limitations of science teaching and learning. Now, even after many years of my PhD, I work with him, completed some great projects and continue with more, which is, a huge success for me.

Salma then wanted to continue this chain of mentor-mentee relationships:

Salma: Like my mentor I want to take a similar approach, so I currently support various school-based teachers, PhD and EdD students. They act as my mentees in turn to support their students [schoolchildren], especially those who possess racially minoritised visible characteristics (e.g., young women of colour).

Similar to Salma, mentoring responsibilities that contribute to the feeling of success was mentioned by Pari. Her view is that with promotion comes more responsibility to support other peoples' successes,

Pari: A promoted post (professorship) is just an indicator of success. But success in your workplace, is being known as an approachable person, able to do my job effectively, achieve my targets, and, most importantly, help others. I think being a professor is just a marker of success. Uh, but that doesn't change what would make me satisfied. And what would make me satisfied is that I'm able to achieve the job's objectives, [which is] more kind of supporting others to be successful. It's more about this responsibility of helping others that I have to do them effectively – that's success for me.

In contrast, Anchal, Leah, Saarya and Yumna felt unsupported and not effectively mentored. Nevertheless, they still managed to complete complex tasks resulting in success for them, for example:

> Yumna: In the engineering sector, my journey as an engineer involved projects where I felt I was just not being supported or I was not skilled enough to be on these projects. But . . . I never felt I was incompetent because I always thought if I was given the appropriate training and presented in a structured way, I could learn. But I went from feeling that way . . . to accomplishing the task – that was success!

Similar to Pari and Salma, Sana, a science teacher, sees her mentoring role as a success for herself, her role in supporting diversity in the STEM sector and developing the young generation to be successful in STEM industries, even though

> Sana: I left labs over two decades ago, still I have the opportunity to support the diverse students in my school, or how we support diversity in the STEM sector and, therefore, that is a success because I didn't just go off from STEM [instead] focused on STEM retention of girls and boys and supported the progression of students into further education.

3. Being altruistic

Seven of the twenty-eight participants indicated that they would feel successful or have felt successful while saving the lives of people and the environment through science. Areeb would be successful if she could do heart surgery – for free – in her small village back in Bangladesh:

> Areeb: People back home are suffering from heart diseases, which could be easily connected with surgery, and because of lack of money, they can't really go and have surgery done if I learn it. [So] I can then go and help them.

For Beena and Faizan, it was the benefit to the planet that mattered:

> Faizan: . . . for the betterment of our planet, I'm always interested in knowing about climate change and how it can be reduced and solved. So, I will start

convincing the general public, and these people will then support different
problems in life and think of ways as [to] how science or scientists can help
in sorting out the problems.

Hanya, too, is very much a climate activist, and she would participate in local
and global activities to support the anti-pollution cause:

> Hanya: . . . lately, I would love to. I wanted to join the rallies against the
> government policies, especially what's going on in my local area, based on
> environmental pollution. But as there were so many important classes going
> on in the school, I couldn't, but I would love to be part of it in the future. I
> never used to think about it much before.

Anchal's ambitions were a mix of the two, changing the climate situation in order
to improve the health of the people:

> Anchal: Certain general topics just put a light bulb in my head that I actually
> really enjoy. So, for example, when I was at university, I actually wanted
> to make a change for the people of Glasgow along with [my] studies.
> You know, to ensure that I'm actually doing something here, including
> promoting and trying to help the climate situation that we're in just now.
> As a group of final year engineering students, we contacted big engineering
> companies to support our project on the air pollution problem in Glasgow.
> And [we] designed electronic bus services, designing charging units on
> the floor where the bus stops, and it charges itself while the passengers are
> getting on the bus etc. This [outreach] work actually continued within my
> working life.

Pari and Amna both view their work as Sadkah Jaria, which is the act of voluntary
work which has a long-term charitable contribution that impacts on the lives of
other people. Amna recited a Quranic verse:

> Amna: '. . . whoever saves the life of one person. It shall be as if he has saved the
> life of all mankind.'

Theme 4. Being involved in the processes

Fourteen of the twenty-eight participants mentioned that achieving success
involves a process. All the secondary schoolgirls in our sample talked about
tangible successes such as good grades, entering a good university or medical
college and taking on particular roles and positions in employment. Interestingly,
none thought that grades are necessarily predictors of long-term success:

Hanya: Because grades don't guarantee that a person is good or bad in science, it is the process of learning and endless enjoyment and not the miseries of GCSE exams!

Ayesha extended Hanya's assertion and criticized the GCSE examinations system and university requirements as the basis for judging a person's capability of entering STEM education. Instead, she would value students being judged on their ongoing thought processes (scientific concepts and practices) and self-motivation:

Ayesha: My perception about having good grades is very different because, in society, this is how they know whether you are successful or not. You have a very good grade in science, so you're successful in science, but actually, it is not true because answering a couple of questions . . . does not exactly tell you about what's in the students' head. Like someone can just memorise everything without understanding the concept . . . and not be thinking [it] through. I don't think that grades actually define one's capability and long-lasting success . . . You might be motivated to succeed in science, but people and institutions don't allow you to do it [science] because of the grading system.

Areeb, Beena and Shahrazad shared thoughts of educational journeys as enjoyable processes. However, they worried that grades could put them off:

Beena: Probably my grades. I have very high ambitions of becoming a successful surgeon, and I'm hoping to achieve that. So, if my grades are not good, that might put me off a bit, and it would be like 'I've worked hard and I didn't get it'. So, it might put me off.

Zahra and Sahar also believed that ongoing learning of science *as an explorer* is a success rather than good examination grades:

Sahar: So, what we did with you [the teacher] was more enjoyable, and at the same time we were learning about different aspects of science such as gravity, [the] structure of [the] brain, radiation, pollution et cetera and so they're fun . . . [So,] you do science as an [ongoing] explorer rather than a competitor of getting good grades.

Leah's key definition of success is 'just keep going for it', she said:

Leah: I think my successes and science is just going for it and just trying – whether that's working in [the] industry as a woman of colour. When I was doing my PhD, I had to keep going through the good and not-so-good experiences in research. But I kept going, [which] has built me up as a strong person and grown my self-confidence in science.

Moreover, some STEM professionals value achieving small successes on a daily basis – that success does not centre around big professional gains such as gaining promotion, grants and awards. So, for instance,

> Yumna: How I quantify success on a day-to-day basis is very different. On a particular day, it could actually be that I had a really great day with my daughter and that is a success, you know as a parent today, I think I was successful. And that could just pretty much define my belief with respect to success on that given day. And on other occasions, it could be that I've delivered a project or an initiative that actually meant I was out of my comfort zone. [Therefore,] I was developing my skillset. Further, there was an intensity, and it was a challenging period, but it's been delivered effectively and purposefully – and that's [a] success. But, overall, success for me is not only centred around my profession.

Moreover, Saarya talked about the accumulative effect of small (micro) successes to achieve long-lasting success through resilience:

> Saarya: Success is working hard to achieve what you need to do. If you work hard, then you get the success you need. Time-wise, it will be quicker for some people, and some will take longer. For me it takes a while to feel success[ful]. Because if you want 'permanent success', you need to work hard to get . . . because I always believe in detail and depth. Once I get it, it's happiness it's huge happiness.

Saarya, in addition, believes that quick success is not as powerful as the success one gets after difficulties.

> Saarya: Quick success is good, but sometimes I think quick success can't get you what you need. You tend to lose momentum. I think my current job has been a huge success because, initially, when I became a science technician, it wasn't an easy job. It was very difficult because you know, like walking in the school and you get the impression that people [do] not want you to succeed. Rather, they are always kind of commenting that 'science technician job is not for you'. Still, I remained in schools, and I found a job – my current job – where they're very supportive, amazing and give me training on what I need to do to establish [myself] as a great science technician. They help me with what I need to achieve, So, that is a success.

Nyla gave examples of her day-to-day micro successes as well as accumulative successes:

> Nyla: So, if I'm working in a lab doing experiments – success would mean having to achieve excellent and consistent results, which are very publishable. Having a good working relationship with my colleagues and scientists is a success, and also [overall] progressing and growing as a professional gives a sense of long-term success.

Anchal and Yumna talked about their resilience in achieving small successes even when they have not succeeded in their higher objectives:

> Anchal: I just keep learning from different people. I learnt my big lesson on gender bias in the engineering industry the hard way. So now I take a lot of notes of my failures as well as little achievements, and whenever I'm steaming in the overall picture [of successes and failures] again, I refer back to my notes.

Anchal added that it is thrilling to feel having full-blown success once you pass through difficult times:

> Anchal: It is all about passing through like kind of tougher time to achieve [the] qualification, job, progression, balance in life etc. So that's there for what success is for me.

Moreover, Yumna gave an example of passing through difficulties where she felt she was not succeeding. Eventually, though, she completed the task successfully and so learnt to imply this learning in future:

> Yumna: You weren't succeeding, but actually you become successful in that domain and then apply what you've learned and better understand its transferability into other sectors than into other roles and other positions.

Salma further supports Anchal's and Yumna's understanding of being successful:

> Salma: The most memorable day of my life was when I was attending my convocation event – sitting in the front row in a red gown and floppy hat. I later received my PhD certificate on stage, witnessed and cheered by a large audience. So, a PhD certificate verifies my success as a Doctor of Philosophy. But then, it just serves as an 'accumulative' and 'multicoloured' indicator, that I achieved from passing through micro-successes and – failures. Such as struggling to write academic essays as a mature student, which I had never written before. And then completing a PhD thesis was

a dream coming true. These multicoloured indicators, both success and failure, don't have an endpoint, for sure, as it carries on showcasing micro-successes and micro-failures to strengthen my ambitions of researching, writing and publishing more.

Theme 5. Continuing with the informal learning of science

Despite being aspired to become scientists from school-going age, sixteen of the twenty-eight participants highlighted their persistence, resilience and intrinsic passion for continuing their learning and exploration of the part of science that interests them through informal means. We believe that being and becoming successful in science is difficult without their self-desire to learn informally.

In the previous chapters and this chapter, we see that the acquisitions of achieving high grades, promotion and grants are seen not to be a solid means to determine whether a person can do science or not. Therefore, participants express their science learning as an ongoing business that they are interested in and eventually feel satisfied with their potential and ambitions of learning science. For instance:

> Ayman: Lots of things make me curious about science . . . because there is so much science that needs to be discovered, and so I always used to think that I want to find something new and develop it further.

Ayman, extended her being curious with the fact that even if she were a boy, she would pursue the ambition of becoming a surgeon, and so she reads books and articles related to eye surgery:

> Ayman: I read a lot about germs around us, which makes me read more about it, and then I get very much interested in the science part of it. I don't think that male or female matters of becoming a surgeon, even if I was a boy. I would like to become a surgeon.

The primary school children, Ayman, Beena and Husna, also evidenced micro successes through informal means. For example, Husna found it satisfying to talk about her ideas of physics aligning with the science fiction characters like *Spider-Man* and *Superman* which previously her class fellows thought was 'irrelevant and too abstract'.

Moreover, Beena talked about *Kelvin Grove Art Museum*'s red steam engine, with self-realization that:

> Beena: I just liked and actually loved the steam engine in the entire museum, but after conversing with you (the researcher) and sharing my interest with

the class, I felt sciencey and now wanted to research more about steam engines.

Meena is very much inclined towards an interdisciplinary subject, chemical physics, which she believes is not taught in school, and so

> Meena: I researched about it in my own time (although) I have not been asked (by anyone) to do this research. This research helps me in my daily life activities to some extent. You know how chemical physics talks about renewable and non-renewable energy sources, smart meters, smart cars etc. and how through linking physics and chemistry can support the medical world too.

Similar informal learning memories were also shared by Khadija, as she started to gain her interest in the study of the brain, senses, learning and emotions by watching a video, and later, she built her interest by exploring more about this topic by reading books, blogs and watching videos:

> Like, I remember watching 'Inside Out' and then talking about it in terms of brain, senses and misconceptions about learning. We enjoyed learning about different emotions that we also have, especially at thirteen/fourteen [of age]. And I really think that my interest in learning more about the brain and how our emotions are directed by it started from watching the film and mainly by . . . [discussing] it with the science teacher in the classroom. And I just became more interested in it as time moved on, but before that, I was not interested in it at all.

In the out-of-school context, Zahra recalled her visit to the *Crystal Museum*, where she got fascinated with the power bikes and continues to learn more about them by watching videos and talking to the science teacher about it after the visit:

> Zahra: I specifically remember the Crystal Museum school trip because that was our first trip, and it was actually very fun. We learnt about energy and how to save energy. And I remember that power bike, and we had to paddle to generate energy. And it was using our energy to lite all the lights, and we were trying so hard to lite all of them that it was really fun.

Similarly, Hanya recalled her experience of visiting *Brunel University's robotics workshops*.

> Hanya: I went to Brunel University, the workshops there really motivated me. We did the robotics stuff and engineering stuff using computers . . . set

up a website and especially liked the computer science activities. I hated computer science, but that interactive activity changed my understanding.

And Areeb likes her freedom towards the learning of science as she recalls science learning at home and in the area around her home and school:

> Areeb: One time I tried making crystals at home on a pencil after looking at a YouTube video, and it actually turned out very good. Only very few broke, but the rest were quite prominent and visible. . . . This morning I was walking on Broadway. and was thinking about cars and friction, air toxicity and associated pollution. Science is just all around you; it is everywhere.

The STEM professionals also mentioned the importance of learning science informally, gained outside formal institutions like schools, colleges, universities or workplaces. For example, Anchal's interest in pollution and climate change has made her read articles and books on air pollution, talk to people from the industries to support her and her group of friends to engineer buses that run on electric power rather than diesel and petrol. This passion continues even today, and she reads and researches a lot on air pollution and designs models of electric buses and cars.

Salma's early passion towards science that became a success in retaining this passion over several years started and continues with some artefacts, magazines, cartoons and TV science-based programmes:

> Salma: My love of science was discovered quite early in life, as early as age six, when a plastic stencil for drawing experiment diagrams caught my eye and a weekly science magazine, including science-fiction-based stories and cartoons. This early interest in science grew over time and was supported and reinforced by a series of small nudges in my life. These nudges have included TV science-based programmes (for example, Dr Who and science shows on the National Geographic channel). I am still a devotee of Dr Who and very much inclined to listen to The Infinite Monkey Cage and use science fiction stories as a pedagogy to support school science teaching and learning.

Moreover, Ambala, Fariha and Zaynab, on full-time career breaks, continue to feel successful by being involved in self-ascribed science learning through informal means. For example, Ambala, at the time of the interview, was out of employment; still, she continually engaged herself with informal learning of science and technologies, and this engagement is a success for her.

> Ambala: See, I read a lot. In that, I'm interested in learning new technologies. So, I do read a lot, and I have subscribed to a lot of these blogs that concern me and my learning of new technologies.

Fariha, in addition, talked about the success she is feeling while sewing a quilt for the first time and linked this engagement as a process to see herself successful in science.

> Fariha: The creative side of me is in this lockdown. I have been sewing, and I am finishing a quilt . . . this is the first time I'm making a quilt, so yeah, creating stuff that I'm doing. It is the science of how you put the patterns on and how it comes to play in the end; everything is science isn't it. But, making a quilt is more of an art form; still, in the end, the experiment of doing it and trying a new thing, for the first time, is science and success.

Moreover, Zaynab has neither studied (after her MSc in chemistry) nor worked in the STEM sector for the last fifteen years. Still, she finds ways to incorporate science to make meaning of her day-to-day housework, such as her current successes in gardening (Chapter 4). Moreover, her accomplishments in sciences translate with her feelings of maintaining a successful bonding with her children through science. As a parent, she feels:

> Zaynab: Understanding maths and science is uncommon among BAME parents compared to reading, writing, and painting. However, advanced science and maths taught in schools are difficult for children, so it requires parents to have some interest and knowledge of it as the interaction of children and teacher is less, so parents need to help a lot. So, I feel successful when supporting my children and establishing a parent-child bond using science as a tool. [As a result,] they see me not as an incapable and silly mother – [for instance] my daughter on the dinner table asked a random question: 'Arc there more wheels? or more doors in the world?' This one question started a discussion on the science materials used in the doors and wheels, history of wheels, pollution and population, gravity and even the science used in building constructions.

In addition, Nyla, as a child,

> used to imagine if there was nothing like a vacuum, what would there be. Like if there was nothing, what would they be like it was just like I really confuse myself with that, like it's just mind-boggling isn't it.

Now with fourteen years of employment gap, Nyla kept engaged with informal self-ascribed scientific critique by picking scientific and non-scientific points in the movies.

> Nyla: I see something in movies like a lab scene and it will just be so full of hazards. And they'll just be incorrect experiments and concepts like in Big Bang – that bothers me, and I pick these points very quickly.

Moreover, Nyla mentioned that one of the most enjoyable parts, though a minimal part of her last employment, was community work involving science communication and public engagement with scientific publications and science in the news. So, she is determined to continue with such a job in future too.

> Nyla: So, we used different media types to communicate science, so obviously, there are scientific publications, but then you have the press releases and news articles. So, for example, I did like a presentation targeted to a (like a) teenage audience, so how would you modify the language? And the way you communicate things for the audience has to get that science across to the public, as it's different to when you're talking between two scientists. I enjoyed that a lot. So, if I had an opportunity, I would do something like that.

Chapter summary

In summary, learning from our participants, we can apply great lessons that the science culture can implement to catalyse the feelings of success in turn to develop confident south Asian women and broadly women of colour in sciences. There are several summary points that consolidate this chapter keeping the entirety of this book's success involving three main building blocks:

1. Science identity (Sci-ID), as personal uniqueness or micro forces and social equity/inequity (or macro and corresponding meso forces).
2. Intersectionality, that is, the intersection of micro and macro forces – with an involvement of meso forces such as family, teachers, formal institutions and informal educational and non-educational contexts.
3. Narratives, that is, the evolving stories intersecting micro and macro forces with the emergence of meso forces.

The most obvious observation to be made is whether responses have involved the intersection of micro and macro along with meso forces or have they focused just on micro forces. In this respect, there were two overarching and interlinked standpoints. One is that successes in science are an ongoing process. Therefore, the participants are not particularly satisfied by some materialist achievements such as good grades, degrees, awards, positions and promotions – authorized by the institutions showcasing the meso forces. Therefore, public laurels have only taken them up to a certain point. It is actually the internal self-satisfaction, enjoyment, success after failure, learning from others or through being *learned* that counts. The second interconnected standpoint is the evolving nature of storytelling, a form that our participants adopt effortlessly in telling us about their journeys of success – along with some accompanied failures. One way or other, they all acknowledge the feelings engendered by long-term successes in science, success that will not simply be given to them as a blessing or gift or that happens accidentally by luck. Instead, to achieve this, they need to work hard and pass through a series of micro successes and micro failures in life. Success in sciences is not a stand-alone landscape but rather more nuanced and accumulative in nature.

The next chapter will pause to collect ideas discussed so far and lead the discussion on pedagogical support, interventions, actions and recommendations.

6

A Consideration of the Arguments So Far and Discussions to Come

In Chapter 1 we introduced three primary metaphors we use in the book. The *diffusion* model which presents the intermingling of permeable cultures at a personal level and in the development of science identity (Sci-ID). Second, the *wearing of science culture* highlights fluidity, uniqueness and subjectivity towards this Sci-ID development. These two metaphors are then associated with *permeability* in developing Sci-ID through engagement, self-perceptions and immersion in the culture of science (Chapter 4). In addition, we have also introduced the *permeable pipeline* metaphor (Chapter 1) in contrast to the *leaky pipeline*, thereby keeping options open for an inward flow of women to enter science education and employment.

In this chapter we pause to refresh our arguments and to progress our views on the (semi)permeable pipeline as a means of giving subjectivity and liberty to our south Asian women participants so that they can

- live a science life (engage, perceive and immerse in (everyday) science),
- develop Sci-ID and
- voice (express) their successful experiences and outcomes.

The permeable pipeline

Like all models or metaphors, the *leaky pipeline* has its uses. We see the point, but we are also wary of its implications. As Rebecca Varney and Kaleb Heinrich (2021) point out, the metaphor is a distortion because it implies the possibilities of plugging the holes (Cannady, Greenwald & Harris, 2014), or worse, that it is possible to compensate for losses by simply increasing the flow rate of students into the pipe (Metcalf, 2010). As Varney and Heinrich note, the metaphor makes assumptions about student uniformity that are not true in any field. The women in our studies do not all start from the same point; they do not *flow* through the system at a constant rate, nor do they all share the same end goal. Instead, these authors offer their analogy of a garden in which to grow interest and allow curiosity in science to blossom. This is not a new idea by any means, and its roots can be seen in Friedrich Froebel's eighteenth-century kindergartens (children gardens) where engagement with the natural sciences was cultivated.

We hold on to – but amend – the pipeline metaphor because we see it as useful in highlighting the fact that there is an interface, a membrane, to be traversed. A pipeline has walls, an outer casing which, however permeable, still exists. This is what keeps the majority of the water in, even while it might *leak in and out*, in both directions. The outer casing constitutes the main ways in which women are channelled towards science and contains, too, the barriers, obstacles to be navigated and negotiated in order to remain within the casing or join it from the outside. Our suggestion, then, is that for the majority of the women who enter the pipeline at the start, this casing acts – on the whole – to provide a secure track that enables them to follow a fairly direct route through and into science-based employment. Many, many women make it because of the pipe's casing. That is certainly true of many of the women we talked to for this book.

But let's be clear, intersectionality matters. It matters because of the effects of restricted access and representation within academic and empirical science. First-generation students and scholars of all races and genders face unique challenges in gaining access to the tacit knowledge and often unseen networks that can be so crucial in fostering success in science. We want our stories to make the tacit as explicit and the opaque as transparent as possible in order to create greater equitability to access. Second, social allies and networks matter – those elements of social capital that mean there is *always* something to be done to enhance inclusion. And third, representation matters. For those who experience marginalization as a result of gender, race, sexual orientation, socio-economic status and so on, they need to be heard and listened to.

Expressing experience

At this point in the book, we talk about inside and out. There are many people who discuss *lived experience* as if it was somehow separate and distinct from, well, just experience itself. It is as if there are two kinds of experiences – experience in general and experience that an individual have personally lived through. In many senses, use of the term lived experience is simply a way to highlight a particular episode, a period of time that is under scrutiny. There is some sense in which we often do need to *bracket* an experience, contain it within a moment in time, so that we can then reflect on it. 'Do you remember the day when I . . .?' 'How about that time that we . . .?' *Bracketing* is a term borrowed from phenomenology, and there is much about discussions of lived experience that follow phenomenological thinking. In bracketing experience in this way, we attempt to treat it as a distinct entity, we look to explore and explain what was happening both inside ourselves and in the wider context. It gives us an opportunity to collect and recollect on a specific issue about ourselves. In essence, of course, there are no discontinuities; all events and happenings occur throughout time, and anyone could be subject to analysis, to both inspection and introspection.

Experience is central to our work. It is what makes intersectionality personal; it is key to how we have analysed our participants' stories. The many ideas behind what exactly constitutes experience have been developed at vast length through texts and tomes worldwide so much so that any review would be several books alone. Our intentions here are much more modest. We want to draw lessons from the intersectional experiences of the many women with whom we have talked and use these as the basis for informing ways forward, ways in which young women might learn to succeed based on the experiences of those who have gone before. There are many implications for researching experience, and we have already mentioned some of these as we discuss our research approaches in previous chapters. Specific experiences – even shared experiences are always individual and different, as are the lessons we derive from them. So, the lessons that the women draw from their own experiences of success are then interpreted by us as we, in turn, learn lessons from their lessons. The messages in the chapters to follow, then, are necessarily distillations of distillations.

An *entre-deux* approach

We can, though, separate *first-person* from *other-person* perspectives. First-person accounts are discrete perspectives and descriptions of what that individual is experiencing or is attempting to do moment by moment. Other-person accounts are different; these are the perspectives of observers who label and portray the events and occurrences as they happen not to themselves but to other people. In this book we adopt a position somewhere in between, in the entre-deux as phenomenologists would have it. This is the hybrid space between first-person and other-person accounts. So, all of the stories, the autobionarratives, we have been given are first-person reports of experience, of our participant women's lived experiences. However, in relaying these to the reader, we have necessarily trimmed and edited, grammaticized and sometimes abridged what the women were saying. That is, we have *storied* their stories; we have interpreted what we think the women were saying and have presented this in the form of a story. We ourselves are neither inside the story nor are we outside of it, hence the entre-deux. As might be expected, we have tried strenuously to remain as faithful as possible to the intentions we can divine in the words and behind them, though in using the caveat as far as possible, we recognize that we are active players in the process and are inevitably interpreting participants' stories through our own *lensed* perspectives. Whenever the possibility has arisen, or has been feasible for us to organize, we have checked our versions of the stories with our participants, to align with what the women themselves were saying. We have then amended our versions where necessary to meet their needs.

Expressing *lived experiences*: Science identity

In our descriptions of self, gender, class, culture, society, science we see these to intersperse and diffuse between each other. What is important in taking these broad sociological features of intersectionality and driving these down to women's personal lived experiences is that we are indeed generating *a model of Sci-ID* – one we have described elsewhere (Salehjee & Watts, 2020). Our model sees a living person as a self-organizing entity. A living person continuously shifts and changes in order to survive and maintain equilibrium. She sees the integrity of her own boundaries, the *who-she-is* of herself, those elements that make her a whole and distinctive person, while at the same time having constant interchanges with her environment. Her boundaries are semi-permeable and so she exchanges material in the shape of thoughts, ideas, interests, ambitions, aspirations, goals, talk, actions, attitudes, cares, concerns, moods and much (much) more with her immediate environment. She has intentions, purposes and agency.

The environment, too, is complex and ever-changing, not least changed by the women themselves. The living person and the lived experience, then, are all part of the same process, of action and interactions between self and environment, circulating back and forth through the membrane that contains the person and makes her self contiguous and coherent. This is not a usual approach. Many of the accounts of intersectionality read as if the woman has been parachuted down into a *social soup* wherein her intersecting gender, heritage, race, social class and abilities are prefixed and preordained. She simply awakens to find herself in the soup, and then she reflects on this world as she finds it. This, though, is really not the essence of the stories we share in this book. There are many ways in which the world can be taken to be, to exist. Our model for Sci-ID argues that there is no pre-given women awakening in pre-given worlds. Rather, there is constant interaction between a woman and her world, based on her past history, present actions and future projects. She engages with herself and her immediate surroundings to realize those of her intentions possible at any one place and time. Her sense of self is embedded in the social world and so her thoughts and feeling may well be her own but are nevertheless related to cultural norms, values and interactions.

So, is it possible to separate a woman from her surroundings? Ours is not a structural functional view that sees society as a given entity serving to exert social forces on individuals' behaviour, not least because this suggests consensus, conformity, passivity and a dearth of personal agency. Ours is an ecological view that understands the woman both as herself and in relation to her background of biological, social, cultural beliefs and practices. To be a person is to be a bounded entity but always in interplay with a situation, a context, a world. We have no experience, lived or otherwise, that is unattached from or independent of these situations. The questions then become, 'to whom do memories, recollections, plans, anticipations actually belong?' 'What exactly is personality' and, therefore, 'what is an identity?' And to be precise within this book, 'what is a science identity or Sci-ID, as we abbreviate it?'

First, we return to our point that science is not just a separate megalithic arcane body of knowledge, of symbolism, argumentation, of practice and institutions. Yes, it can be all of those things, but some science has also diffused throughout culture and social life sufficiently to become what James Corburn (2005) calls 'street science'. There has long been a sense that health concerns, environmental problems, pollution, climate change, agricultural practices, morbidity, energy policies and much more cannot be left simply to the decision-making and action taking of experts and professionals. According to Corburn, 'street science' challenges the idea of science as a universal truth-speaking language and emphasizes instead the interdependence of science and historical contexts, of science and politics, of science and local knowledge. It represents a rapprochement between scientists seeking generalizable, rule-bound, risk-assessed, causal certainties and local residents' stories, anecdotes, perceptions and particularities. This rapprochement is a two-way science street so that, just as scientists listen to and pay attention to the idiosyncrasies of everyday life, everyday people listen to and pay attention to the meanings and methods of the science they encounter. If there is science diffused throughout everyday culture, then some of this will permeate through the membrane that contains the person. All women come into contact with some science in some shape or form. In this book we are examining the ways in which women construct their own scientific realities through stories of their *lifeworlds* and using their own contingent knowledge and explanations.

Second, memories are malleable, aspirations are adaptable. This certainly comes through in the women's stories, the differences of recalled events between a participant and her siblings – the shift and changes in ambitions over time. So, a woman's Sci-ID is seldom static but swings up and swallow dives with various turns and occasions. As we noted in Chapter 1, these are seldom straight-line changes where consequences follow events in some linear fashion; rather, they are complex churnings as moods and memories, actions and achievements combine to nudge and transform Sci-ID in one way or another.

Expressing successes in science

Revisiting Figure 1 (Chapter 1) and the science lives of twenty-eight multiaged women, their strong Sci-ID and their expressions of science successes (Chapter 5). These expressions of successes highlight participant women's intrinsic passions wherein multiple micro forces outweigh large-scale macro forces and their interactions with meso forces through their self-motivation, perseverance and resilience towards science.

Moreover, this self-motivation, persistence and resilience towards science become stronger over time since not only does science interest them intrinsically but they also see it as important to their own lives and to society. Moreover, despite their busy day-to-day educational and/or professional scientific practices, the majority indicated that they continue to learn science through semi-formal and informal means. Their sense is that such informal – non-institutional – learning is often as – if not more – important to society as that which is taught in formal educational settings. Furthermore, for some participants, their strength in continuing with learning science allows them to challenge any other failures in science and any other inequitable societal expectations. Moreover, the five themes in Chapter 5 represent descriptors, goals, ambitions and states of being that indicate:

1. Success is finding contentment and happiness.
2. Success is prospering against the tide.
3. Success is having role models, mentoring and being mentored, in being altruistic.
4. Success is working hard within the process.
5. Success is having an appetite for continual learning.

Some intersections in life, such as intersections of nationality with self-identity, gave rise to feelings of being privileged, certainly in comparison with their parents or with non-UK based south Asian women. This was a source of awe and wonder and, at the same time, discussed with a degree of humility. *Going against the tide* was also an expression that recognized the intersections of heritage, religion, gender, race, family and teachers, colleagues and so on with their own self-determination. In those quotes and comments, the main focus was on making a permanent life in Western society while, at the same time, taking a secure place within the sciences. Allied to this comes the opportunity to stand out in the community, to make a statement, to act as a role model or mentor for other UK-based south Asian scientific women and young girls. Some of them depicted this role modelling as their ultimate responsibility for other women from minority backgrounds. Along with this came a duty to support others and participate in charity work. Success is not always about fighting against the society and being liberated but is (more) about successes in serving society, communities, individuals and self. Being successful is viewed less of a struggle and more as an ongoing progression of self-commitment and self-satisfaction in creating a climate of acceptance, equality, equity, diversity and inclusion. This also exhibited very positive intersections with heritage, religion, gender and nationality.

That said, not all of our participants shared a clear-cut view of these large-scale intersections. These successful women from minority groups viewed *oppression* as a societal term and did not perceive themselves as being oppressed at the personal level and did not view the entire south Asian community to be sitting at the crossroads of oppression. Success did not centre on the intersections of oppression but rather on the efforts of south Asian women who took the challenge to promote equity, justice and dignity for all. Most discussed the impact of micro forces. Success comes by being self-motivated, hardworking, self-reliant and able to balance home and work, make a home for their children, fulfil professional obligations through scientific talks and so on. We saw such reliance on micro forces when participants shared their viewpoints of science successes as an enjoyable process – the abstract nature, the curiosity of finding the unknown, the challenges they enjoy and so on. Like many young women, they envision becoming scientists, doctors and engineers, but their successes in science are powered by their self-motivation.

Dispositions for successes in science

Our women participants have exhibited a range of dispositions as they reach these *states of being*, to feel that they have a significant Sci-ID, that they have experienced small and large successes in science, that they have enjoyed, reaped the benefit from their science lives. If we can decide and delineate what dispositions are needed in order to stay inside the pipe, or to re-enter it from the outside, then we can make some inroads into what constitute *dispositions for success in the sciences*. In this respect, our plan has been to scour the women's stories for hints of the attitudes, abilities and strategies they have found useful in order to arrive at what they think constitutes success. Therefore, this is an exemplary list, is certainly not exhaustive, but is drawn directly from what our participants have been saying. If these skills can be genderized (we are not sure they can), then it might be possible to see these as *women's skills*. Skills alone, however, are not sufficient; there are other qualities that are required. As we outline in Chapter 5, these women have needed drive and ambition, strong self-belief in their abilities, clear personal and social values, robust self-confidence and self-affirmation, healthy intellectual and emotional resilience. We re-emphasize these attributes here as themes of *dispositions for personalized successes* and list the ten that provide some examples of how science successes are broadly expressed.

We have used the term *dispositions* because we shy away from the many (many) publications to be found on *mindsets for success*. At one level, there is much to be valued in these texts, and researchers such as Carol Dweck (2006) have made considerable contribution to the discussions on women and science through her delineation of mindsets. Our reservations surround the interpretations of this good work wherein we are offered *recipes for success* as in 'develop a mindset for financial success' (Anderson, 2013); 'the power of positive selling . . . build a mindset for success' (Schiffman, 2012); 'grow a mindset for academic success'; and so on. As we have made abundantly clear in earlier chapters, we see

Table 9 Dispositions for successes in science

Dispositions for Successes	Personalised Successes
1. Recognizing and engaging in culturalization	1. Success is finding contentment and happiness
2. Success is prospering against the tide	2. Ignoring or evading the demands or requirements of others, circumventing unsupportive advisors
	3. Resisting *the system* wherever possible
	4. Forging a positive science identity, consciously demonstrating abilities to counteract doubt
3. Success is having role models, mentoring, in being altruistic	5. Being wary of and combatting isolation using peer networks
	6. Finding safe spaces to foster whole selves, seeking and find environments that enable success
	7. Being altruistic, engaging in activism
4. Success is working hard within the process	8. Being strong, committed, resilient and persevering
	9. Making partial agreements, manipulating situations, bargaining and negotiating with people in *the system*
5. Success is having an appetite for continual learning	10. Remembering and reigniting a passion for learning science

no single recipe that leads inexorably to success, nor do we see that increased sales, financial rewards or academic achievement are of themselves single indicators of success. By using the term *disposition*, we want to encompass a wide range of feelings, attitudes, emotions, states of being, of belonging, recognition, self-satisfaction, of positivity, creativity and energy towards science. Table 9 summarizes the dispositions for successes, mentioned in this chapter and earlier chapters, in broadly ten points and align it with the five personalized successes in science themes presented in Chapter 5.

We have already highlighted some dispositions in terms of micro forces, attitudes and abilities that would potentially keep the women within the permeable pipeline. The question remains, though, 'how best to help women reach these states of being, these desirable points in life?' 'How to help them along – or back into – the science pipeline?' Given all we have said – and that they have said – about the nature of success, there can be no single recipe, no one specific route that would ensure success for all of them. In the chapters to follow, we do discuss some of the pedagogic lessons that we draw from what the women have been saying. More of that in a moment.

More than a word or two about pedagogy

Much of the literature in this field gives the impression that pedagogy is the work of teachers, while learning is the work of students. This is not how we see things here. The roles that teachers play entail, in our view, a multitude of issues and dimensions both explicit and implicit, and learners in turn possess a vast array of means to acquire knowledge and understanding, both intended and unintended. We begin with a small example: One of us (MW) is standing with his wife on the broad ridge across the south of England known as the North Downs. She is admiring the beautiful day and the view across the landscape towards the south coast and asks him quite casually, 'Why do clouds have flat bottoms?' With his background in science, MW knows the answer; his wife, of course, knows him very well and expects him to know why clouds might have certain shapes and how they behave, expects him to give her a manageable explanation. After all, they are husband and wife and have been in situations like this countless times before. So, 'what is *pedagogic* about this particular very commonplace event?'

First, we intend to circumvent the debates around the etymological roots of the word *pedagogy* as in *paidagogos* – the slaves in ancient Greece who *walked with* children to school and *walked with them* through their learning. The converse is *andragogy*, the study of adult learning, although this is seen to be much more self-determined than is pedagogy. We plump for a more contemporary and generalized use of the word *pedagogy*, one that moves past its use in exclusive reference to children and yet retains the original sense of the word as leading or guiding to learn. Paulo Freire (*Pedagogy of the Oppressed*, 1972), for example, famously used it to discuss adult literacy rather than child education. His points are well made, although educational institutions seem to have monopolized its use; pedagogy has a much wider meaning – and is not exclusively about children, teachers, schools, colleges, universities or other formal settings.

Nor, we maintain, is it about *top-down instruction* – from whatever source. This has become a common usage of the term *pedagogy*, one that really entails *instructional science* such that teachers are given step-by-step instructions on how to teach. Instead, we see that it must encompass a wide variety of social sites that range far and beyond formal educational institutions. It involves a wide range of activities that include socializing, contextualizing, enculturalizing, criticism, challenge, creativity and development – only some small part of which constitutes *telling* – or *training* – through direct instruction. In this vein, we take as our starting point a quote by Basil Bernstein (2000), who wrote that pedagogy is a sustained process whereby somebody(s) acquires new forms or develops existing forms of conduct, knowledge, practice and criteria from somebody(s) or something deemed to be an appropriate provider and evaluator. (p. 78)

There is much to be absorbed here. For example, it puts the onus on the process of acquisition – it refers to someone *acquiring . . . from*, rather than 'a provider' *providing . . . with*. That is, pedagogy is not of itself about *telling* or *instructing* and Bernstein inverts here a common sense of pedagogy as necessarily being the 'the art, science and craft of teaching' (Smyth, 1987; Watkins & Mortimore, 1999). Therefore, in our 'what are clouds' situation above, it is MW's wife who initiates the exchange – it is she who seeks to acquire rather than MW himself offering to provide an unbidden out-of-the-blue definition of cloud formation (not that he isn't prone to do so on occasions). Bernstein also proposes that the provider is *deemed to be appropriate* and, in this case, MW clearly passes that test. This is a pedagogic moment, then, in the making.

Bernstein's quote says nothing about learning as such. Gert Biesta (2009) coined the deliberately clumsy term *learnification* to chastise educationalists for turning everything about education into measurements of learning, for turning education into a 'learning industry [. . .] the translation of everything there is to say about education in terms of learning and learners' (p. 38). Yes, in Bernstein's form of pedagogy there is certainly acquisition of knowledge, but there is also mention of forms of conduct, of practices and criteria – which we take to include judgements, mores, morals and values. That is, education – and the role of the pedagogue – is about much, much, more than just cognitive aims and objectives; it also includes, for example, personalization, socialization, disciplinarity, evaluation and accreditation – as well as the political, economic and cultural aspects of the educative systems being used. As Henri Giroux says,

> Pedagogy is not simply about the social construction of knowledge, values and experiences; it is also a performative practice embodied in the lived interactions among education, audience, texts and institutional formations. Pedagogy, at its best, implies that learning take place across a spectrum of social practice and settings. (Giroux, 2004a, p. 61)

'Does MW want his wife to *learn* about cloud formations?' Well, yes, but only in so far as this forms a part of his (and her) concern for her general well-being, her feelings, sensibilities, her science literacy and her broader understanding of the way the world works. 'What might be that broader understanding, exactly?' Well, staying with clouds, there is clear pedagogic intent behind issues, for example, of weather systems, changes in temperature and the likelihood of rain, of longer-term issues such as global warming and climate change MW's attempt to enlighten his wife on the mechanisms behind cloud formation could be cast in terms of general science literacy. Alexander (2004, p. 11) defines pedagogy as follows:

> Pedagogy is the act of teaching together with its attendant discourse. It is what one needs to know, and the skills one needs to command, in order to make and justify the many different kinds of decisions of which teaching is constituted.

Different pedagogy is needed to teach people to type accurately than to sprint quickly or to paint original works of art. By the same logic, we do not expect principles of pedagogy to be universal and suggest that their formulation and application evolve differently in varied educational contexts. The underlying assumption is twofold in that learning is seen as occurring through interaction between individuals within specific communities, hence situated and local. But it is further refined by the role that teachers are given in providing creative and stimulating facilitation for learning, a co-constructivist approach.

That said, it is well established that practitioners have difficulties in surfacing and articulating pedagogical values and beliefs. Practitioners are not always able to identify and articulate effective and successful aspects of their work (Turner-Bissett, 1999). In order to support teachers in locating their voices Jensen et al. (1997) maintain they need opportunities and time to recount the anecdotes and stories of the daily activities in which they are engaged. In that work, a process of stimulated recall was aided by the use of the video recording. Engaging in a dialogue with a knowledgeable research-partner, supported by reflection on their own practice, promoted deeper thinking and conceptualization in a way reminiscent of Vygotskian thinking. In focusing on a recent image of practice, Jensen et al. created opportunities for drawing out and revisiting the pedagogical dilemmas that typified each practitioner and for reaching out beyond their current stage of understanding.

So, in brief, our view is that the pedagogical task requires educators to focus on achieving two basic pedagogical principles. The first is based on providing a supportive environment where the learners can engage, be motivated, see point and purpose in what is taking place. It is a milieu that provides enculturalization and accreditation in relation to their aspirations and ambitions. The second is based on developing practical learning activities.

A pedagogy for success

Our pause for thought so far leads us to make a definitive statement: we develop here something we call a pedagogy for success (PfS). We see this PfS to be an organic progressive change process centred on enhancing minority inclusion into science. The inception of PfS is heavily influenced by our own directions and all of the stories we have discussed so far. It stems from our own academic research endeavours, through teaching and learning, and in careers and employability at school, university and community activities. In this sense, PfS blends our own voices with those of all of our participants as they discuss the successes in their science lives. In 2002, Lynne Rompelmann published *Affective Teaching* where she proposed three components to strengthen a pedagogy of success. Our comment here is that this was seen as a pedagogy aimed at ensuring academic success rather than success more broadly and so is both highly focused within schooling and academia while also being very general about all subject areas. Her three components were opportunity for response, feedback and consideration for the person. The first component considers equity in the opportunities that students have to respond, the provision of individual support for students and high expectations in terms of reasoning. The second involves evaluating, correcting, praising, providing reasons for the recognition and active listening. The third component includes proximity, courtesy, respect, a caring approach and limits to behaviour. While not dismissing these three components, not least because they clearly have merit in themselves, this is somewhat away from the broad direction in which we travel. Ours is a pedagogy *for* success not *of* success, and this small preposition makes a big difference.

One central issue we raise at the start lies in enhancing a sense of becoming and belonging. This relates to our first principle mentioned earlier; it is part of creating a *culture of success*. Research into belonging sees it as an essential human need and motivation. However, in education, particularly in the field of science learning, the impacts of belongingness on academic success have often been overlooked. With schools and universities becoming increasingly diverse, knowing how to support students from non-English-speaking backgrounds is integral for institutions and science educators – we need to enhance their sense of belonging in science. In PfS we posit five key elements: learner identity and academic success; meaningful student-teacher interactions; a reciprocity between educators and educatees; positive peer relationships; and broad and relevant experiences that meet academic goals. Pedagogical approaches that help increase belongingness for science learners need to create more welcoming and productive environments at schools, colleges and universities.

In essence, our PfS is an attempt to develop, foster and build upon dispositions for success. Dispositions, in turn, reinforce a pedagogy for success. As educators, we know that working with people who are well disposed to what they are doing is infinitely easier than working with those who are ill-disposed. So, fostering an ethos of success works well when falling on receptive ears. Equally, those who are well disposed towards feelings of success will shape and structure the prevailing pedagogy – this is what we intend by the expression *reciprocity between educators and educatees*. We see that the two work together to feed off each other.

So, while we discuss the main features of PfS later in the text, we do see it as underpinned by our attempts to engender a sense of successful becoming and belonging in science, opportunities for women to express that growth of belonging, occasions to value both one's own wearing of culture and the culture of science, along with understandings of participation within the enterprise and community of science.

Features of a pedagogy for success with women learners

Here we reconsider the figure we use in Chapter 4 drawn from Yujuan Luo's work (2022) with respect to the five key elements of PfS mentioned earlier. This gives us six *learning situations*.

We use these six learning situations as a means of exploring ways in which we can intervene to support success, to delineate a PfS. We are interested in five particular features of PfS and the pedagogical morphing that happens with shifts in the physical environment. These features are not original and focus on a series of pedagogic decisions and are drawn from a range of writings concerning the workings of pedagogy, for example, Marilyn Cochran-Smith and Susan Lytle (1999) on the relational web; Declan Kennedy and Aine Highland (2007) on learning objectives; Mark Nissen (2006) on knowledge flow; Tara Fenwick and Paolo Landri (2014) on experiential textures; and Tamir Sheafer (2007) on evaluative tone. These decisions, then, are:

1. *The web of relations*: In each of the six learning situations in the figure, we must make decisions on how to shape the relationships between teacher and learner. These decisions include the overall *culture* of the learning space and how to enable and respect the sharing of power.

It shapes the ways, for example, in which a sense of belonging can be generated. Communal opportunities in STEM can be an important lever in increasing STEM positivity and motivation (Diekman, Weisgram & Belanger, 2015).

2. *The learning objectives*: In each situation there will be a different focus on learners' needs and goals, their learning objectives. Decisions in this case will weigh pedagogic processes that interchange between teacher-determined objectives and learner-initiated learning. So, for example, this might provide prompts to understanding of people's science lives, the nature of Sci-ID, the multitude of science-related careers.

3. *The flow of knowledge*: This involves the direction of the flow between teachers and learners, between learners and learners. They are decisions on when to *hold in* and teach or relinquish responsibility and generate collaboration with and between learners, moves from teacher-telling to exchanging with *more-knowledgeable others*. Here lie opportunities for learners' voice, for expressions of culture, for gathering feedback and giving stories of success. These opportunities will arise differently in each of the six learning situations depicted in Figure 4.

4. *The experiential texture*: These are organizational decisions on resources and materials, managing learning engagement, maximizing the opportunities unique to the immediate environment, moves – for example – from serious work to play learning and back again. Again, the formal or informal context of the situation, say, will impact upon this experiential texture.

5. *The evaluative tone*: Evaluating self and collective effectiveness and outcomes. This, too, is shaped by the situation. So, there are commonly very clear criteria and expectations allied to evaluation in formal learning situations where is accreditation part of the situation, and this is often framed as formative and summative assessment. On the other hand, commendation, compliments and praise are more likely in informal contexts. Social and collaborative situations might bring approval and applause, while personalized situations are likely to deliver moments of self-satisfaction.

We both have strong practical experience of teaching in higher education and state education, and we use some of these experiences as we discuss interventions, using PfS, with women in the next sections. As before we introduce them before we learn from them (Table 10).

Table 10 More participants

Name	Place of Birth	Self-Designation
Arshi	England	Biochemist, full-time mum
Cara	India	University undergraduate, physiotherapy
Carolina	Uganda	University undergraduate, science education
Maria	Indonesia	University undergraduate, biology
Sasha	Bangladesh	University undergraduate, biological sciences
Shari	India	University undergraduate, physiotherapy

Arshi is a twenty-five-year-old biochemist and mother of a two-year-old toddler. She is a 'first in the family scientist'. Her migrant parents did not know what subjects and careers she should or could pursue. Nevertheless, they always supported her decisions and never forced her to take any particular educational career or route. Looking back, Arshi's Sci-ID was strong from a very early age; she used to do her 'own little experiments, for example, mixing up bath products with shampoo in the bathroom, spending a large proportion of her time in gardens – even in winters wrapping plants with fabrics and so on'. Despite being interested in science from a young age, her realization of being a science person really began at seventeen (her first year of college) when, along with her friends, she applied to attend a Nuffield Science industrial placement. During this placement, she felt like a 'true scientist' working alongside 'actual real scientists'. At the end of the placement, she firmly decided to carry on with laboratory work 'for the rest of my life'. Arshi never found herself disadvantaged in her science education and professional life. At the moment, she feels that her Sci-ID is on hold as she is on a 'career break' to look after her young family. However, this break does not stop her from engaging with science as she continues to read scientific papers that interest her, including pathogenicity research papers. She remains 'very much interested in the current news on the Covid pandemic' in that it reminds her of the course she did on science communication. This has led her to think 'the Nitty-Gritty of science to what scientists have said on TV and presented to us [public]'. Arshi has now started to apply for positions as a biochemist and looking forward to being back in a biochemical laboratory shortly.

Carolina's parents emigrated from Uganda to settle in the UK; she was a child when they moved country. She has undertaken all of her education in schools in the west of London and chose her university place in the same area so as to be close to home. She is the first in her family to go to university and describes her family as intensely supportive and extraordinarily proud of her achievements;

they call her the 'shining light' of the family. She commutes daily between home and campus even when she may have no lectures scheduled that day; she makes the point that working in the library gives her space and time to settle into work, something that is very hard to manage in the hustle and bustle of home life.

Sasha's family originates from Bangladesh; they are small traders and own a small corner supermarket in the local area. She has worked in the shop since childhood and knows the business intimately. She also knows that the business will pass not to her but to her brother, younger than her but still the oldest son. She has mixed feelings about this, some resentment of the wielding of patriarchal traditions while at the same time enjoying being successful in science at school and now at university and revelling in her course in physiotherapy. She is always looking for clear learning objectives and teaching activities which interest her. Sasha has undertaken several work placements at the local hospital and sees herself eventually taking a role within a hospital department within the national health service (NHS).

Cara was born in India and moved to England at six with her parents. Her science identification was apparent from a very early age, well before university. There was never any doubt at school that she would continue with science after age sixteen (the compulsory age of science education in England) because she excelled in science examinations throughout her time there. Currently studying physiotherapy at a west London university, she enjoys group works more than lecturers – but prefers to choose the group members she trusts, as this allows Cara to discuss science openly without the fear of making mistakes.

1.   *The web of relations*

How are decisions made about relationships between teacher and learner? Clearly this depends on which of the six learning situations we are discussing. In formal university classrooms where purposive learning takes place, we have both used our experience of what works to create strong working relationships with our students. Needless to say, what works in some university classes fails miserably in others, but this, too, is part of our own teaching experiences. We most certainly learn from the mistakes we make. In general, though, students in formal situations appreciate the devolution of responsibility as they grow in their relation to their lecturers and tutors, as Carolina suggests:

> I have really enjoyed the course. The lecturers have all been fantastic. You know that they really do know what they are talking about, and they work with you in

such a good way. You get this big confidence in what you are doing so that you kind of inherit their passion for the science they are doing. I guess they wouldn't be here at all if they weren't passionate about science. It has really washed off on me.

Relationships with the students in formal situations are commonly built on an appreciation of what motivates them. As we discuss in the next chapter, if we can find the right *nudge*, then it is quite possible to move students in the direction of success in science. They can depend, too, on the kind of work being done. So, for example, relationships are different in the laboratory than they are, say, on field trips and excursions outside of the campus. There are different codes and different dynamics in different situations, as Maria says:

> It was great fun on the field trip. Oh, we did some serious biology alright, but we were also able to joke around and have some fun. The weather was good for a change though it was actually quite cold on the beach itself – the water was freezing! But that didn't stop us all feeling cheerful! You get to know people so much better that way, the lecturers were so much more free and easy. We were all good to go with what we were doing.

Undertaking sub-littoral biology on a cold beach – even though it was high summer – shifts the tacit codes and dynamics between teachers and students. There are no recipes for creating the right pedagogic relationships but for both Carolina and Maria, the relationships worked and fostered greater interest and, we would argue, success in their relationships with their lecturers, their co-learners and with science.

In other learning situations, for example in informal and personalized learning situations, then relationships are necessarily different. In the pen portraits described earlier, even after a formal start to her science life, Arshi has become an informal personalized learner so that she keeps abreast with her own professional field through her own devices. After her career break, she is looking forward to returning to laboratory work and, to do so, must demonstrate to herself and to others that she is still engaged in her specialist interests.

2.   *The learning objectives*: Differentiating learners' needs and goals, their learning objectives versus teaching objectives, weighing pedagogic moves from teacher-determined to student-initiated learning

Wherever possible we see it as important for the needs of the learners to dictate the learning objectives. This is a central principle behind the objectival direction of PfS. While learning objectives for a school lesson are commonly predetermined, lessons are also opportunities to tie particular concepts to instances and examples that the student already knows and understands. It is so much better when they volunteer ideas, primarily because we believe that interest and engagement (particularly that which stems from pro-activity and independent thinking) are two important ingredients to success. Sasha says:

> I like to know that there is a real direction to what I am doing. It gives me a sense of purpose and shapes my thinking. I like to know what is coming up, how it all ties together, what skills I am expected to master – everything like that. I think I am one of the only one who has actually read the module guide they provide with the course! . . . Actually, I can think of other times when I kind of wander about inside what I'm doing, sort of drift off and browse rather aimlessly. So I guess it is not all driven by objectives!!

3. *The flow of knowledge:* The direction of the flow between teachers and learners, between learners and learners

Each of the six situations in Luo's diagram illustrates different forms of knowledge flow. For example, in social and collaborative situations, the knowledge is commonly shared and jointly collated. There are many instances within science community circles where this happens and is the basis of most group work, networks and collaborations. No one person has a monopoly on wisdom, and each member of the group contributes to greater or lesser extent. Conversely, unless deliberately engineered otherwise, lectures, seminars, presentations tend to be led from the front and the flow of knowledge is fairly clear. That deliberate engineering, of course, can take place in formal lectures and again is the basis for groupwork, breakout discussions, paired problem-solving, team-based learning and so on. Cara makes her point by saying:

> I really like groupwork. OK, I much prefer it when we get to work in our own chosen groups rather than be randomly assigned with other people you don't know so well. When you are with the people you trust then it works really well. You can be open and make mistakes, you don't look so much of a fool. And we share everything. And you know you can chase people who are not delivering with no hard feelings. No offence taken, know what I mean?

Learning informally (i.e. without strict rules) trades on a collective interest to collaborate and to co-manage activities, rather than being *led from the front.*

4. *The experiential texture:* The organisational decisions on resources and materials, managing learning engagement, maximizing the opportunities drawn from the immediate environment

There is an enormous and still growing literature on something called *the pedagogy of place*. This work brings together the kinds of learning that is possible in an immediate context, such as a classroom, a field centre, a laboratory or a science museum. However, researchers in this field are also very interested in the impact of culture in the sense that any physical or geographic space brings with it a range of cultural expectation – no place is culturally neutral. In this way, the experiential texture is a means of drawing on the affordances offered by a particular location. Each different location provides different opportunities and different affordances.

We must immediately recognize that there are physical locations and, of course, virtual ones. Some recent work has explored the use of virtual reality headset to work with students of dentistry so that they are all able to explore the same mouth, the same issues of dental decay all at the same time, without a physical mouth or set of dentures being present in the room. Something similar can be said for the learning of a language through the use of smartphones (Luo & Watts, 2022) without ever visiting the country of origin of that language. In that work we used interactive activities and video clips, YouTube, TedEd, BBC, WhatsApp and so on as starter activities and complements to more formal aspects of language learning. Shari echoes this:

> The lecturers all made mini-video-lectures of their own research. They were short, you know, like six or seven minutes, and they talked about their work, they were great! They were posted on the department's website. I picked upon some of the words they were using and then went onto Google to see what they were talking about! And one lecturer has written her own textbook and so that was easy, I could just look up most of what she was talking about. They invited us to comment on their video clips and so we got together in groups to tell them what we thought. It was safer that way!

5.   *The evaluative tone*: Evaluating self and collective effectiveness and outcomes

Who evaluates success? The direction we have taken from the start of the book is that success means many things and appears in many shapes and guises. Quite clearly there exist formal criteria in some circumstances that decide whether a learner has successfully achieved a pass, merit or distinction in her work. At other times and in other cases, the feelings of achievement and success lie deep in the core of the individual, her own feelings of self-satisfaction and self-worth. A PfS must encourage both, to strive for other-recognized goals while also charting one's own small steps and longer milestones.

The infusion and diffusion of dispositions for success

These five features of our pedagogic approach indicate the ways in which we like to work, the ways in which we like to frame our educative endeavours. But we have learned much more than this from our readings of the women's stories, their autobionarratives. In Chapter 5 we isolated five main themes from what the women were saying – their descriptors, goals, ambitions and *states of being* that indicate success. These were:

1. Success is finding contentment and happiness.
2. Success is prospering against the tide.
3. Success is having role models, mentoring and being mentored.
4. Success is being altruistic.
5. Success is having an appetite for continual learning.

To learn from the themes in these stories is to embed these descriptors of success within PfS. That is, when we are educating for success, this is what it can mean. Needless to say, not all of our women participants voiced all of these descriptors, nor – had they been in conversation with each other – might they have actually all agreed that all of them constitute descriptors of success. That, we see, is simply the nature of the beast – success has many facets and multiple meaning. In this section of the book, we want to return to our metaphor of diffusion or, more specifically at this point, of infusion. What is the difference? Not much, we distinguish the two here as a point of emphasis: As verbs, the difference between *to diffuse* and *to infuse* is that diffuse is to spread over or through as in air, water or other matter, especially by fluid motion much in the manner we have already described, while infuse has a greater sense of intervention – to cause one component to spread through another, to insert or fill. That is, we want to use infusion to imply that we are introducing something and then to cause it to diffuse. To be specific, we want to infuse our PfS with certain dispositions, dispositions towards success.

Chapter summary

We summarize this chapter using Figure 6, portraying the infusion, diffusion and disposition towards success, incorporating what we have already maintained in the previous chapters. That is a continuum from weak to strong engagement and immersion with science, wearing of science culture (along with other intersecting and permeable cultures) and Sci-ID. This then leads to the

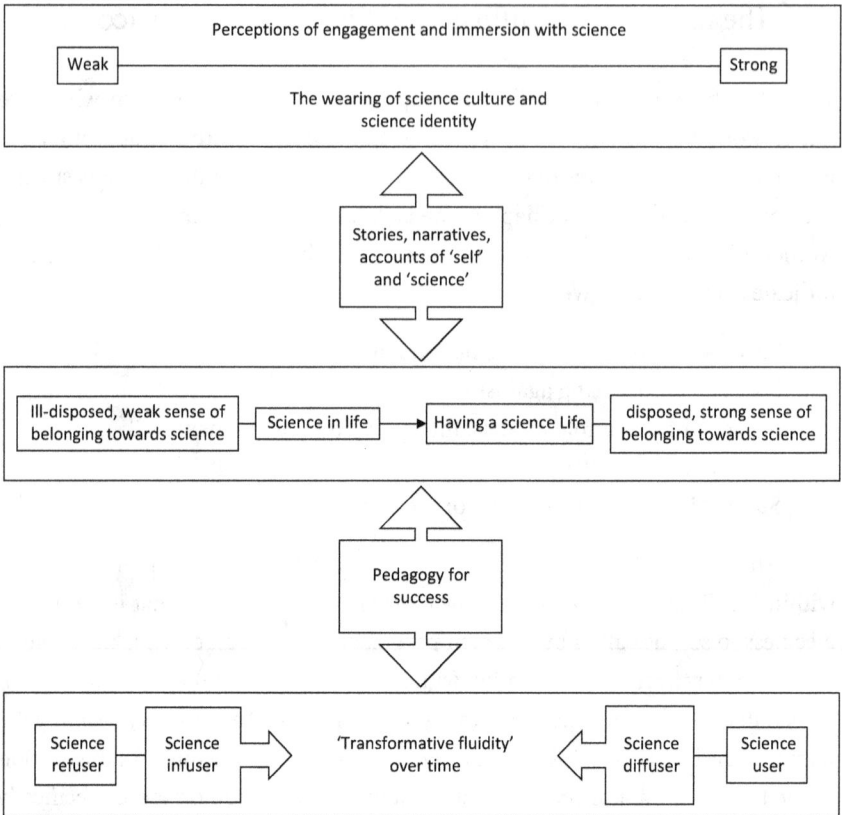

Figure 6 Infusion and diffusion of dispositions for success.

expression of experiences through science stories accumulating to present ill-disposed or strong dispositions for successes in science with having a science life (Table 9) in an individual's everyday life. Next, we established that there is fluidity in perceptions, engagement, immersion, wearing of the science culture and Sci-ID. Therefore, PfS can support:

1. Science refusers, ill-disposed with weak sense of belonging towards science to become science infuser and then science diffuser, that is, movement from science in life to having a science life.
2. Science acceptors, disposed with strong sense of belonging towards science, are already science diffusers; therefore, PfS will further strengthen their sense of having a science life.

The sequence implied in this figure links the wearing of the culture of science to transformations in Sci-ID over time. We see this as simply part of the complexities of life – few people can boast a firm and fixed view of themselves as scientists. While this may well be true for some, maybe those who are working, for example, within well-established research teams in the pharmaceutical industry, or who are medical specialists, it is less true for others. 'How would a PfS impact upon a woman who is wholly committed to science and already has a powerfully strong Sci-ID?' As with all educators, we are pressed to intervene pedagogically in educational affairs. The answer, though, is probably very marginal. As educators, Saima and Mike have both encountered steadfast students of unswerving ambition, and their efforts to help have neither been seen nor deemed necessary. There is little either one of them could have added to one's story of success. The women represented in this figure, though, are different. We have had much more success with those who are more flexible, willing to countenance new ideas, are open to suggestion, can be *nudged* and *triggered* towards science.

Where we have heard women's autobionarrative stories, we have been able to glean something of their dispositions. So 'where does our PfS take us in these cases?' The following chapters look to answer this question and deals mainly with intervening in the science lives of people (south Asian women), so they can remain within or re-enter the science pipeline.

7

A Classroom Study of Small Steps to Support Success

In our book *Becoming Scientific: Developing Science across the Life-Course* (2020), we used Jack Mezirow's transformative learning theory as one of the foundations of our theoretical framework. We will detail Mezirow's theory involving large transformations in the next chapter. The aspect transformative learning theory in this chapter will involve learning experiences that strongly support studies of teaching and learning in academic institutions' meso-social contexts (Salehjee & Watts, 2015), envisaging 'disorienting dilemmas' (Mezirow, 2000; Illeris, 2014) as aggregated effects from numerous small-scale transformative experiences rather than one large-scale life-changing event (Pugh, Bergstrom & Spencer, 2017). Similarly, Pugh's (2020) recent work builds on several 'micro-changes' in students' lives through school science learning to appreciate everyday science in an out-of-school context. Our understanding is comparable: our belief is that teachers and educators need to offer a series of learning experiences that can enhance and enrich everyday lives of the students so that they become 'forcefully active learners, pursuing personal lines of enquiry . . . and become autodidactic' (Watts, 2015, p. 353).

Aligning with Pugh's micro changes and aggregation of these changes, in this chapter, we implement pedagogy for success (PfS) to plan, implement and evaluate small nudges in a school context to have aggregated benefits on schoolgirls' learning, engagement and immersion into science. We draw on the previous six chapters to suggest a compilation of action points that are drawn from the stories and our discussions so far. We add, too, a compendium of associated reading and viewing. The doers of the action points are certainly not just students and teachers; we suggest that there is something here for everyone. By focusing on the science lives of young south Asian women we raise many broad agendas for science education that go beyond issues of equality and diversity. As we noted earlier, our intended audience comprises students, teachers, lecturers, educators more widely, practitioners in youth, adult, further and higher education. And not forgetting parents, siblings and members of extended families.

Pedagogy for success and small science nudges

In this chapter we explore our *case study girls* responses and narratives concerning their school science education. We also use Derek Bell's (2014) seven 'elements of successful intervention', which usefully describe the main features for the design and implementation of science education interventions. These seven elements include: (1) having a clear *purpose* for the interventions, leading to (2) impactful *outcomes*, (3) for suitable *people*, (4) working in the right *context* which in turn leads to (5) measurable and demonstrable *outputs* and (6) robust *process* leading to (7) effective *implementation* (p. 43).

In our case we align our *PfS* with Bell's *purposes*, *people* and *process* elements (Table 11).

Our case study school is situated in Scotland, and the intervening science activities were partially funded by the UK's Royal Society of Chemistry and supported by the University of Strathclyde, School of Education. In this school

Table 11 Pedagogy for success

Bell's (2014) Elements of Successful Interventions	Pedagogy for Success (Chapter 6)
1. Successful interventions have a clear 'purpose' which:	• focuses on learner's enjoyment, intended to stimulate curiosity and interest in science (*experiential texture*) • considers academic success using the school science curriculum with freedom of choosing content and teaching resources (*objectival direction*) • evaluated the changes in the girls' dispositions towards science, shifts and movements in their science identity (*evaluative tone*) • is a reciprocity between educators and educatees (*knowledge flow*)
2. Successful interventions are undertaken by 'people' who:	• have broad relevant experience of the teachers, students and researchers who meet academic goals (*objectival direction*)
3. Successful interventions establish 'processes' which:	• imply positive, open and discursive peer relationship and meaningful student-teacher interaction (*relational web*)

Source: Bell (2014, p. 43).

one of us (SS) was working alongside the usual class teacher, with whom she designed a series of *science nudges* to promote the development of science identity (Sci-ID), science literacy and a positive disposition towards science success in a mixed group of Muslim south Asian boys and girls. Although the class was mixed, here we discuss the outcomes of the study in relation to the girls only – there is time and space elsewhere to discuss the data related to the boys. As to be expected, we learned lessons from our own successes – and our failures – in doing this work, as we explored any development and *migration* that took place in the girls' Sci-ID within this group.

Being a school, this case study represents formal education in science. In looking at the key features of PfS, the *relational web* is quite clearly constituted by the formal, traditional, relationship between teacher and learners in an established institution. SS has an easy-going manner and so elements of that formality were open and discursive rather than stern and forbidding. The learning objectives within the class were drawn from the stated national curriculum for science, filtered through the ways of working within the school, the schemes of work organized for science and the materials available for teaching. SS was given a considerable amount of freedom to work with the class teacher and the class, and so she added to the *standard science objectives* for this level of education through her own project designs. The *flow of knowledge* was not all one way from teacher to students. Certainly, there were core aspects of direct teaching science to the group but many of the activities that SS initiated required the girls to generate their own ideas, research their own topics and bring in their own science materials. These were then shared throughout the class so that the flow was also group to group and student to student. It was certainly in the *experiential texture* of the class sessions that SS and the class teacher made a difference. The learning experiences they designed were unorthodox, geared towards light-hearted fun and enjoyment, intended to stimulate curiosity and interest. This is not to say that the usual diet of science at this school could not be fun and interesting, just that these activities were designed to be so. There were elements of *gamification* that introduced the sense of *playing* with ideas, of following personal interests, of introducing art and poetry to science. Being a school and part of the formal system for science education, the overall *evaluative tone* was one of tests and examinations. Beside this, though, SS had her own approach to evaluation since part of the purpose of the case study was to look at any changes in the girls' dispositions towards science, shifts and movements in their Sci-ID.

Becoming successful in science, as we have pointed out throughout the book, is not limited to completing a degree in science and becoming fully fledged scientists but entails becoming successful in developing science literacy including features, such as curiosity, engagement, relevance, focus, thinking, argumentation, imagination, problem-solving and developing science self-efficacy. In our previous work (Salehjee & Watts, 2020) we described periods of time when people's Sci-ID changes. This can involve a movement towards science or, indeed, away from it. We called this a *migration* into or away from the Sci-ID development. Here, we extend these theoretical and empirical frameworks of Sci-ID migration in two ways. In this chapter, we focus on the south Asian women's Sci-ID migration by capturing and presenting their science learning experiences. We have described these small *experiential movements*, small migrations, as their responses to *science nudges*. Not all the nudges we discuss here are equally effective or, put another way, we see some as rather more successful with some women than others. In this respect, we want to chart the *how and why* of these small movements in enabling women to become increasingly successful in science. In particular, we want to highlight those nudges that have led them to reflect critically on their science and non-science life choices. In the next chapter, as mentioned earlier, we consider much larger-scale actions and events that trigger much more significant *transformations* in women's lives. We look to discuss these triggers through the lens of intersectionality in order to highlight how these life-changing incidents were perceived by our participants.

Case study: A co-educational school in Scotland

Bell's elements of the intervention mentioned above, are to give us a direction to implement and evaluate our aim of *immersing* the girls in the science that happens in their everyday school and home lives. Our intentions were to see what just works for these women Aligning with Bell's remaining four elements of successful interventions (Table 12).

Beginning with Bell's *suitable people* in the *right context*, our case study features students from a co-educational school in Scotland that caters for some 200 Muslim students. Many come from *point-five migrant Scottish nationals*, a designation that simply means one of their parents was not born in the UK. The aim of this project was to increase students' dispositions towards, and acceptance of, science, of being scientifically literate and growing their acceptance of *being sciencey*. We collected data that explored and compared young women's conversations about being sciencey (or not) in different social settings (at school, home, in after-school clubs, etc.) and how their

Table 12 Pedagogy for success – part 2

Bell's (2014) Elements of Successful Interventions	Pedagogy for Success (Chapter 6)
4. Successful interventions take into account the 'context' by:	• evidencing the need of interventions in the first place in the independent Muslim School (*experiential texture*) • building on the strengths and limitations to mitigate small changes as nudges among the students (*objectival direction*)
5. Successful interventions depend on effective 'implementation' which:	• is fluid and allows 'changes in circumstances' (*objectival direction*) • relies on constant reflections and students' feedbacks (*knowledge flow*) • evaluates the 'progress, failures and achievements' in becoming sciencey (*evaluative tone*)
6. Successful interventions result in 'outputs' which:	• are based on main purpose and 'objectives of the intervention' (*evaluative tone*) • 'include short-, medium- and longer-term criteria appropriate' to individual students and learning contexts (*evaluative tone*)
7. Successful interventions bring about change through their 'outcomes' which:	• 'impact on engagement, teaching and learning' (*evaluative tone*) • 'improve' or transform 'existing practice' are fully evaluated and provide feedback for future interventions (*evaluative tone*)

Source: Bell (2014, p. 43).

identifications of gender, ethnicity, class and religion have informed their engagement with science knowledge and skills, and these characteristics have shaped their educational and career aspirations and choices. The class comprised thirty eleven- to thirteen-year-old Muslim south Asian students', seventeen girls and thirteen boys. The conversations we initiated enabled us to design, implement and evaluate the impact of four broad science nudges. We talked to the girls about their feeling and approaches of being sciencey, both before and after exposure to the science nudges.

The headteacher of the school allocated the class teacher an additional three hours each week for the full academic year to give time to work alongside SS and design specific activities that would align with certain curricular topics. During some of this additional teacher preparation time, we conducted discussions with the teacher through face-to-face conversations, telephone calls and emails, supporting him in designing, planning, delivering and reflecting on topics such as *materials, the periodic table, physical and chemical changes* and *diet and nutritional values of organic and inorganic substances.* We conveyed to the class teacher our own directions for these activities to improve scientific engagement and sciencey-ness among the Muslim south Asian girls.

Storytelling as science nudges

At the core of our science nudges was the use of storybooks. The decision to do so emerged from informal conversations with the class teacher and his students, where story reading and writing sessions were seen as a favoured part of school life. Engaging school-aged girls in science through storybooks and other media, such as film and documentaries, is seen by some researchers to be enormously valuable (e.g. Rennie, 2014). Using fiction books and characters, it is said, can help to tease out scientific concepts. An example would be using the *Iron Man* to teach chemical and physical properties of ferrous compounds. Similarly, stories provide a mediating platform that can help students link to fictional characters, such as watching the *Inside Out* film about a young girl, Riley, and then reflecting on the evolving nature of learning and emotions in a science classroom (Salehjee, 2017).

Therefore, with a clear *purpose* for an effective *implementation* the class teacher, with support from SS, embedded three stories in the science classes in eighteen weeks, building in problems and activities in and around the normal diet of science lessons. Students were supported mainly by their class teacher and occasionally by SS in communicating scientific interpretations and practices entailed in the stories and characters, performing classroom-based science investigations and connecting scientific knowledge and skills to their everyday out-of-school lives. Modes of students' learning included reading children's stories through the lens of science, writing stories, science poetry, designing artefacts, keeping a research journal (scrapbook), engaging with problem-solving classroom-based activities and reflecting on the beliefs and opinions about the use of science in everyday lives. Some key details of these science nudges are:

Story 1: Charlie and the Chocolate Factory

This *nudge* involved reading some of the book's chapters and discussing the use of scientific vocabulary followed by problem-solving activities to investigate and evaluate (1) the design of a chocolate boat and chocolate bridge to test for strength and stability; (2) we used acids and base, and dilution tests,

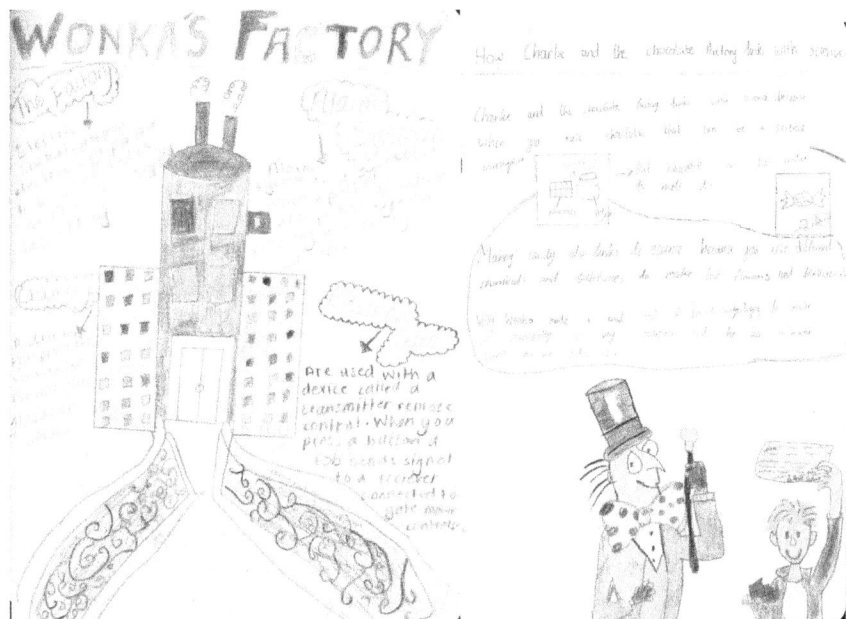

Figure 7 Everyday science: *Charlie and the Chocolate Factory*.

using blueberries; and (3) performing chromatography using coloured chocolate buttons. Students were then asked to link scientific vocabulary and investigations with their everyday lives. This was achieved through oral and poster presentations (Figure 7).

Story 2: The film, The Wizard of OZ

Here the students were asked to identify and discuss the use of scientific vocabulary and actions presented in the film. They were asked to familiarize themselves with (1) properties of some metals including iron and tin, (2) the process of rusting of iron and (3) misconceptions of Tin Man rusting. The students then linked scientific vocabulary and episodes in the film to their everyday lives. This was presented through annotations, written accounts on misconceptions and discussions with peers.

Story 3: The making of 'bread' – stories compiled by the students themselves

This nudge story involved (1) student-led conversations about breadmaking with parents, siblings and friends, followed by a bout of internet research. They were required to note scientific terms, types of bread, nutrition values, recipes, and the history of breadmaking; (2) students investigated different types of bread under microscopes and tested for organic and inorganic molecules using iodine and flame tests. They then (3) presented their work in the form of a book including self-narrated short stories, poems, pictures, facts and highlighting scientific vocabulary and concepts.

Our research approaches

Aligning with Bell's *measurable and demonstrable outputs*, we gave the girls numerous opportunities to tell us about their in- and out-of-school science lives through a sequence of short conversations and through opportunities to recall, reflect and write their thoughts and perceptions about being sciencey. We also asked them to reflect on social structures that have shaped and reshaped their Sci-ID (Salehjee & Watts, 2018). We sought to understand their science lives through the opportunities they offered (McAdams & McLean, 2013). The stories were collected over one academic year. We also used *science status questionnaires*, *science nudges evaluations* and *informal conversational interviews* as means to evaluate the implementation's impact on the girls' dispositions and acceptance of science in their lives, a shift in their ability to think and act as a scientific literate person and a movement towards the feeling of being sciencey. Our data collection methods were:

1.   The science status questionnaire

We used a science status questionnaire both before and after the science nudges by asking all thirty students to complete the statements below:

1. *I want to study .... subjects after the age of 16 because*
   ....
2. *I want to pursue .... career in the future because*
   ....
3. *I engage with science in .... (indicate places) by ...... (write how you engage with science in these places) ....*
4. *I feel 'sciencey' because*
   ...

2.   *Science nudges* evaluations

The class teacher, Mr Mark, used students' accounts to assess their performances formatively and made evaluative notes on the use of children stories as part of his teaching. At the end of each science nudge we asked students to rate each one using stars (*) from one to five, where one * meant poor and five * meant excellent. Students were also asked to write their views (if any) in the given comment box.

3. Conversational interviews

We gathered additional data through numerous day-to-day conversations and, in particular, we engineered informal semi-structured conversational interviews with all the girls. All the seventeen girls came forward to take part to discuss their social structures' impact on becoming sciencey and scientists (or not). Our research approach adhered closely to our university's ethical guidelines regarding permissions, freedom of expression, confidentiality and security of data.

The participants

Table 13 The seventeen participant girls

	Place of Birth	Self-Designation
Alia	Dubai	Schoolgirl secondary
Afreen	Oman	Schoolgirl secondary
Benish	England	Schoolgirl secondary
Dunia	Maldives	Schoolgirl secondary
Dilshad	Iran	Schoolgirl secondary
Faiza	Scotland	Schoolgirl secondary
Falak	England	Schoolgirl secondary
Halima	England	Schoolgirl secondary
Hannan	Scotland	Schoolgirl secondary
Isra	Pakistan	Schoolgirl secondary
Lakshmi	Scotland	Schoolgirl secondary
Maha	Spain	Schoolgirl secondary
Meera	India	Schoolgirl secondary
Raheema	England	Schoolgirl secondary
Shyla	Scotland	Schoolgirl secondary
Uma	Scotland	Schoolgirl secondary
Zarnish	Pakistan	Schoolgirl secondary

More pen portraits

Alia is an eleven-year-old girl, passionate to become an ophthalmologist in future. She was born in Dubai and moved to Scotland with her family at the age of seven. Her parents are non-scientists and runs a small business in Glasgow. They always appreciate Alia's passion of becoming an ophthalmologist. She loves school science, informal science and her determination of becoming an eye surgeon initiated from the age of nine/ ten after meeting her grandmother's eye surgeon in Dubai. To achieve her passion, she gives extra attention to school science and in spare time learn about the structure of eyes and watch eye surgery-based teaching videos on YouTube. Alia views herself as an independent Scottish young woman and so don't see her gender, religion and immigrant status as barriers to achieve her passion of becoming an ophthalmologist.

Benish was born in England and is eleven-year-old. Both parents were born in Pakistan. Her mother owns a restaurant, and her father is a lawyer, all now living in Scotland. Her parents bring science kits for her to play with, which she thoroughly enjoys, and she is also seen as a good science student at school. Currently, she appreciates out-of-school science much more than the formal education of science, as she can see science in the stories she loves. Moreover, Benish believes that the fantasy-based ideas in children's stories could become true in the future with the advancement of science. Despite her engagement with scientific learning, she loves writing stories. She is determined to proceed with it in future, though very recently Benish has shown some interest in becoming a mechanical engineer.

Hannan is eleven-year-old, she was born in Scotland, her mother is an Egyptian-born British doctor and father a Pakistani-born schoolteacher. Hannan enjoys conversations with her mum about hospital work but certainly has no aspirations to become a doctor. What she likes about her parents is the 'hard work' and 'goal setting' in their working lives. Science at school is enjoyable, for Hannan, when she is engaged with practical work. Hannan's wish is to open a café. She might take biology and physics subjects at school but, beyond that, she intends to specialize in business studies and home economics. Religion for Hannan is essential in her life, and almost every day, her father shares the stories narrated in Quran with her. These stories, she believes, are very powerful and learning for everyone, Muslims and non-Muslims.

Halima is twelve-year-old and the youngest of four siblings. She was born in England and moved to Scotland at the age of three. Her father is an immigrant from India; he is a computer engineer and Halima sees him as her role model. She is well supported by her father and rest of the family in developing herself as a science person. She is a high achiever, loves school science and is always involved in discussions about science and society at home and school. Halima's passion is to become an aeronautical engineer and to serve the country by joining the Royal Air Force (RAF), but sometimes she worries that her south Asian and Muslim identity would be problematic in becoming a RAF engineer.

Outcomes

We look at outcomes of our science nudges in terms of three *migrational shifts*, beginning with the short questionnaire:

1. *Shifts in considerations of education and career*

The first two questions on our science status questionnaire were aimed at noting any shifts in the girls' intended career choices. At the start of the study, most of the girls (fourteen of the seventeen) preferred non-science subjects to science – their favourite subjects being English and physical education (PE). The majority said they would choose these subjects beyond the age of compulsory schooling and so were looking towards pursuing non-science-oriented education and careers as soon as they had the choice to do so. At the end of the one-year project, the figures had flipped; now, thirteen of the seventeen girls had changed direction, preferring science to non-science education and careers (five of the thirteen) or wishing to pursue with both science and non-science subjects with some aspirations of becoming scientists (eight of the seventeen). We must note that this increased interest in science did not reduce interest in English or PE. Rather, our sense is that the stories acted as a bridge between English and science and simply improved their interest in both subject areas. The remaining four girls remained steadfast, preferring the same non-science subjects and choices, with no apparent change of direction over time.

2. *Becoming more scientifically literate*

The change in their perceptions before and after the science nudges showed a marked increase in girls' opinions about their family (from five to twelve), about children's stories (from two to seventeen) and places other than home and school (from zero to seventeen). These nudges initiated cognitive development in their meaning-making within science, allowing them greater ability to explain their understandings of science. We can see some of the girls becoming self-enquirers in their learning experiences in science. This encompassed both their in-school and out-of-school activities as they understood the wider application of science, for instance:

> Dunia: I do karate in school, which is body balancing strength and flexibility – that's science.
>
> Zarnish: In the school assembly, sometimes we talk about good eating habits and the correct way of drinking a glass of water in three sips.

These learning experiences generated curiosity and problem-solving capacities and understanding the relevance of science in the context of family life too, such as:

> Afreen: I made the dark-chocolate boat at home with my sister. . . . Yes, we talked about floating and sinking too . . . Surprisingly there was no difference in floating and sinking using white or milky chocolate, so the colour doesn't matter. My sister is older than me, so she knew the words . . . hmm . . . you know, density and concentration.

Some of the girls talked about social contexts other than home and school and so were allowing their science learning to emerge from, and merge with, wider everyday experiences, for instance:

> Afreen: In the Spring Fair, I learned about diffusion, dilution of coloured henna in water, all the art stuff and then applying lemon-sugar mixture after the henna is dried to make the colour darker and keep it to stay on your hands for longer.
>
> Dilshad: I have learned a lot from these stories – like trust, jealousy . . . friendship, teamwork. Team working is a skill that I can use in school, and even in my Scout sessions, we see how we work with each other as a group.

Overall, we not only saw students' engagement with science as a *degree of immersion* into science – their reflections on their science learning experiences within everyday life gave us an indication of self-motivation towards becoming more scientifically literate.

3. *Feelings of 'being sciencey'*

The class was asked about the extent to which they see themselves as a sciencey person. We gave no clear definition of what we mean by *sciencey*, simply allowing them to make meaning of the term themselves. Before the science nudges, almost half (eight of the seventeen) did feel that they were sciencey, the other half not so. Delving deeper, we came to understand that, for most, their perceptions of being sciencey were restricted to school science and, in fact, actually entailed achieving *good grades*, rather than any broader view. However, after the science nudges, the changes were twofold: first, all the seventeen girls felt that they were becoming sciencey and, second, their perception of being sciencey included a broader sense of what was entailed by science. They showed understandings of science not only through school science but also from the experiences gained at home, through mainstream media and social events. For example, completing the sentence 'I feel sciencey because I can . . .', some said:

Falak: Engage with the learning of science more (than before) from books, internet, and science centre.

Halima: [Observed that] science is around us in the real world and even in the fantasy world.

Benish: Talk about science with my friends and older cousins.

Alia: Feel that it's (science) not only science we study at school . . . and so not that difficult after all.

Dunia: Plan stories linking to science . . . and it helped me to see science at home, in the park, while I am travelling through car, train and plane.

In addition, these girls began to see what it means to be *sciencey and becoming a scientist*, as one of them stated:

Isra: A sciencey person is someone who is very much into science, being nosey . . . so uses science in living a healthier and happier life. And scientists are (people) who do a job and earn money from this job. So, I see myself as a sciencey person but not a scientist.

No student criticized the activities, and all the stories and accompanying activities were rated three star or above. Girls were happy (all seventeen) to do more of these activities in the future. We were heartened by this, and we saw that the four main changes in the girls emerging from these evaluations included their increased interest, engagement so that, for example, Maha, Meera and Raheema said:

Maha: Science is everywhere, I found out so many words in the *Charlie and the Chocolate Factory* book . . . At home, I am reading *Percy Jackson* and the *Sea of Monsters* – it has lots and lots of science in it too.

Meera: Now I also look into the library books and try to make hypotheses. And I've tried some research work at home. Like, you know, in stories there are witches that have broomsticks so it means it [broomsticks] need energy to fly - so that's science too, and so it can't be magic. I'm thinking a lot about it nowadays.

Raheema: My mum was a bit shocked when she found out that I am . . . writing a story, a poetry and making bread for science. But she helped me along with my older sister, and we made different types of bread like chapatti and flat bread on the stove and scones in the oven. We were using the same flour but different amounts of water and added some baking powder in scones to rise . . . We all enjoyed, learned science and . . . ate delicious bread.

They talked, too, about misconceptions in the stories such as:

Zarnish: Roald [Dahl] has used a lot of science in the story, like melting, heat energy and suction force – some fantasy as well. Like Mike's TV got smaller and Augustus got too much stretched like rubber – but it's not scientifically proven. Some science in *Wizard of Oz* is incorrect, too, like rusting of Tin and not Iron.

We certainly enjoyed their curiosity and their own recognition of being curious about phenomena both in the stories and in everyday life:

Uma: Lots of things makes me curious about science now, models of bubbles, liquids, and solids, because there is so much of science that needs to be discovered by Charlie [from *Charlie and the Chocolate Factory*] and by anyone like him. And so, I always used to think that I want to find something new and develop it further.

Lakshmi: Well, yes, it sounds strange, but I have started to think a lot about particles including rain, hail, snow, dust, like in *Wizard of Oz*, that are around me. And that makes me read more about it and then I get very much interested in the science part of it.

Finally, we turn to the informal semi-structured conversational interviews that we conducted with the seventeen girls. The science nudges fostered conversations that portrayed increasing aspirations towards science in these girls' lives and illustrated changes in their viewpoints towards a growing identity with science. That is, we mapped the Sci-ID migration as the girls' Sci-ID slowly drifted towards a greater disposition towards science and some glimpses as to how they might be successful in science. The girls we interviewed responded to three main questions:

Q1. What are your future educational and career aspirations?
Q2. Can you think of a storybook character as an interpretation of you being a sciencey person?

Q3. Do you think, being a young Scottish, south Asian and Muslim person will impact upon (1) you being sciencey? (2) your future educational/career choices? Please say how and why.

After the science nudges all the seventeen girls we interviewed perceived themselves as *being sciencey* and exhibited willingness to strengthen their *sciencey-ness* during the interviews. Their responses led us to categorize them within three themes: Being sciencey (1) with aspirations to become a scientist, (2) some aspirations to become a scientist and (iii) no aspirations to become a scientist (Table 14).

We have chosen four of the seventeen interviewees to detail their accounts in response to our third question, their sense of any impact of ethnicity, gender, nationality and religion on their ways of thinking. We enjoy these responses because all four accounts indicate the capacity of science nudges to shift and change their dispositions towards being sciencey. We indulged ourselves in some member-checking processes by asking the four girls to subsequently check and amend their accounts in order to maximize response validation.

1. *Being 'sciencey' with aspirations to become a scientist*

Table 14 The impact of structural influences on being sciencey/becoming scientist

| Names | Age | Perceived Structural Influences | | Themes: Being Sciencey |
		Privileges	Barriers	
Alia	12	Scottish nationality	Gender inequity	Aspirations to
Halima	13		South Asian inequity	become a scientist
Isra	12	Nationality		(five of seventeen
Uma	12	Gender equity		girls)
Zarnish	13	Gender equity	Gender inequity	
Afreen	11	Religious freedom		Some aspirations
Benish	13	Gender equity		to becoming a
Dilshad	11		Gender inequity	scientist
Faiza	12	Scottish nationality		(eight of seventeen
Falak	12	Scottish nationality		girls)
Maha	11	Gender equity		
Meera	11	Scottish nationality		
Shyla	13	Gender and religious inequity		
Dunia	12		Gender inequity	No aspirations to
Hannan	11	Religious teachings		become a scientist
Lakshmi	12		Gender inequity	(four of seventeen
Raheema	12	Scottish nationality		girls)

Five girls aspired to become scientists – ambitions they had, they said, from an early age.

Alia – a future ophthalmologist

Alia was born in Dubai and now resides in Scotland. She loves school science, portrays a strong inclination to become a doctor from a young age and said:

> I always knew that I would like to become a doctor but was not sure which doctor and, from the age of nine or ten, I have become very much more persistent with myself that I'm going to become an eye surgeon.

Alia's parents were born in Pakistan and currently run a small business in Glasgow. Although non-scientists, they have never discouraged her from becoming a scientist, have always motivated her to do what she wants in life. She discussed how she identifies herself as a female ophthalmologist, which she can achieve *with no barriers*. She was determined that if gender ever became an obstacle, she would fight for it much in the way of *Jo*; Jo is the central character in the story of *Little Women*:

> I don't think that being a male or a female matter in becoming a surgeon – if I was a boy, I could become whatever I want. So, my gender should not affect what I do. And if it might affect my decision, then I will fight for it. Like Jo from the *Little Women*. I love the character of Jo because she's a strong woman. I like the book because it shows how independent women are and why women should fight to get what they want. My country [Scotland] allows me to fight against such things to achieve my passion.

After the science nudges, she read the book *Charlie and the Chocolate Factory* in a new light and said:

> I never thought that there can be so much science in such a book, I enjoyed bringing in my science knowledge from my science books to read the story.

She also reflected on her appreciation of other subjects:

> I am interested in geography and literature but not to such an extent that it will make me take it up further in life. Basically, because of the links between geography and science, we learnt about pollution, and I liked that as it is really about science. Now stories and literature too.

Halima – a future aeronautical engineer

Halima was born in England and then, from the age of three, became resident in Scotland. She is a high achiever in science and 'always wanted to become an engineer', in particular, 'an aeronautical engineer' – ever since she was five/six- years-old. Her father is a computer engineer and her mum 'stays at home and busy all the time'. She believes that her father has influenced her in wanting to be an engineer. Halima exhibited clear Sci-ID development along with family's support. She did, though, worry about her being south Asian:

> I think like a scientist. I literally enjoy fixing things at home with a feeling that I can do it because I have the (science) skills to solve problems. Nothing can stop me there. Plus, my dad is a kind of a scientist. So, nothing will go wrong. The only thing that I think of is that I would like to join the RAF [Royal Air Force] as an engineer serving my country, but then my [heritage] . . . brown skin, black hair and eyes might become a problem because people might judge me differently. I hope not!

There was no movement away from science – Sci-ID migration was towards greater identity formation – over one schoolyear, although Halima's appreciation of science in life broadened after the science nudges:

> Now I can see more of science around me . . . My favourite is *actually A Storm in a Teacup* because it's all about physics. It's mostly everyday life that what happens in a teacup when you put in milk and tea. And what happens when the popcorn pops in the microwave, and how fireworks work. There's so much stuff and it is really quite interesting . . . so I resemble the stormy teacup.

Moreover, it is not only science that Halima likes; she also appreciates the use of languages and arts but was clear that this would not be her direction in life:

> I like drawing, and stuff in English and French languages. I want to learn them so that if I go abroad, I will be multilingual and (so it) will help me in future. But I always see myself . . . as an aeronautical engineer.

2. *Being sciencey but with some aspirations to becoming a scientist*

Eight girls gained confidence in doing science but unsure to become professional scientists. We describe Benish's story here, who exhibits an ambivalence about science.

Benish – a future story writer or a mechanical engineer

Benish was born in England; her mother owns a restaurant and father is a lawyer, all now living in Scotland. Both parents were born in Pakistan. Before the science nudges, she was inclined to become a storywriter but after the nudges showed some inclination of taking science. She said:

> English is my favourite subject and I enjoy it, and I love writing, I can write non-stop, it just comes naturally to me. But sometimes things vary and all the time – and I feel like I'm getting better at science.

Benish believes that her parents would like her to choose whatever career she wants and would not influence her (or her sister) in becoming a writer or engineer:

> If my sister become an engineer, that's not a problem. Being boy or a girl doesn't matter – it's what I'm interested in – not the fact that I am a girl.

Her mother bought her 'science kits' so that she could design experiments with her younger sister. She thoroughly enjoyed this, making her think she was quite a sciencey person:

> When I was younger, my mum brought different kinds of experimental kits for us almost every week, and now at home I design experiments with my sister and make different kind of models. Like recently we made a model of kidneys by looking at a YouTube video. My mum and dad never sit with us and do these things with us, but they always provide all the materials and whatever we ask for.

After the science nudges and conversations about learning science, Benish acknowledged that she is inquisitive about out-of-school science – especially 'engineering stuff':

> Thinking about science comes from a variety of places. So, when I see something, science related, I start thinking about it and I like to expand on it. Then when I come across something new, something interesting in science, I keep researching about it. But if I don't get interested into it, I don't expand on it. For example, in the *Kelvin Grove Art Museum* the red steam engine fascinated me a lot, I took pictures of the information related to the engine and researched an article online and expand on it further by looking at recent engines – so my depth of knowledge about it grows as well as my interest in it.

Nevertheless, her storytelling propensity seemed to win out over science:

Alice in Wonderland is my favourite book, because it's very well written and is full of jokes. There is fantasy and the story just changes very rapidly. After learning science from *The Wizard of Oz* story, I started to see Alice differently. There are a lot of emotional things in it – happiness, sadness and confusion – and there is a lot going on in every chapter. One minute someone is dying and the next minute someone is dancing, and then they are saving themselves from disastrous creatures. So, when I think about it, stories do not only contain things that we know but also what we don't know, the things that are fantasy might become [scientifically] true one day. For example, the thing about liquid potions that made Alice smaller and bigger – could be real potions of drugs one day, who knows?

3. *Being sciencey but with no aspirations of becoming a scientist*

Four girls come under this category.

Hannan's story – a future café owner.

Hannan, introduced earlier in the chapter, is born in Scotland, her mother an Egyptian-born doctor, her father a Pakistani-born schoolteacher. Her wish is to open a café. She might take biology and physics subjects at school but, beyond that, she intends to specialize in business studies and home economics to benefit her 'dream café'. She portrayed a very strong Muslim identity, and she is the only student from our study who talked about the way the school supported her religious beliefs:

> I fit in this school well – like a jigsaw, because when I'm here it makes me practice my religion more [as compared to my previous school] and it helps me to become a better Muslim, so that I have a better connection with God. In my previous school, I was not that religious, and I was a very different – a completely different person. I started wearing hijab [headscarf] here, I think I am more modest here and I think that I am a better person now.

She also linked her Sci-ID with religion and believed that being a Muslim would benefit her being sciencey in the future:

> In the Quran you learn science from different stories. Like you know holy water Zamzam actually responds to you. So, when a Muslim person says Bismillāh [in the name of God] the water forms beautiful snowflakes – ice crystals. But when a person swears on water, then it results in a very ugly snowflake. So, water does actually respond to what you say and who you are.

Hanna's academic and professional choices did not change over time but her feeling of being sciencey was much increased. Before the nudges, her view of being a science person related to 'paying attention in the classroom', 'having good marks in science tests'. Later, her perceptions of science broadened to non-obvious practices:

> Some things that I link with science - like school science experiments – are very obvious. That was before but now I can see science where it is not very obvious. And I can see that everything could have science in it. So, I knew that sound is important and it's around us but then doing science from a story which is not obvious does make me picture science more clearly . . . I read *Charlie and the Chocolate Factory* before, but I never thought of bringing science into it. And now I see that there is a lot of science – and me doing the project and doing science makes me feel sciencey.

The class teacher

Quite clearly, while we were busy supporting the science story work in the classroom, the class teacher, Mr Mark, was instrumental in bringing the work to fruition. When we looked at the evaluations of the activities themselves, the class teacher was very positive, for example:

> I can see more learning, engagement and critical thinking skills developing among students.
> The use of scientific vocabulary has become part of their day-to-day school routine.
> Without proper laboratory facilities, we managed to link school science with everyday science, which has broadened students' [scientific] understanding and practical skills.

In contrast, Mr Mark did find that:

> the chocolate boat activity and designing a super-hero(ine) costume was too open-ended and challenging for some students.

Some reflections on this case study work

The lessons we learn from the project centre on the changes in perceptions of being sciencey secondary school context. We are interested in these shifts in identity as indicators of greater dispositions towards science and, therefore, of greater likelihood of future success in science. As a case study of a class of students, our capacity to generalize is very limited. We can, though, highlight several areas of interest whereby we can make inferential judgements about the value of such work. Overall, following Bell's elements required for successful interventions and its alignment with PfS, we feel that the outcomes from one academic year's work were very positive. We could see increases in students' scientific knowledge. As we have illustrated in the quotes earlier, this was not just in mainstream curriculum science but in appreciation of the science around them in everyday life. That is, the beginnings of an appreciation of their own science lives. This was not an either-or exercise – either have fun with science or reject it and have fun with English, it proved to be an additive process so that the girls were at the same time reading and writing stories while also performing associated science experiments. To a greater extent, they were able to engage in scientific discussions through linking some scientific terms, predictions, ideas, concepts and misconceptions with the children's stories we used and eventually to their everyday lives. Their confidence in doing and appreciating science grew over time, as did their ability to see themselves as being sciencey. This successfully challenged their prior perceptions of being sciencey as simply being a measure of high achievement in science tests and examinations.

We count our science nudges, then, as a qualified success and are heartened that so many could move to a greater appreciation of science in their lives. Our goal was not to persuade all these students to become career scientists but simply to work at modifying perceptions, encouraging curiosity, to seek a broader remit for science, invite them to keep an open mind on matters scientific and reflect on their growing identities. This certainly seemed to have worked for a substantial number of the girls. We have no way of knowing at this point of time how long-lasting are these movements towards science nor what future experiences may yet impact upon them that either enhance or reverse the changes we have discussed here. For certain, we believe that such science nudges should continue to feature in school science to increase – or at least maintain – impact on students' aspirations and, hopefully, impact upon their out-of-school science lives as well.

As we have noted in previous work (Salehjee & Watts, 2020) that there will almost certainly be some unmoveable people at both ends of a spectrum of change. Five of the seventeen girls were already determined to become scientists, and, at best, the science nudges simply reinforced their personal aspirations. Similarly, for four of them, becoming scientists was simply not going to be part of their future world. In these cases, the activities simply washed over them and made little or no difference to their attitudes or predilections of becoming scientists. We do feel that the nudges helped them to realize that they can be sciencey without becoming scientists. In the middle of our sample are eight girls who have showed some spark of interest in becoming scientists after the science nudges. Needless to say, we cannot predict that they will continue with science education or head towards science careers. Who knows? There is always a possibility that, at some future point, they decide to retrain away from their current roles and take on responsibilities that require elements of science in their work. That is, if they experience some *positive and forceful nudges in life*. In this case, we are also heartened that in our effort of making students sciencey we did not turn off any of the students – we had no reports of anyone being adversely affected by the activities to actually set them against science.

It is certainly true that the science nudges, the science learning experiences, were all of a kind, designed in collaboration with the class teacher and based upon literacy activities through books and films. This deliberately traded on the declared interests of members of the class. The stories chosen were not of themselves (science stories) but were popular texts, and these were then used to explore how they might be read *with science in mind*. As Olga V. Kritskaya and John M. Drix (1999) have argued, such texts can support reflection, can provide a catalyst to seeing (science) within stories and give opportunity to reflect on personal insights, perceptions, practices and conversations. Therefore, we found further Sci-ID formation with the learning experiences, science nudges, accommodating new learning though strengthening their Sci-ID.

Chapter summary

The thrust of this section of our work is that accumulated small nudges towards science can aggregate and work to change young people. Through our own and the class teacher's observations, we see that the students enjoyed the chocolate activities the most – although we consider that the independent activities on breadmaking were also of considerable significance. That said, we do see all the activities as having an *accumulative impact* and that neither the chocolate activities nor bread activities alone have the capacity to stimulate meaning-making, engender critical reflection and can promote movement in their learning (Mezirow, Taylor & Associates, 2009). In many cases, these changes through nudges have pushed these students to critically reflect and evaluate the scientific practices around them, practices that are not restricted to school science.

In intersectional terms, the structural influences of *being Scottish* were generally seen not as a barrier but as a *privilege*. It was seen to be an enabling factor in *becoming scientific*. Similarly, *religion* was indicated by many as an advantage in being sciencey. These students' *south Asian parents*, even most parents with non-science backgrounds, were reported to be *supportive* to their children's educational and career decisions, and so these girls saw themselves as having independent choice in their school subjects – be those within science or not. It is certainly the case that *gender* was seen as a *privilege* for some, although it was also seen as a *barrier* for others. In this sense, our results fail to match exactly the work of other authors in the field. For example, our case study did not portray immigrant status as a barrier. Nor, in this sample, do south Asian parents dictate their children's future, nor do these young women feel less privileged in science – and being female and Muslim was seen as a barrier for a few, but certainly not for all. We construct the outcomes of the case study as a re-emphasis of the position we expounded in 1 and 2 show that intersectionality can be driven down to the individual and that these structural influences can be read in terms of the unique and personal interpretations of the individuals.

Our final comments here relate to our PfS, aligned as it is with Bell's (2014) seven 'elements of successful intervention'. Between ourselves as researchers, through SS's onsite involvement with the class, through the sterling organizational work of the class teacher and through the active collaboration and endorsement of the headteacher and senior management of the school, we managed – for a whole academic year – to engender a wonderfully science-positive environment. And, in our view, that science-positive environment certainly paid dividends. The *relational web* that was created meant that the teacher-student relationships became more dialogic, discursive and conversational. Prevailing courtesy, consideration and respect were easily retained even while the fabric of formality was more relaxed and engaging. The *objectival direction* for each part of the year was clear and structured yet was reached in a way that fed into the girls' personal interests, their home lives and their increasing recognition of their own science lives. The *knowledge flow* became multidirectional so that it was not simply a case of teacher-telling, but the activities gave rise to considerable student autonomy so that they, too, could inform the class teacher of what was happening. The group work problem-solving activities meant that peer-to-peer interactions were common, and the girls learned from each other. In addition, we see it as important for these girls to have the opportunity to discuss their reflections and self-perceptions in relation to their gender, ethnicity, race and class as these benefit (or not) the development of their Sci-ID. Most important for us, the *experiential texture* of the science lessons changed in a very significant way. The activities were enjoyable and engaging, and this drove the increasing interest and engagement with the science in and behind the stories. We think it is clear from the many things they said, as we illustrate earlier, that the girls appreciated the warm feel of the lessons. Science lessons were not seen as boring, they were not clouded in mystery, they were not rigidly framed around arcane concepts and remote ideas. Finally, the *evaluative tone* became shared, so the girls were themselves judges of progress, of success in what they achieved. It is true that this was not a formal examination period for these girls and so there was a greater degree of freedom in how the science curriculum could be framed. Nevertheless, they were most certainly able to make evaluative comment on their own progress and on the value of the science lessons they had experienced.

8

Life Changes and Transformations

In this chapter, we make use of Jack Mezirow's (1991) transformative learning theory and, more fixedly, its iteration by Knud Illeris (2014). Mezirow's theoretical framework is useful for understanding the personal stories, the ways in which individual lives develop and transform in journeys from early science through compulsory science education, then onwards to crystallization as a scientist. In this chapter we leave formal schooling behind and consider the life-changing events that can happen in-between stages of education and beyond, well after it is finished. There are clearly many different kinds of transformative experience and events in women's lives, from single deeply salient events that shape their ambitions and *life directions* to numerous instances that impel women towards – or away from – a study of science. To this extent, we leave behind the idea of the aggregation of numerous small changes – nudges – in favour of a few large life-changing ones.

In our book *Becoming Scientific: Developing Science across the Life-Course* (2020), we used transformative learning theory as one of the foundations of our theoretical framework, in adapting Mezirow's theory, we mapped the *science identity (Sci-ID) migration* of seventy multiaged women and girls from various ethnic and social class backgrounds. The transformative learning approaches were embedded in our empirical work in order to capture individual's formation and transformation in Sci-ID over the course of their lifetime. Needless to say, we were not present for the entire duration of their lifespan; instead, we relied upon their own accounts of what had taken place at important moments in their lives. In this chapter, we continue with the discussion of Sci-ID migration we began in Chapter 7, but we root it even more firmly in transformative learning theory in relation to success. The main components of this migratory movement involve significant science learning experiences – experiences that are largely energetic, and correspond to individual's perceptions, emotions, meaning-making and actions in relation to science and, in particular, to science success.

So, the individual absorbs and engages with these energetic science learning experiences gained from their surroundings and reach out to grasp them on an ongoing basis. We attempt to cover both the formation and transformation of Sci-ID migration as a means of discussing Mezirow's theory. As our recent studies (2017, 2018, 2020, 2021) have highlighted some individuals' migration involves *formation*, that is, strengthening their Sci-ID further. These individuals are principally women already with a clear direction in science, and their science learning experiences – small or large – in their lives support them further in developing their Sci-ID. Some, however, have undertaken a more *transformative* route into a Sci-ID. These are women who were either science *hesitant* or even *science refusers*, where their initial learning experiences led them away from science – but their lives have later involved formation of identity into science. In the next section we look at the basics of transformative learning theory, followed by the representation of transformative science learning experiences of four south Asian women, Anita, Elif, Pavina and Vikki, by focusing on their stories of Sci-ID migration and their eventual stories of science success.

Transformative learning theory

In aligning transformative learning theory with identity transformation, Mezirow (2000) adopts the position that identity is fluid and is subject to change over time. However, his idea of fluidity requires some form of 'disorienting dilemma', a possible intense life experience that leads to dramatic change. He allows, too, that there can be instances where transformation happens slowly and silently, usually when accompanying micro-transformative experiences (Heddy & Kevin, 2015). We make two points here.

First, we do not see major changes happening in one's life *without some* small nudges having already happened to suggest that direction. That is, when a major event occurs and a radical rethink is required in life, it would be very unusual for a woman to suddenly strike out in an entirely capricious venture without any previous notions, inclinations or thoughts. It is not that a sudden whimsy might not catapult a woman into an entirely new life; it is that the new life might very well have had seeds of possibility sown previously in her thinking. In our terms, there are no transformations without nudges. This gives part of the rationale for why we have discussed nudges (Chapter 7) before transformations (Chapter 8). Second, in this chapter we leave behind therefore any discussion of *slow, silent, micro-transformative* experiences and focus instead on *rapid, loud, macro-transformations.*

In our view, the primary link between Mezirow's transformative learning theory and Illeris's (2014) identity model includes the *meaning-making* process whereby individuals negotiate their understanding of self in a way that shapes (transforms) their identity within social and cultural contexts. They describe this process of meaning-making as an intense, thoughtful journey of constructing the meaning of oneself through life experiences. In his 2000 work, Mezirow began this direction by distinguishing four principal processes that describe the core component of meaning-making. These are:

1. Elaborating Existing Frames of Reference
2. Learning New Frames of Reference
3. Transforming Habits of the Mind (or meaning perspectives)
4. Transforming Points of View (Mezirow, 2000, p. 22).

Taking these in turn, a 'frame of reference' encompasses 'structures of culture and language through which we construe meaning by attributing coherence and significance to our experience' (Mezirow, 2009, p. 92). A frame of reference consists of 'two dimensions – habits of mind and resulting points of view' (Mezirow, 2009, p. 92). 'Habits of mind' are the specific ways in which an individual thinks and feels, thoughts and emotions that result in a set of codes by which everyday life can be recognized and discussed. Specific habits of mind result in specific 'points of view'. We all have points of view concerning our lives and these may be informed by beliefs and attitudes, sustained as memories and actions. For Mezirow, frames of reference form the basis upon which we judge future-related actions (Mezirow, 2009). For example, gender and ethnicity discrimination acting as a code might result in a point of view that science employment is 'not for me because I am a woman of colour'. Or, conversely, as we have heard some of our participants say, 'I am determined to enter into science because I am a woman of colour'. These beliefs can remain in one's perception as memories that, later in life, act as a comment, a point of reference, on moments of decision-making. We understand the continuing meaning-making within day-to-day life as being similar to Erik Erikson's identity crisis (1968) and Mezirow's sense of 'critical reflection' (2000, 2009).

When an initial frame of reference is found to be inadequate in accommodating some new life experience, it can be replaced with a new one. This commonly entails adopting a fresh meaning perspective that heralds changes in habits of mind, a perspective that is 'more inclusive, discriminating, open, emotionally capable of change, and reflective'. In other words, a perspective that is 'more developed' (Mezirow, 2000, p. 7), which results in a transformation in points of view. These cover the last two of Mezirow's processes. The new frame of reference generates new bouts of meaning-making and new habits of mind, which in turn spawn new points of view. This elaborates the process of the continuing conflicts in day-to-day (educational and professional) life leading to learning 'new frames of reference' and eventually leading to self-development (D'Amato & Krasny, 2011).

It is not uncommon in Mezirow's work, and in the work of the legions of researchers who have followed him, for a person's critical reflection on an existing frame of reference to be initiated through conversations. Something a friend says, a one-off conversation with a passing stranger, a professional review with a colleague, a teacher, a counsellor – a conversation such as that can prompt an individual to examine the frame that condones or rejects some life experiences through 'continuous effort to negotiate contented meaning' (Mezirow, 2000, p. 3). The meaning-making process in a person's learning depends upon such critical self-reflections, specifically on the experiences that have taken place within a particular educational frame of reference or context.

Learning experiences, critical reflections and (trans)formative forces of change

Mezirow (1991, 2000, 2009) has long written about life-changing trans-formative experiences/moments as 'disorienting dilemmas' leading to critical reflections – that can sometimes be dramatically large – as in the case of Anita to come – generating expressions such as: 'I was shaken to the core!', 'It was a life-changing moment', 'I'll never be the same again!'. In a similar vein, Kevin Pugh, Cassendra Bergstrom and Bryden Spencer (2017) have used 'transformative experience theory' derived from Dewey's (originally 1929, now republished 1988) work to focus specifically on a chain of learning experiences that can result in critical reflections – involving transforming 'motivation', 'free-choice' learning, 'expansion of perception' and 'experiential value' of science to enrich everyday experiences among individuals (p. 369). In addition to large dramatic experiences, we see chains of learning experiences and associated critical reflections in many of the women's stories. So, whether one or an accumulation of a few large dramatic and/or a series learning experiences, the resulting critical reflection processes should be *intrinsically*

Learning experiences	**Transformative learning experiences**	Learning experiences	Learning experiences	**Transformative learning experiences**	Learning experiences

Critical reflections

Trans(formative) force of change

Accommodate new or more focused learning experiences

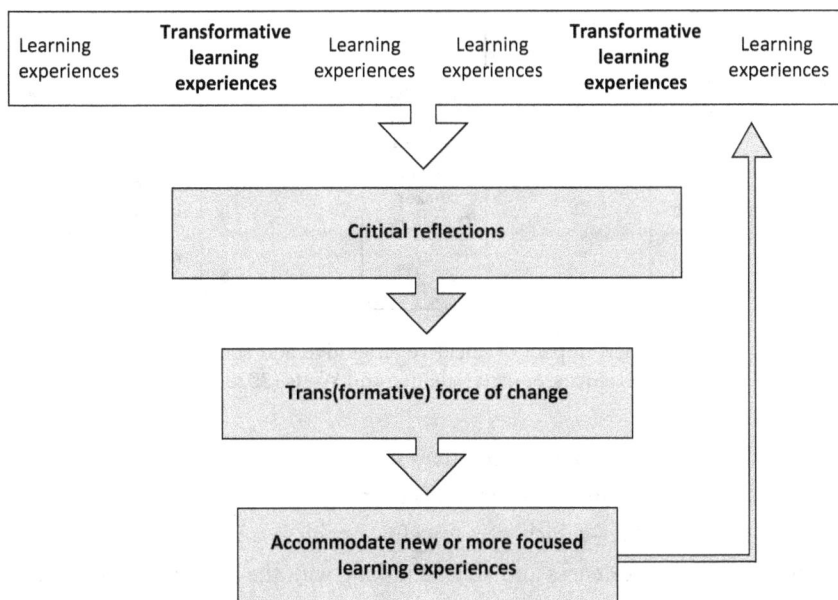

Figure 8 Our take on the (trans)formative learning adapted from Mezirow (2000).

forceful, leading to self-examination of pre-held assumptions and are often created through conversations with others and self – leading to what we call the (trans)formative force of change.

We acknowledge that not all the science learning experiences will change a person's perception of self-ability and self-motivation towards critical reflective processes. As Illeris (2014) makes the case that learning practices need to be of 'higher order' and require considerable energy to create changes – especially if those changes interfere with strong pre-held affiliations towards something. These *transformative learning experiences* include events, triggers and interventions initiating 'discourse leading to the critical examination of normative assumptions underpinning the learners . . . value judgments or normative expectations' (Mezirow, 2000, p. 31) (see Figure 8).

Learning experiences: Affective, cognitive and social dimensions

Pugh, Bergstrom and Spencer (2017), in advancing their concept of the chain of learning experiences, believe that these learning experiences broadly correspond to behavioural (we use social instead), cognitive and affective dimensions. Similarly,

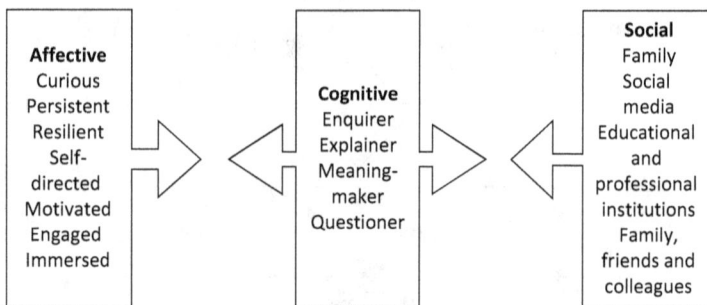

Figure 9 The combined impact of affective, cognitive and social dimensions on the chain of learning experiences. *Source*: Salehjee and Watts (2020)

we see transformative experiences that support the migration of people, for instance, Anita, into nursing that requires the transformative forces of change – to become a *super mother* – which were forceful enough to support Anita's upcoming science learning experiences and actions linking with the affective, cognitive and social dimensions. So, the transformative force of change accommodates new or more focused learning experiences corresponding to the existing meaning preceptive. Some qualities of these intrinsic forces of action towards science, drawn from our recent studies, under the three dimensions of affective, cognitive and social, are presented in Figure 9 (adapted from Salehjee & Watts, 2020).

As we have discussed in earlier chapters, the social dimension, for us, represents meso forces influenced by intersecting large macro forces with associated social categories (e.g. south Asian family and community, academic and professional institutions and (mis)recognition of south Asian women) playing a vital role in the migration ((trans)formation) of Sci-ID. However, these social aspects are not separate from the affective (micro level) dimensions, rather has a strong bond with it, as illustrated by Avraanidou (2020):

> identity as a landscape of becoming by placing emphasis on *recognition* and *emotions*, as core features of identity, through an intersectionality lens. These constructs intertwined, I argue, can give meaning to the process of becoming a science person or forming a science identity, and at the same time shed light on issues related to power, inequality, racism, and exclusion. (p. 323)

The cognitive dimension is no doubt influenced by both the meso-social and micro-affective dimensions. For example, as we detail further in the narratives later in the chapter, first Anita made meaning of her growing disposition towards science through enjoying and feeling good when watching mid-wife-oriented television dramas and through her experiences as a young mother. In our second narrative to come, Vikki's meaning perspectives were changed through heartfelt self-questioning of her own abilities and immersion in mathematics. Her excellent examination results reversed all her previous self-doubts when she was reassured that her grades were better than those of her peers – albeit White male class fellows – who she had thought were so much more superior. In this sense, we tie our understanding of this learning chain with Mezirow's – previously discussed – critical reflection processes. From our empirical studies we see that self-reflective processes need a person to be self-enquirer, self-questioner, self-ponderer and has the ability to self-reflect on existing explanations of their (science) lives.

Emotions of feeling incapable – such as those of Anita and Vikki – were part of the conversations with some young south Asian women in our previous (2017) study – where young women really did not feel able to make meaning of science because 'science is too difficult' and 'not for me' and they could not muster sufficient self-confidence to become engaged in science because 'formulae, terms and models don't make sense to me'. In their 2019 study, Emily Dawson and colleagues captured the actions of a group of minoritized girls in a science museum where, rather than enquiring about and questioning the exhibits in the gallery, some of the girls spent their time taking a series of *selfies*. Dawson et al. labelled this an instance of 'cool girl performance' – illustrating minimal intellectual interest in a particular social context (museum). Although we would rather see this as the cool girls' unwillingness to make any kind of cognitive or micro-affective investment in the science surrounding them. Quite clearly, this meso social context was problematic for these *cool* girls, even while other girls in the museum group seemed determined to exhibit their cognitive abilities by coming forward to ask and answer teacher's questions. Dawson et al. refer to this second group as having donned a 'masculine performance' cloak. Here again we see that the micro-affective involvement of wearing a cloak of masculine performance, to show their cognitive ability in a museum-based meso-social context, is predominant.

Transformations in women's lives

Let us return our attention to the transformations in the lives of south Asian women. The meaning-making processes leading to the transformation of a frame of reference could come about through a woman's own critical analysis of her life. If, as a result of that reflection, she feels the need for radical action then that reflection would act as a key instigator of change (Mezirow, 2009).

Our intention here is to delve into these transformations and then explore the implementation of a pedagogy for success (PfS). Before that, we present some participants (Table 15).

Table 15 Six more participants

	Place of Birth	Self-Designation
Anita	India	Nurse, proud mother
Elif	India	University undergraduate, biology
Jala	England	University undergraduate, physics
Pavina	Bangladesh	University undergraduate, forensic science
Preet	Sri Lanka	Social worker at a hospice
Vikki	England	University student, mathematics

And some further pen portraits:

Anita is a thirty-six-year-old children's nurse who views herself as a proud mother of eleven- and eight-year-old girls. She completed her school education in India, and while she was in her first year of college, she married a British-born man of Indian heritage. So, she moved to England at the age of seventeen. Education after school 'paused for seven years', during which time she had two daughters. Anita was divorced after these seven years of marriage. The reasons given by her ex-husband were that he found her incompatible with himself, that she was deemed 'incapable' because of her limited education and inability to work and because of her failure to give him a male child. After her divorce, Anita's academic, professional and personal life transformed. She became a strong, qualified, career-oriented mother. Returning to education was not easy, but she aspired to become a nurse. In part this was because she believed she had gained some learning from her own time in the hospital as a patient. She also greatly enjoys watching television serials based on nursing. Four years after her divorce, Anita began working as a qualified nurse and currently supports her family independently.

Preet always believed in her abilities and viewed herself as a 'brainy person'. Reflecting on this, she acknowledges herself to be a 'sciencey person . . . always used to be too proud of my abilities . . . my parents used to call me "doc" at home'. But then her life changed because of a health scare. At eighteen, she underwent emergency surgery for an inflamed appendix but, in her words, 'nothing serious'. As life happens, the surgery took place on the day Preet was due to sit an A-level chemistry examination. So, lying on the hospital bed in both frustration and anger, she felt helpless and realized that her overconfidence and pride needed to be re-configured. This self-reflection led her to work on becoming 'modest as a person'. Later, She carried on with her science A-levels subjects and enrolled to take biological sciences at university. After completing her BSc degree, she took on a voluntary role as a Punjabi to English interpreter at a nearby hospital. The hospital patients there were either new to the country or elderly. She then decided that she wanted to work in the national health service (NHS), not as a medical doctor but as someone who could support vulnerable and elderly patients. Currently, aged forty-five, she works as a social worker at a hospice in London.

Jala is the first in her family to go to university. She became switched on to physics at secondary school when her physics teacher set up an out-of-school visit to the National Space Centre in Leicester. She was wholly taken by an exhibition of the work on Major Tim Peake's six-month mission in the International Space Station and became absorbed by the way his duties were carried out in a low-gravity environment and the kinds of experiments he was conducting. During our conversations, Jala returned to this day at the Space Centre as having been hugely decisive in her choice of physics at A-level, and then at university. She has, she said, been back to the centre on many occasions and it still fascinates her. In her words, 'I am not so sure it was a turning point, but that day was certainly a consolidation of all of my thoughts and ideas up to then. When you're a young girl, you have all sorts of dreams and fantasies. But that day, Tim Peake's messages from space, and he played the guitar up in the space station, really stopped all the other directions in their tracks.'

Vikki shared her mathematics life with us, which includes some transformative learning experiences leading to critical reflection of her pre-held assumptions and a transformative force of change. We first met Vikki when she was twenty-one-years-old and then more recently at twenty-four. She belongs to a British Sri Lankan working-class family and is the first in the family to study at university. Her negative feelings, assumptions and beliefs about her own abilities and how other people (class fellows) see her have transformed over time. This realization took more than a year, and currently, at age twenty-four, she feels like an able woman mathematician and supports young women to see themselves as 'not less in any way from other students and just keep doing their best'.

As we heralded earlier, we begin these discussions by delving first into the narratives of four of these women, Anita, Vikki – whose pen portraits are described earlier – along with two others, Pavina and Elif. We will explore Mezirow's four principles, discussed earlier in this chapter, more thoroughly through their stories.

Anita

As described in her pen portrait, Anita is a single parent of two young girls. The background to her divorce was that she deemed unable to financially support her husband and his extended family and preferred to stay at home to look after her two young daughters. Her reluctance to work was also because she had not continued her studies after seventeen and had never before been in full-time employment. An additional allegation from her ex-husband was that she could not provide a *son* to continue the family name; 'sadly this gender-biased taboo still exists in some south Asian families'. The divorce was strung out over time; it extended beyond a few weeks or months. Moreover, Anita had faced a long series of adverse experiences over the previous five years of her marriage, so her initial *frame of reference* was very much enforced and reinforced by her husband and his family – of being 'useless', 'unsupportive' and 'illiterate'. After the divorce, now single with two daughters, the officers in social services recommended, among other things, that Anita return to her studies.

Anita found continuing education very difficult after a seven-year gap – so she was recommended to meet an employment counsellor, a meeting that Anita believes was a 'life-changing experience'. The counsellor supported her

> in thinking about my daughters and in being their 'super girl' [and so] this shifted my thinking from being a hopeless wife to a super mother.

Anita's conversations with the counsellor involved a series of critical reflections about her self-abilities and the need to support her daughters – resulting in learning new frames of reference. Her self-reflections changed her perceptions of her own meaning and direction of life – commensurate with Mezirow's changes of meaning perspectives and transforming habits of the minds. In Anita's case, her shift in meaning perspectives evolved rapidly after these conversing with the employment counsellor and through self-reflection of her own abilities. Her entire story portrays transformation of emotions and contemplations with her family, her interactions with educational institutions, career counsellors and, of course, herself.

Meeting the counsellor and Anita's progressive migration from 'hopeless' to 'superstar' did not happen instantly; it took a protracted series of meetings with the counsellor. Nevertheless, there were a series of seeds, periodic moments of reflection on self and exploration of the importance of her existence/positionality that led her to boost her ability and find the meaning of her life. One of the critical self-reflections she shared with us is:

> It took me a while to see myself as a person who can think independently because, during my married life, the female side of my existence was always discussed – sadly in a very negative way . . . I was less intelligent than my husband – which is WRONG . . . it was my fault that I had no son – again scientifically WRONG . . . I cannot lead my own life, again WRONG WRONG. But I stupidly accepted all these [misrecognitions] until I was left to survive with my daughters alone. God saved me!

We see that her intention of being a good mother was very evident even before the divorce, but the ongoing learning experiences in her life supported her in regaining her confidence. Anita is now thirty-six-years-old and a proud mother of eleven- and eight-year-old Meera and Mina and really enjoys her role as a nurse. She makes the following points:

> The seven-year gap in my education was huge – as we talk, I believe that I had no interest in any [educational] discipline and profession, no clue whatsoever, no childhood dreams that I can think of. I became more religious after the divorce and every day asked God to show me a direction – so he really did. There was a struggle in choosing a career for myself but with prayers and meditation I started to think about what I already know. This included my knowledge about difficult pregnancies, my own included, about childbirth from my own experience and my devotion for *No Angels* and *Call the Midwife* dramas on TV [laughs] . . . I believe this guided me to take up a children's nursing as a profession. And there are absolutely no regrets – None at all!

Viki

At age twenty-one, Vikki chose a mathematics course at university because of her self-interest. On one occasion, she said, 'even in my dreams, I am doing maths and never feel tired of doing calculations.' Vikki's early learning experiences at university, though, made her doubt her intellectual abilities. These experiences included being the *only south Asian woman* and *only one of the three women* in her first-year class of fifty students, leaving her to believe that men are better intellectually, especially in mathematics. Her impression was also that White women have a better upbringing and strong support from family and friends – unlike her own experiences. Moreover, she believed that her White class fellows view her as 'much less capable than them – although this was not true'.

Despite these feelings, believes and impressions, Vikki achieved the highest grades in some of the mathematics modules. Achieving better grades reinforced 'my madness towards mathematics' – another transformative learning experience but one opposing the previously held disposition – and this made her self-reflect critically on her intellectual abilities. So, Vikki decided that despite her differences in ethnicity and gender, she was as capable as any other of her class fellow. This resulted in a transformative force that powered a change in her habits of mind. Again, this change did not happen quickly. Instead, her meaning perspectives took a full academic year to develop. It was at the end of that year that she felt comfortable with taking a new look at what she achieved – and could achieve – regardless of what other class fellows might think about her. One moment stood out for her, a six-word sentence to her by a male classmate when she topped the statistics course. He simply said: 'We knew you could beat us.' On reflection, Vikki realised that 'they [her male class fellows] all *knew* but It was actually me that doubted my abilities'. So, according to Vikki, a six-word appreciation became the tipping point of her self-realization, and since then, there are 'no doubts and no feelings of being less competent than others'. Currently, at the age of twenty-four, she is working as an intern in a university supporting first- and second-year students as they work on their basic mathematical skills. Vikki mentioned:

> Mostly, the female students come and speak to me outside of the teaching time, during break times, in the cafeteria or library. They share similar fears and feelings of inability that I used to have three years back, [like] 'the others are much more able than me', 'I believe I have made a wrong decision', 'I think I need to change my course', etc. . . . So, I make sure to build their confidence and make them realise that they are able, probably more so than the others, and can progress in maths just as I have.

Pavina

Pavina is currently a university undergraduate who had little initial interest in the sciences beyond A-level and had studied sociology both at school and for the first year of her university degree programme. Like Vikki and others, she is the first in her family to go to university and is very much, she said, the family *pin-up girl* for academic success. Her brothers and sisters have all visited her university campus to 'see just what it is she does all day'. When her sister announced that she wanted to be a beautician, Pavia immediately pounced and talked about physiotherapy, about restoring people to *beautiful health*. Her younger sisters, too, have taken a liking to the look of university life and are working hard to follow in her footsteps. Her parents are busy working people, and she feels a strong responsibility towards her younger siblings ('Sometimes I'm like another mother to them').

In the summer of her first year, her best friend was killed in a car accident and ('stunned and horrified') Pavina took a year out from her studies ('My head was all over the place'). When she returned, she had fully re-evaluated her direction and enrolled not for sociology but for a forensic science degree. It was very hard, she said, to make up lost ground not only in recapturing the science she had previously studied at school but also in regaining her discipline for study. Her friend's death, though, 'had to mean something', and so Pavina set about transforming her own life in response. The university was understanding, and she was full of praise for the support she received through both the staff on the course and her classmates.

> My tutors were really great. They could see I was driven to succeed, and they gave me lots of help and opportunities. I didn't do well in the first set of exams and had to re-sit them. But by then I was getting back into the swing of things and although the grades on those exams were capped, I got into my stride, and I made sure I safely passed the next ones.

During our conversations she was hesitant and rather circled around her reasons for this significant change in direction. Clearly it was triggered by the death of her friend but there seemed to be more to it. Eventually she said:

> The man [the other driver in the car accident] just got away with it. He was going too fast, and we all think he was on his phone at the time, and he was guilty of careless and very possibly dangerous driving. It takes a split second, that's all, and it ended the life of my beautiful friend. He wasn't hurt, he made all sorts of claims in court and basically walked away scot free . . . [A long pause] . . . If it happens to someone else, I want to be someone who digs up the full story, gets to the truth.

As with other stories, Pavina's was not a sudden transformation in her life. Yes, the accident clearly triggered a full-blown rethink of what she was doing but the year away from academic studies was a long period of reflection. In that year she had earned money as a barista in a coffee bar, observing the lives of other people and ruminating on what she herself wanted to do.

There's still a bit of the sociologist in me when I am watching other people. But I decided that sociology would never take me right into the heart of the matter, I needed something more direct, more . . . hands-on . . . more . . . effective. So, the switch to the sciences. I love the lab sessions, I'm really into it now.

Elif

Elif says of her psychology degree that it lasted just three months. Almost as soon as she had graduated from university she married and began a family. From that point onwards, she says, she never used her psychology degree again. When her daughters were six- and four-years-old, like Anita mentioned earlier, she went through a messy divorce and became a single parent after her husband decided to return to India. He sank much of their shared assets into an ill-fated business and then he began work in a fairly low-level occupation to survive. Elif herself worked in an insurance office for many years, to the point when the girls reached school examinations age. She then decided she needed to do something that would *fulfil her potential*. With that, she enrolled in a course in botany at the Royal Botanical Gardens at Kew in London, as one of the premier institutions for plant biology in the UK, and then went on to undertake a further intensive period at the Royal Horticultural Gardens at Wisley in Surrey. She opened her own garden and landscaping business shortly after and is now a full-time horticulturalist.

We asked if she could pinpoint the catalyst for change in her life:

> Not just one thing, I don't think. It all just seemed to come together at one time. I had visited Kew many years before when I took the girls there and wandered around in awe an amazement, thinking 'Oh gosh, I'd love to work here!'. I got some money after my dad died and so I suddenly had the means to do it and I thought, what the heck, just go for it.

She draws clear approbation from the pride both daughters show in her achievements:

> They say things like 'Mum, I always knew you had it in you!', and 'Mum, you really change who you are as soon as you talk about plants!'. It's an odd feeling! It always used to be me feeding them with confidence and assurances, and now they do it to me. They are getting on with their own lives but their pleasure in what I do is important to me. I want them to think their mother is a success, that she actually knows what she is talking about! They want the company to be a success and want me to have a proper professional life.

What does Elif see as markers of success?

> First, good reviews on my website. Second, I love that feeling of people saying 'Wow!' when they see what I have done to their gardens. I have just landed a nice contract for work at a big stately home near us and I'm so excited. I got that through word of mouth, and that kind of behind-the-scenes recommendation really means a lot. I'll have to be in top form and I have been drafting ideas already.

Her work in plant biology seems a long way away from her original degree in psychology.

> If I'm honest, back then I really didn't know what I wanted to do and so a plumped for a degree I thought would open doors for me. As life happened, I never used it. I don't know where the biology came from . . . neither of my parents have any science . . . it's not in my family anywhere. But I love it! Really do! I've gone from being one person to being another one altogether. And the truth is that it is not all biology. I have to know a lot about building materials, you know, various kinds of stones, the properties of porcelain tiles, different timbers, sand cement and gravel. So, its botanical science and materials science all mixed together.

Transformative learning – a heutagogy for success

All these examples of transformation have a pedagogic component. As we have already discussed, ours is a fairly broad sense of pedagogy, and our PfS has spacious capacity for inclusion. There are different pedagogues – leaders towards learning – mentioned in the lives of these four women so that, for Anita, for example, it was her careers counsellor, whereas for Vikki it was her classmates. However, while other people feature very clearly in these women's transformative learning, it is also their own personal micro-agency that proves a key driver of change in their science lives. In each story there are elements of meso level discussions on formal education, training and instruction, and there are also very evident themes of micro level self-determined learning, of self-direction even while determining with others the attainment of science goals through informal personal means.

These themes represent a heutagogical approach to these women's science lives (Hase & Kenyon, 2015). The essence of heutagogy is the greater emphasis placed on what a learner wants to learn rather than what a teacher wants to teach. The heutagogical educational process rests to a great extent on the choices made by the learner rather than those of the pedagogue. It still requires the presence of a pedagogue but much more in the role of the facilitator, guide, enabler – a learning chaperone – who supports the emotional commitment, direction and ambition of the learner. While there may be formal sessions and formal assessment along the way, as in training to be a nurse, a botanist or a forensic scientist, there are also ways to manage this, to negotiate affairs such as presentations or placements in as flexible a way as possible to suit the learner's needs.

So, in the (partial) absence of formal assessment, 'what are the indicators of achievement, the markers of success in these self-determined transformations?' The first of these is self-satisfaction, that is, hitting the affective (micro) dimension first and then intersecting with the cognitive and social (macro and associated meso) dimensions later. This is not just in reaching particular stages in a process or goals that have been set; it entails satisfaction too in the process of learning. Autonomous learners, transformed from their past experiences, become increasingly skilled in research, acquiring, practising and developing various components of their learning. They become adept at planning their own studies, stetting their own learning objectives, developing their own learning preferences as they work. Second is the increasing sense of choice to experience: choice is empowering. Even where choices and decisions work out less successfully than might have been hoped, the lessons are learned and future choices shaped accordingly.

In the cases we discuss here, the *relational web* of PfS was that created by the learners themselves. These women took charge of their learning lives and generated their own *relationships* within the various structures open to them. They established their own goals and directions in discussion with their mentors, tutors, lecturers, counsellors and facilitators. As in the discussion of the schoolgirls in Chapter 7, the *knowledge flow* became multidirectional so that it was not simply a case of working with a *more knowledgeable other*, but the learning activities gave rise to considerable learner autonomy. Important, too, has been the *experiential texture* as their science lives changed in significant ways. Engagement, engrossing, immersion, challenge, self-fulfilment were just some of the terms they used as they talked. Finally, the *evaluative tone* became shared, so the women were themselves judges of progress, of success in what they achieved. It is true that this was not a formal examination period for these women and so there was a greater degree of freedom in how the science curriculum could be framed.

Illeris's (2014) version of transformative learning theory is very much of this ilk. As we said earlier, it represents the *meaning-making* process whereby individuals negotiate their understanding of self – and self-as-learner – in a way that shapes (transforms) their identity within meso-social contexts. These negotiations overlap self-perceptions and permeable cultures where large-scale social categories of gender, ethnicity, social class and religion intersect. Illeris describes this process of meaning-making as an intense, thoughtful journey of constructing the meaning of oneself through life experiences. In this chapter we have adapted this by adding the *construction of the meaning of one's success in one's science life.*

One more point can be made here. We reiterate our belief that transformation can only really be successful where there have previously been nudges. This is not such an outlandish statement, in that, in each of the cases described earlier, transformation into science must have had at least some preparatory thinking, some early disposition to lay the ground for the shift of direction to follow. The women we have talked to have been very clear and astute about their lives and not particularly whimsical or scattily impulsive – at least not in the discussions we shared with them. They have moved away from their past preoccupations and into science clear-eyed and determined, a clear-eyed determination that speaks of myriad minor nudges that have preceded the move.

Chapter summary

We cannot close this chapter without a consideration of the role of intersectionality in the stories we have shared. First, 'does Anita see her ex-husband's rather fixed cultural family ideas as a barrier or as a challenge to spur action?' 'Did Vikki see her largely male mathematics class as a *gender hindrance* or as a springboard for self-confidence?' These are hard questions to answer, and our initial response would be *perhaps a little bit of both – but with the challenge winning through!* In general terms, a sociologist would point to our very small and very selective sample – these successful women form just one sliver of all south Asian women in Britain. This is certainly true, and we have not attempted a large-scale and comprehensive survey of the science successes of south Asian women. That is a project, maybe, for another day. Meanwhile, the women whose stories we present here *are* south Asian women, they *have* made changes in their lives, they have taken a very positive view of science and they have been willing and able to chart success in what they have achieved. No, we cannot make sweeping generalizations about *all* south Asian women; we can only listen, look and learn from those who have granted us the time to talk.

9

The Summary of the Book

The start points to any educational research are the ontological questions: 'What does it look like?' 'How will you know it when you see it?' The answers depend to a very large extent on what *it* is. In our case the questions become 'What does science success look like?' and 'How will we know science success when we see it?' The questions we have pursued in this book relate to the nature of science and the successes of south Asian women. And our first response is that success in science can look quite different and multidimensional – in our case it can be quite different from the perspective of a south Asian woman, for example, to that of a White male. In fact, definitions of success can be radically different. As we have seen throughout the chapters, *success* can range, for example, from clear achievement in school grades to feelings of making a difference in a local community, from gaining a good university degree to becoming accepted by peers and work colleagues, from feelings of self-worth to a sense of fun and enjoyment. We know about these successes because they are contained in the stories women have told us, the stories we have relayed here in as faithful a fashion as we can muster. Success in science relates to science identity (Sci-ID), to perceptions and understandings. It is a disposition to grow as a person and accomplish goals, to trust in oneself and one's ability to succeed. It can take different forms in different cultures – and it takes hard work. And the hard work involved is different for different people at different times, and so the work undertaken by a south Asian woman will look different to that undertaken by her White male counterpart. Therefore, this book provides learning opportunities for those who do not identify themselves as a person from a minority ethnic group and/or who identify themselves as a women but living in a multicultural Western country such as the UK and so study, work and live their (science) lives with women from ethnically minoritized communities.

Success in science at a young age can be understandably parochial, often – but not always – lying within the narrow ambit of the school, the curriculum, the grade system, with peer approval, parental support and so on. We saw some of this in the responses of the girls in Chapter 7. This has also been discussed in the past, for example, by Nancy Brickhouse (2012) who comments on perceptions of success in young children during their in-class and immediate out-of-school science programmes. Whereas in-school science commonly rewards the simple accumulation of facts and concepts, out-of-school science values the applications of science – the *doing* of science for a collective purpose. This accumulation is geared through self-interest and a willingness to learn science. As women grow older, this willingness remains intact and propagates in their personalized belief system, self-satisfaction and self-integrity – all of which they gain from large and small successful experiences and events over their lifetime. Therefore, measures of success, either personal or social, are much more difficult to measure as time goes by and as women reach adulthood. Yes, in mainstream science there are accepted markers such as publishing a seminal paper in a highly rated journal, giving a keynote presentation to an important conference, acquiring significant funding for a major research project, leading a research team and the like. But, as our women participants have outlined, there are many other ways of viewing success. Maria Varelas (2012) makes the point that discussions of success allow women to talk about who they are, who they want to be, how they want to be recognized by others, why they might act in certain ways, how they perceive opportunities and obstacles and, of course, how they recognize, experience and express their successes. Success is an emotional state. Feeling successful is an affective process, it is having a positive feeling, it can be ephemeral or long-lasting. It engenders science confidence, it fosters feelings of pride, it generates excitement and announces the impact being made in a competitive world.

In choosing women participants, south Asian women in Britain, we have focused on the shifts and changes in their dispositions towards both science and success and we have looked to give voice to their lived experiences. Some of their stories present a series of *work-life balancing acts* as women overcome hardships in life. In other cases, science has helped them adjust that balance or even to provide the springboard that allowed them to leap out from their current circumstances into a different world. Nowhere do we underestimate the hard work and difficulties involved in any of this. One prevailing cultural trope is that south Asian women who go to university or pursue a career damage their marriage prospects. However, the young south Asian women with whom we interacted saw no such issues and exhibited clear dedication in developing or continuing their careers in sciences. Some mothers changed their careers as scientists or discontinued employment altogether because of family responsibilities, but nevertheless they still purposively engaged with science in formal and/or informal ways.

A second cultural trope is that *you cannot be what you cannot see*. That is, aspirations to success fail where there are no role models for young women to look up to; they cannot see themselves achieving positions where they cannot see themselves represented. Or, put another way, achievement is so much more difficult where there are no role models to follow. Role modelling is still a very positive means of enthusing young women into the sciences. It is not the only way, of course, and throughout the book we have been in praise of the many families who have both sparked and then kindled the *flame of science* in so many young women. While there are instances where south Asian parents have more elevated expectations as compared to White parents, our participant south Asian women all spoke about their freedom to choose their own routes into education, careers and to home life. In turn, our participants appreciated their parents' hard work and struggles and generally saw their parents' expectations as reasonable and realistic. Lack of parental knowledge about education, careers or university did matter to some but the majority found their parents very supportive of their future decisions. As Stephen Ball, Meg Maguire and Sheila Macrae (2001) suggest, the tightness of the 'framed field of reference' significantly depends on level of parental education. We can say, though, that these young people have tended to ignore or resist this frame. They have demonstrated the skills required to *percolate the intersectional barriers*. In this book we have discussed how many south Asian women exercise their personal agency through *self-feeding*. By this we mean that their initial fledgling Sci-ID can be increased through small successes in science, so feeding a growth in Sci-ID which in turn enables even greater successes and even greater sense of identity. Greater Sci-ID allows women to move more easily and more quickly through the holes in the *intersectional barriers*.

Women exist in a world where they construct themselves at the very same time as the world is constructing them. Understanding changes in the development of Sci-ID lies neither in the individual alone nor in the social context alone but in the interactions between the two over time. Similarly, our participant south Asian women self-define success even while the world around them ascribes success to what they do to achieve success. The person exists as an intricately complex and multidimensional entity within a socio-cultural milieu, dimensions that involve their ideas and thinking, their affective and emotional states, their actions and intentions, their heritage and family circumstances. Our ecological model of Sci-ID depicts ways in which individual learning processes, needs, aspirations, ambitions, perceptions and understandings interact in a reciprocal manner with the demands, expectations and responses of social contexts such as families, schools, universities and employment. We have already noted Mills's thoughts on identity being that point where the *individual realm* meets the *public sphere*. While each woman in the previous chapters is unique, there are sufficient commonalities in their sciencelife experiences to allow us to draw themes and ideas from what they say.

Across the book, we present accounts from more than fifty south Asian women, a good number but still a tiny sliver of a sample given the approximately one and a half million south Asian women with UK citizenship. We did not cover immigrant south Asian women who are currently immersing themselves in the UK culture, some of whom are educating themselves and/or working in STEM sectors in order to obtain the UK citizenship. This means that the under-representation of the UK-based south Asian women is still prevalent. Both school-based learning and informal multimodal and purposeful approaches to becoming enthused about science learning were evident in the stories. Moreover, traditions where religion (especially Islam) acts as a dividing force in becoming a science person are lifting and dissipating. We see how women in our study connect religious or non-religious beliefs with science, the culture of science and other everyday cultures in which they live their science lives. Therefore, there is still more to be explored, and initiatives are needed to minimize the widespread and existing under-representation of south Asian women in the field of sciences and the resistance of women in appreciating science and having a science life as scientifically literate UK citizens. The book has enabled us to sharpen the discussion of *nudges* and *transformations*, Sci-ID and point to a *pedagogy for science success* both in formal (educational institutions) and informal settings.

A feeling for the incumbent

In Chapters 1 and 2 we made insertions into the grand theory of intersectionality because we want to retain the overarching messages of the theory while at the same time driving this down to the individual level, to the messy complexities of women's everyday lives. In Chapter 3 we veered away from Bourdieu's sociological thinking for very much the same reasons. His exposition of habitus moves towards a sense of the individual in society but nevertheless, for us, lacks any sense of the real, raw, personal accounts of women – in our case south Asian women – as their lived experiences are revealed. That is, these overarching theories lack any feeling for the people they discuss. Our collecting of stories, of autobionarratives, has been an attempt to embrace various ways of knowing science, knowing success, of exploring hybrid perspectives from different cultures, finding fruitful ways of presenting these. This has been our attempt to explore a feeling for learning and for learners.

Our reading of intersectionality provides a myriad reason for why women do not or cannot enter science, for why the so-called leaky pipeline continues to leak unabated. However, somewhere against this backdrop of societal and cultural negative barriers and hindrances there exists a strand, a bubble, of positive success. These are the success stories of women who have remained within the pipeline or who have re-entered it further down the line. They may have remained or re-entered in part or in whole, whichever part or whole of science they have chosen to develop for themselves. In hearing and probing these stories, we have looked to explore what it means to be successful in science, what are the characteristics of this bubble, what are the dispositional features that allow and enable women to be successful. And we have sought to this from the actors' point of view with some feeling for the women to whom we have talked. We have looked to understand how the successful learning of, engagement with, involvement in various parts of science takes place in and out of formal educational settings. Before discussing our participants' (south Asian women) accounts of their meaning and dispositions of successes, we will reveal our explorations and findings of the science lives of these south Asian women with respect to their Sci-ID development and the ways they balance and wear science culture along with other cultures.

South Asian women's science lives and science identity

Throughout the book we have encountered women who engage with science in many different modes. In our view, this is because there is so much infiltration – diffusion – of science throughout the culture of everyday life, plus the fact that there are so very many facets of science with which people can engage. We have signalled this permeation of science in life by examining women's *science lives*, exploring the many ways that women encounter and involve themselves in science of many kinds. As we noted near the start of Chapters 1 and 2, differences in social structures reflect on personalized science lives. At the same time, personalized *stories of successes* in science do happen – and these we have celebrated throughout the book.

One goal of our research studies has been to encourage women to look at and appreciate their science lives. We have asked the question in several ways, but the broad gist has been, 'How well do you get along with science?' and their science autobionarratives have taken us there. The first point we make here is that these science success stories are not manufactured, they are produced from something, they spring from the real lives of real women where science is an ever-present feature of their everyday living. Certainly, different events will elicit different stories and different aspects of science, depending clearly on the event, the questions asked and the storytelling disposition of the woman concerned. There is always more than one story to be told of any event, and a science story is a natural part of these women's lives alongside stories of their professional duties, caring roles, early childhood, marital history and so on. These stories interweave and interlace, and science is just one more of those perspectives adopted as the need arises.

Second, their stories seldom give the impression of stark polarity: 'There is me, and then there is science.' There is little evidence of a *gap* to be spanned, a serious divide to be bridged, where science seems a wholly separate entity, a discrete bubble, within life. On the contrary, the stories they tell argue for a considerable penetration of science in their everyday lives. Or, put the other way, while these women can *switch hats* during the course of their everyday lives, science is one of those hats along with the many others – aesthetic, moral, political, religious, cultural – that they have available to choose from.

Identity in general is a personal designation of self, allied to aspects of social structures and, while it is embedded in social experience and institutional practices, it is also an expression of personal agency. Although we gain insight from examining and theorizing through large societal and group-level theories through sociology, cultural studies, history or politics, our view is that there is a need for many more accounts of individual moments of agency, of individual, personal positions to enrich our understanding of the lived experiences of science education and careers. An ecological perspective on Sci-ID draws attention to the relationships between internal emotions, preferences, beliefs, personal-cultural history and the external situation, context and broad environment.

There are different timescales involved in personal lives than in grand sociological vistas, and so even though a science life might last for most of a human lifetime, there are points of distance followed by periods of fascination when a woman becomes vitally engaged in science. In Chapter 7, we tracked the exploits of young south Asian women as we nudged them towards science through shifting their dispositions towards matters scientific over the period of an academic year, entangled as these matters were with contemporary youth literature. This was a relatively slow and gentle *baking of the science cake* with this class of schoolgirls. In Chapter 8 we charted the rather more abrupt transformations in women's situations that led to enduring change in their science lives. We must assume that some of this change had been brewing in the background, but that it then took a significant trigger for these women to take a serious rethink and change the direction of their lives.

As we have noted, our own deliberations on the nature of identity, and Sci-ID in particular, follow a very long and very august line, and our additions to that enormous body of work arrive through the self-authoring of south Asian women as they shape-shift through transformations of their own cultural meanings for science and the science meanings within their own cultures. Given the kinds of timescales we have been discussing, we privilege the study of identity over months-long and years-long periods of time. That said, from our Chapter 3 on the influence of families, we might add that we also have some signals from across generations.

Our ecological sense of Sci-ID allows women to have a say in what they are and what they do. They are certainly influenced by the intersecting historical, social, cultural, institutional and familial structures that surround them but refuse to be limited by these. In many cases they simply do not see that these structural social forces actually apply to them. In this sense, families are important in supporting their goals and ambitions, as a milieu for negotiation or even a challenge to work against. Many of our women participants have been the first in their families to take up a university place, or to move into science by other routes, and this has commonly been a source of enormous family pride. In many cases they have then proved to be the beacons that then light the way for their siblings or their own offspring. Their own Sci-ID, then, is shaped over a generation, as is their example to others.

As important for us is that Sci-ID can flex both towards and away from science. We understand these periods of withdrawal over years to be times when the woman is flooded with other preoccupations – such as raising a family, caring for others, making her way in business. However, the model of the semi-permeable pipeline does allow for re-entry, and the stories in Chapter 8 illustrate how this re-entry can take place. There is a core to Sci-ID that holds still while the outer membrane waxes and wanes.

Balancing and wearing cultures

This book uses cultures as one of the basic means of discussing intersectionality and Sci-ID. Despite its extensive use, we do not claim to capture all the facets of what might constitute a culture. We do, though, aim to story the intersection of the culture of science with other everyday cultures, specifically south Asian family cultures in the UK. Chapter 3 discusses how south Asian family cultures are not always stereotypically strict and unsupportive as depicted in the media. Indeed, from the many stories we have collected, family culture is predominantly viewed as supportive of a successful science life. This takes us well away from fixed perception of a *typical* south Asian family – we rather suspect there is no such thing. Moreover, as we clarified in Chapter 5, the intersecting macro forces and associated meso forces in society can impact different cultures in very different ways. Cultural impact is dependent not only on social norms and customs but also, according to our studies, on how the individual south Asian woman acknowledges and gives importance – gives weight – to these norms and customs in their personal lives. For example, sometimes women acknowledge negative societal dispositions as they approach them but then do not allow these to impact their science lives. Other times they give importance to such negative dispositions as an impetus to boost their agentic strength, to work against them. At other times, being told or discouraged from doing something acts as a spur to action, boosts their strength and determination. Sometimes they push away such negativity and take alternative routes to science success.

The balancing of cultures in one's life is evident in the stories we present in each of the previous chapters. We have demonstrated how individuals can be immersed in the culture of science in one moment and context, such as a science-oriented context, and can then switch to attend religious duties within their community in the next. Moreover, as we discuss in Chapter 4, a formal science context is not always necessary for a woman to be immersed in science; this immersion can so readily take place in informal contexts such as gardens, kitchens, living spaces, shops, hospitals and so on.

The theory of intersectionality reassures simultaneity and acts as a reminder for us to not to single out and consider just one subject at a time – the effects of multiple subjects are clearly evident in the stories we have presented – where our participating south Asian women work to balance the demands of different cultures simultaneously within different social contexts. The fact that we present this complexity of these cultures to be permeable, diffusible and as an intermingling balancing act. One point was clear – all of our participants have wanted to succeed in the sciences and so have worked hard towards achieving small or large, single or several, private or public successes. The number, size and exposure of their successes depend to a large extent on their personalized interest, self-determination and motivation – often triggered by life experiences in their everyday formal or informal lives.

Along with balancing cultures, we have also discussed the concept of *wearing science culture* – whether it is worn heavily with agentic conformity and strong Sci-ID, worn lightly with weak agentic conformity and weak Sci-ID or somewhere in the middle. Moreover, discussing the heavy, moderate and light *weight* of other intersecting cultures supports our understanding of why some south Asian participants express strong Sci-ID and others not so – when asked about their science engagement, immersion and journeys. Therefore, focusing on just one culture, or seeing science culture as separate from other everyday cultures, or relying on ethnic reductionism is criticized in this book. Instead, a diffusion of the elements of the science culture supports our better understanding of an individual's Sci-ID strength, science life and developmental journeys.

Autobionarratives

People, south Asian women in this book, tell many different stories about themselves. Their stories concern themselves and the many people who populate their lives, the roles they adopt, the issues at play, the settings and the circumstances, the values being enacted. It is through these stories that they make sense of themselves, assert who they are, make sense of others and make sense of science. We are honoured to have been trusted with these stories, and they form the main planks of all the chapters of the book so far. We have respected these stories and, in our entre-deux approach, have abridged their words verbatim or *storied* them as best we could. In some cases, this has simply meant *editing for meaning* so that the usual vagaries of spoken speech, the half-finished sentences, the *umhs* and *ers*, the laughs and coughs have been filtered so that readers can see more easily what is intended. In some case we have added the on-verbal paralinguistics, the shrugs, handwringing, eye rolling or even the tears, where this has happened. Where we have felt that our editing has been rather more than that, where we have summarized or précised stories in our own words, we have gone back to the woman concerned and undertaken as rigorous an approach to respondent validation as is possible.

It would be wrong to think that the stories we present in this book are the *cream of the crop* and that we have left an enormous amount of negative counter data simply *lying on the cutting room floor*. It is clearly the case that we have not reported all of the data from all of the women we have spoken to; there has simply not been sufficient room to do so in any depth and richness. Yes, indeed we have reduced the many hours of recorded conversations to manageable portions in the chapters here. But the direct answer is that, as do all reporters with a degree of integrity, we have read and re-read our transcripts and worked hard to balance the comments we make with the words of the women involved. The have spoken very eloquently of the science in their lives and we have sought to capture both their feelings and fluency.

Our direction throughout has been that enabling these stories to be told also empowers the women to position themselves in terms of their own lives, their professional lives and their relationships with science. While we did ask about issues of family and gender, we generally resisted any mention of age, race, class, heritage, culture and the like, allowing our respondents to shape their answers in the ways that they wished. Positionality refers to how one is socially located in relation to others and the ways in which power works between the people involved. Allowing the women to express themselves as they saw themselves sometimes resulted in discussions of power relationships – but often did not, the narrator content simply with defining self and science as a *stand-alone project*.

Meaning and dispositions of successes in science lives

Jo Bostock (2014), in her book *The Meaning of Success*, has celebrated stories of successful women working at the University of Cambridge. Her book's core understanding of the meaning of successes is that there is 'no one meaning' of success, success 'is not a single thing' and 'inner integrity is the driving force' for success, so

> success comes from within at least as much as from any external recognition.
> This is an important lesson for us all, men and women to remember. (p. 7)

Our multiaged ethically minoritized women participants, who do not belong to the elite institutions, such as Cambridge, have also delineated several meanings of successes in their lives. These meanings resemble Bostock's understanding of success in several ways. Still, they are different in the aspects of balancing and wearing cultures in different social contexts. We agree with Bostock that the learning we gain from books that voice women are not only for women to learn, but they are also equally important for other genders and people from different ethnic, national, class and religious communities.

Chapters 5 and 6 represent meanings, goals, ambitions and *states of being* that our women participants believe is success:

1. Success is finding contentment and happiness. So, it is about self-realization of growth, total commitment, enjoyment, fulfilment and personal satisfaction, regardless of age, position, context and time. Contentment also in considering oneself privileged compared to their immigrant parents and self-satisfaction in having better and more opportunistic life choices and authority in choosing educational and career paths compared to women living in south Asian countries.

2. Success is prospering against the tide and sometimes rising above it. Therefore, it is about confidently dismantling the stereotypical and intersectional societal-oriented challenges, for example, guarding science, gender, ethnicity, nationality and religious identities in formal institutions, being persistent in achieving science-based ambitions despite the feelings of isolation in higher education and professional contexts and working additional hours to balance work and home lives.

3. Success is to have role models, mentoring and being mentored. Perseverance in becoming and being immigrant scientific women role models for younger family members, students, women at the workplace or women and girls in general who share similar visible characteristics. In this role-modelling view, success is also about appreciating life-changing motivational mentors and the mentoring process because personal success is also about supporting others to succeed.

4. Success is having an appetite for continued learning. Specialized science education is never enough. Success is about continuing with the thirst for learning more from others and learning drawn from multiple literacies and multimodal approaches to accessing and synthesizing scientific concepts, facts, processes, information, affect and values towards generating meaning and understanding.

5. Success is working hard within the process. Accepting success as an ongoing process could lead to gaining institutional appreciation, laurels, positions and certificates. The road to success is not like a walk in the park and does not come over several weeks of perseverance; instead, it demands self-commitment of the highest level and includes ongoing challenges and failures, which are learning opportunities to work better, onwards and upwards.

6. Success is being empowered to be altruistic, intrinsically empowered to improve the lives of people and the planet through actively seeking

learning from ever-evolving scientific knowledge, involve in scientific practices that matters to them, people around them and/or people from around the world. Being altruistic becomes the purpose of science lives, which supports willingness to continue with science rather than just acquiring institutional endorsements of an award, degree or promotion as their sole purpose of their lives.

Zooming closely into these six descriptors, our women south Asian participants have constituted some fundamental dispositions for success in their science lives which we believe could apply to any person. First, they have a solid skillset of personal engagement, critical being and consuming purposive change on an ongoing basis, so they do not vision success to have an endpoint; rather, it is ever-evolving with a view that learning from others never stops, so they consistently strengthen their learning from others even after achieving a good position in their professional lives. They reinforce where they start their journeys from, what worked or didn't in their science lives and then utilize those learnings as they climb the hierarchical social ladder.

Second, they acknowledge the issues of societal misrecognition, unacceptance and lack of appreciation towards them and/or women with protected characteristics, for which they go against publicly and/or locally and reboot their agentic potentials regularly. And so, they do not doubt their own abilities and/or are misrecognized by others as oppressed and jeopardized; instead, they take on the agentic responsibility and prove themselves as problem solvers to the issues of science and associated societally credited influencers (ethnicity, gender, nationality, social class, race and religion, etc). Third, from time to time, they believe that working hard is the key to success, and their belief system is that success depends on the availability of choices which will not be given to them on a plate; instead, they have to grasp these opportunities themselves. So, they don't give up science, even if they are not studying or working in a formal scientific setting, and continually learn science and grasp various learning and working opportunities without much help from others, act scientifically literate, have a science life and strengthen their Sci-ID over time.

Issues of validation

Throughout the chapters, we have at different points referred to the various approaches we have used to validate the stories we have collected. In the main, during the *harvesting* of stories, we have used respondent validation. That is, we have usually précised the stories being told and then taken these back to the respondents and asked, in essence, 'is this a fair reflection of what you said?' 'Can you see yourself in what we have made of you?' A very large part the answer has been 'Yes, that's fine, I am happy with what you have said'. In a few instances, the women have asked for small changes – usually along the lines 'Did I really say that? Oh, wow, can I please soften it a little.' We have always accommodated to their wishes; it is their story after all.

We did not follow this route with the class of girls in Chapter 7. In part this was because the data collection took place over a period of a year, with multiple data gathering methods and data gathering points that we used in and around the classroom. We were, though, in regular conversation with the girls, they were happy to share their thoughts and ideas with us and we – often verbally – confirmed with them the directions we were taking. On the whole, along with respondent validity, we feel very confident that the various parts to our studies have both contextual validity and theoretical validity. The first of these simply means that the questions that drive the studies within the book are worth asking. That is, 'are the science lives of south Asian women in Britain worth exploring?' Our answer, of course, is yes, for the multitude of reasons we offer in Chapter 1. Our overriding sense is that these stories of success can help us create the conditions for science success for many other under-represented groups, not just south Asian women. Where these women lead today, may many others follow in their wake.

We are also clear that our work has theoretical validity. Intersectionality is a broad umbrella though not all *intersectionalists* might be happy with the way we have driven down from the social to the personal. In Chapters 1 and 2, we made four insertions to the theory in order – in our view – to narrow the gaps between theory, empirical research and educational practice. Inersectionality is a strong, appropriate and applicable theory suited to the forms of research we have been conducting and very much suited to the sample of participants with whom we have been working. There is a fourth form of validation that we now need to address here (da Silva Lopes, Pedrosa de Jesus & Watts, 2016), which is consequential validity.

There are different forms of consequence to be derived from the work we have been doing. First, we might ask, do these studies help us understand 'how south Asian women succeed in science, coming as they do from under-represented groups in society?' That is, 'are the understandings we have gleaned of any consequence at all in the greater scheme of things, and are these understandings valid?' We are confident this is the case. We have looked to offer a neater sense of *personal intersectionality*, a fresher ecological approach to Sci-ID, a real-world view of a woman's *science literacy* embedded within her *science life*, an appreciation of the many modes that comprise science success, an exploration of a pedagogic approach to engendering such success, consideration of the nudges and transformational triggers that form part of that pedagogy and, above all, a platform for these women's autobionarratives, their science success stories. Are these valid consequences from the work we have done? We certainly believe so.

Second, we might ask supplementary questions: 'So what?' 'Where does this go from here?' 'Can these outcomes be replicated elsewhere' and, more to the point, 'can we (re)create these conditions in order to ensure science success for all future generations of women, particularly those form under-represented groups?' That is, 'what are the consequences of these understandings?' We answer these questions in the following ways:

1. We do not see success in science simply as the attainment of the highest accolades that institutions of science can bestow. We are not concerned with *fashioning* a new cadre of Nobel Award scientists making new scientific discoveries. On the contrary, we would be content if more and more women appreciated the science that already exists in their lives. There are innumerable science phenomena that are diffused throughout everyday culture, and we want that women do not close the door on learning about and understanding these. Given this science *open door* policy, we would be very content should women return to science – in a purely amateur or professional capacity – throughout their life course.

2. No pedagogic process can *ensure* success, be that the training of an elite athlete, a neurosurgeon, a Michelin star chef, a fighter pilot or a concert violinist. There is too much of the person involved, too much of the individual, her engagement, motivation, resilience, perseverance to be certain of anything. What we have set going with PfS is the preparatory groundwork, making sure that the relationships between pedagogue and learner are fitting, that the objectives are shared, agreed and obtainable, that the provision of resources is appropriate and that the pedagogic process is designed to enable learners to participate actively in their own assessment and evaluation. We see these elements to be important whether science education takes place within the formal structures of schools and universities or wholly outside of the formalities of the educational system.

3. It is particularly difficult, of course, to intervene in the pedagogic processes that take place within homes and families. In this respect, we

particularly enjoy those stories where some science success is achieved and then taken back within the family grouping. Much of the science education literature on young people's aspirations towards science makes the point that having a scientist somewhere in the extended family can act as a strong and positive role model for those that follow. For many of the south Asian women in our samples, though, they *are* the sole role model in their families; it is they who are paving the way, being the stand-out science person. They are the first in the family to study, work at and achieve in science, to be the family *beacon of success*. The old saying is that success breeds success – in this case not just for the individual herself but also all those within the ambit of her family, friends and community.

4. We noted a moment ago the mix of timescales within which we have worked, varying from the momentary to a year-long study. This is both a strength and weakness; we need many more similar studies to enable us to connect the dots between the three, evaluations of the short-, medium- and long-term pedagogic interventions that make a difference. This would allow us a sharper picture of women's science trajectories over the full scope of their science lives. Without this time-lapse perspective, our understandings will always be limited. As we argued at the end of Chapter 7, we see no abrupt transformation without a multitude of prior prods, pulls, pushes and we need a clearer sense of how these small nudges aggregate and accumulate to produce the *final straw* that precipitates a wholesale move into a science-related arena.

5. Our previous point does bring us round to formal, school-based science education. Surely it is here in the decade between ages five and fifteen that many of the seeds are sown or otherwise. It is here, surely, that the open door should be established so that young women see possibilities rather than hurdles, school science is seen as hospitable rather than inhospitable. We fully accept that not all school students will become scientists – at least not at this early stage of their lives. However, the goals of science literacy stand firm; young people deserve answers to questions on a wide range of topics, only some of which appear on examination syllabuses. The science teachers we know squeal and protest at this point. In Britain, a secondary school teacher may have classroom contact with some 200 students (both motivated and the disengaged) spread over the age range eleven to eighteen. They have insufficient preparation or marking time, they are pulled in numerous administrative and bureaucratic directions, their teaching is heavily scrutinized and policed by both school insiders and outsiders, they

have little enough time to breathe let alone provide a wonderfully enriched and inclusive science literacy curriculum. Without deep delving into the shape and form of science-teacher identity is a separate issue, we must agree, and so we look outside of the school system for fuller answers.

6. There is throughout society a cadre of people who are, in one form or another, professional communicators of science. Scientists themselves, speakers, writers, presenters, medics, technologists, policymakers, museum and gallery staff, programme makers – and many more – all have a role in communicating science. There is much to be learned from the expertise and skills involved in cleverly crafted messages, whether these emanate through a well-written book, an environmental science centre, a news broadcast, a science podcast, a government public health warning and so on. They, too, are door openers. There is much to be done here to bring together message makers with classroom teachers.

7. Where success is concerned, clarity is power. Knowing what success looks like to the woman involved is a critical component in achieving any kind of improvement. Success is relative, depends on others around her and the circumstances in which she is looking to achieve ('Given the circumstances, this counts as a big success'). While success is related to achievement and aspiration, it is also mutable so that sometimes a failure can be reframed as a success. Future successes depend on past successes; therefore, a Sci-success-ID is predicated on previous science successes and continues to develop with accumulating science successes.

In keeping with the overall tone of our discussions in the book so far, we feel a deep satisfaction with having reached this point in our deliberations – arriving at this point in the discussions marks a success in itself. The external reviews of the book are, of course, yet to come. Whatever is said, we end here with our own feelings of success as things stand at the moment. We fully understand that there is much (much) more work to be done and so part with a final reminder: the road to success is always under (re)construction.

References

Abbas, T. (2004), 'After 9/11: British south Asian Muslims, islamophobia, multiculturalism, and the state', *American Journal of Islam and Society, 21*(3): 26–38.

Advance, H. E. (2020), *Equality in Higher Education: Statistical report 2020*, retrieved from: https://www.advance-he.ac.uk/knowledge-hub/equality-higher-education -statistical-report-2020

Afshar, H. (2008), 'Can I see your hair? Choice, agency and attitudes: The dilemma of faith and feminism for Muslim women who cover', *Ethnic and Racial Studies, 31*(2): 411–27.

Ahmad, F. (2001), 'Modern traditions? British Muslim women and academic achievement', *Gender and Education, 13*(2): 137–52.

AHRC (2021), *Science in culture theme*, retrieved from https://www.sciculture.ac.uk/

Aikenhead, G. S. (1996), 'Science education: Border crossing into the subculture of science', *Studies in Science Education, 27*(1): 1–52. DOI: 10.1080/03057269608560077

Alexander, R. (2004), Still no pedagogy? Principle, pragmatism and compliance in primary education, Cambridge Journal of education, *34*(1): 7–33.

Anderson, C. (2013), FundaMENTAL WEALTH Principles: Developing a Mindset for Financial Success, New Jersy: Pearson eDNA Press.

Anwar, M. (1998), *Between cultures: Continuity and change in the lives of young Asians*, London: Routledge.

Archer, L. (2018), 'An intersectional approach to classed injustices in education: Gender, ethnicity, "heavy" funds of knowledge and working-class students' struggles for intelligibility in the classroom', in R. Simmons & J. Smyth (Eds), *Education and working-class youth*, Cham: Palgrave Macmillan. https://doi.org/10.1007/978-3-319 -90671-3_7

Archer, L., & DeWitt, J. (2016), *Understanding young people's science aspirations: How students form ideas about 'becoming a scientist'*, London: Routledge.

Archer, L., Dewitt, J., & Osborne, J. (2015), 'Is science for us? Black students' and parents' views of science and science careers', *Science Education, 99*(2): 199–237.

Archer, L., DeWitt, J., Osborne, J., Dillon, J., Willis, B., & Wong, B. (2010), '"Doing" science versus "being" a scientist: Examining 10/11-year-old schoolchildren's constructions of science through the lens of identity', *Science Education, 94*(4): 617–39.

Archer, L., DeWitt, J., Osborne, J., Dillon, J., Willis, B., & Wong, B. (2013), 'Not Girly, not sexy, not glamorous: Primary school girls' and parents' constructions of science aspirations', *Pedagogy, Culture and Society, 21*(1): 171–94.

Archer, L., DeWitt, J., & Wong, B. (2014), 'Spheres of influence: What shapes young people's aspirations at age 12/13 and what are the implications for education policy?', *Journal of Education Policy, 29*(1): 58–85.

Archer, L., Hutchings, M., & Ross, A. (2003), *Higher education and social class*, London and New York: Routledge Falmer.

Archer, L., Moote, J., Francis, B., DeWitt, J., & Yeomans, L. (2017a), 'The "exceptional" physics girl: A sociological analysis of multimethod data from young women aged 10–16 to explore gendered patterns of post-16 participation', *American Educational Research Journal, 54*(1): 88–126.

Archer, L., Dawson, E., DeWitt, J., Godec, S., King, H., Mau, A., & Seakins, A. (2017b). 'Killing curiosity? An analysis of celebrated identity performances among teachers and students in nine London secondary science classrooms', *Science Education, 101*(5): 741–64.

Archer, L., Moote, J., Macleod, E., Francis, B., & DeWitt, J. (2020), *ASPIRES 2: Young people's science and career aspirations, age 10–19*, London: UCL Institute of Education.

Archer Ker, L., DeWitt, J., Osborne, J. F., Dillon, J. S., Wong, B., & Willis, B. (2013), *ASPIRES Report: Young people's science and career aspirations, age 10–14*, London: King's College London.

Aschaffenburg, K., & Maas, I. (1997), 'Cultural and educational careers: The dynamics of social reproduction', *American Sociological Review, 62*(4): 573–87. https://doi.org/10.2307/2657427

Atkinson, D., & Sohn, J. (2013), 'Culture from the bottom up', *Tesol Quarterly, 47*(4): 669–93.

Avraamidou, L. (2020a), '"I am a young immigrant woman doing physics and on top of that I am Muslim": Identities, intersections, and negotiations', *Journal of Research in Science Teaching, 57*(3): 311–41.

Avraamidou, L. (2020b), 'Science identity as a landscape of becoming: Rethinking recognition and emotions through an intersectionality lens', *Cultural Studies of Science Education, 15*(2): 323–45.

Bakan, D. (1966), *The duality of human existence: An essay on psychology and religion*, Washington: Rand McNally.

Baker, M. (2010), 'Choices or constraints? Family responsibilities, gender and academic career', *Journal of Comparative Family Studies, 41*(1): 1–18.

Bakhtiar, L. (2011), 'The Sublime Quran: The misinterpretation of Chapter 4 Verse 34', *European Journal of Women's Studies, 18*(4): 431–9.

Ball, S. J., Maguire, M., & Macrae, S. (2001), *Choice pathways and transitions: 16–19 education, training and (un)employment in one urban locale*, Swindon: Economic and Social Research Council.

Barnes, M. E., Truong, J. M., & Brownell, S. E. (2017), 'Experiences of Judeo-Christian students in undergraduate biology', *CBE—Life Sciences Education, 16*(1): ar15.

Baumann, G. (1996), *Contesting culture: Discourses of identity in multi-ethnic London* (Vol. 100), Cambridge: Cambridge University Press.

Beck, U. (1992), 'How modern is modern society?', *Theory, Culture & Society*, 9(2): 163–9.

Beck, U. (2002), *Individualization: Institutionalized individualism and its social and political consequences* (Vol. 13), London, Thousand Oaks and New Delhi: Sage.

Beechey, V. (1979), 'On patriarchy', *Feminist Review*, 3(1): 66–82.

Belkhir, J. A. (2009), 'The "Johnny's Story": Founder of Race, Gender, Class Journal', in M. T. Berger & K. Guidroz (Eds), *The intersectional approach: Transforming the academy through race, class and gender* (pp. 300–8), Chapel Hill: University of North Carolina Press.

Bell, D. (2014), *The perceived success of interventions in science education-a summary: A report for the wellcome trust*, London: Wellcome Trust.

Bennett, T., & Silva, E. (2011), 'Introduction: Cultural capital—Histories, limits, prospects', *Poetics*, 39(6): 427–43.

Bernstein, B. (2000), Pedagogy, symbolic control, and identity: Theory, research, critique (Revised Edition), Lanham, Boulder, New York, Oxford: Rowman & Littlefield.

Bhopal, K. (2010), *Asian women in higher education: Shared communities*, Stoke on Trent: Trentham.

Bhopal, K. (2011), 'Education makes you have more say in the way your life goes': Indian women and arranged marriages in the United Kingdom', *British Journal of Sociology of Education*, 32(3): 431–47.

Biesta, G. (2009), 'Good education in an age of measurement: On the need to reconnect with the question of purpose in education', *Educational Assessment, Evaluation and Accountability (formerly: Journal of Personnel Evaluation in Education)*, 21(1): 33–46.

Bird, A., & Reese, E. (2008), 'Autobiographical memory in childhood and the development of a continuous self', in F. Sani (Ed.), *Individual and collective self-continuity: Psychological perspectives*, Mahwah: Lawrence Erlbaum Associates.

Blake-Beard, S. D. (1999), 'The costs of living as an outsider within: An analysis of the mentoring relationships and career success of black and white women in the corporate sector', *Journal of Career Development*, 26(1): 21–36.

Bly, A. (2010), *Science is culture: Conversations at the new intersection of science+ society*, New York, London, Toronto, Sydney, New Delhi and Auckland: Harper Collins.

Bostock, J. (2014), *The meaning of success*, Cambridge: Cambridge University Press.

Bourdieu, P. (1986), 'Forms of capital', in J. Richardson (Ed.), *Handbook of theory and research for the sociology of education* (pp. 241–58), New York: Greenwood Press.

Bourdieu, P. (1990), *Sociology in question*, Cambridge: Polity Press.

Bourdieu, P., & Passeron, J. C. (1977), *Reproduction in education, society and culture*, London: Sage.

Bowleg, L. (2008), 'When Black+ lesbian+ woman≠ Black lesbian woman: The methodological challenges of qualitative and quantitative intersectionality research', *Sex Roles*, 59(5): 312–25.

Bradford, S., & Hey, V. (2007), 'Successful subjectivities? The successification of class, ethnic and gender positions', *Journal of Education Policy*, 22(6): 595–614.

Brah, A. (1979), *Inter-generational and inter-ethnic perceptions: A comparative study of South Asian and English adolescents in Southall*, unpublished Ph.D. Thesis, Bristol: University of Bristol.

Brah, A. (1996), *Cartographies of diaspora*, London: Routledge.

Breakwell, G. M., & Beardsell, S. (1992), 'Gender, parental and peer influences upon science attitudes and activities', *Public Understanding of Science*, 1(2): 183.

Brickhouse, N. (2012), 'Meanings of success in science', in M. Varelas, *Identity construction and science education research*, Netherland: Sense Publishers.

Brown, B. A. (2004), 'Discursive identity: Assimilation into the culture of science and its implications for minority students', *Journal of Research in Science Teaching*, 41(8): 810–34.

Brown, J., & Talbot, I. (2006), 'Making a new home in the diaspora: Opportunities and dilemmas in the British South Asian experience', *Contemporary South Asia*, 15(2): 125–31.

Bulbeck, C. (2010), '(White) feminism and foreigners: My quest for connection-musings spurred by the festschrift in my honour', *Australian Feminist Studies*, 25(66): 493–503.

Business in the Community (BIC) (2015), *Sector factsheet: Ethnic minorities in Science, Technology, Engineering and Mathematica (STEM)*, retrieved from: http://race.bitc .org.uk/sites/default/files/rfo_sector_factsheet_set_vfinal_new_2.pdf

Business in the Community/Diversity (2011), *Race for Opportunity Ethnic minorities in STEM – update*, retrieved from: https://issuu.com/bitcdiversity/docs/factsheet_stem _updated_1_

Cahill, C. (2004), 'Defying gravity? Raising consciousness through collective research', *Children's Geographies*, 2(2): 273–86.

Campaign for Science and Engineering (CaSE) (2014), *Improving diversity in STEM*, retrieved from: https://www.sciencecampaign.org.uk/static/uploaded/50c4b928 -d252-4ce8-825065f92d8deca3.pdf

Cannady, M. A., Greenwald, E., & Harris, K. N. (2014), 'Problematizing the STEM pipeline metaphor: Is the STEM pipeline metaphor serving our students and the STEM workforce?', *Science Education*, 98(3): 443–60.

Cappellini, B., & Yen, D. A. W. (2016), 'A space of one's own: Spatial and identity liminality in an online community of mothers', *Journal of Marketing Management*, 32(13–14): 1260–83.

Carastathis, A. (2016), *Intersectionality: Origins, contestations, horizons*, Nebraska: University of Nebraska Press.

Carbado, D. W., Crenshaw, K. W., Mays, V. M., & Tomlinson, B. (2013), 'Intersectionality', *Du Bois Review, 10*(2): 303–12.

Carlone, H. B., & Johnson, A. (2007), 'Understanding the science experiences of successful women of color: Science identity as an analytic lens', *Journal of Research in Science Teaching, 44*(8): 1187–218.

Carlone, H. B., Johnson, A., & Scott, C. M. (2015), 'Agency amidst formidable structures: How girls perform gender in science class', *Journal of Research in Science Teaching, 52*(4): 474–88.

Census (2011), *Census National Statistics*, London: Office for National Statistics (ONS), retrieved from: https://www.ons.gov.uk/census/2011census

Chan, C. D. (2017), 'A critical analysis of systemic influences on spiritual development for LGBTQC youth', *Journal of Child and Adolescent Counseling, 3*(3): 146–63.

Chan, C. D., & Erby, A. N. (2018), 'A critical analysis and applied intersectionality framework with intercultural queer couples', *Journal of Homosexuality, 65*(9): 1249–74.

Charleston, L. J., Adserias, R. P., Lang, N. M., & Jackson, J. F. (2014), 'Intersectionality and STEM: The role of race and gender in the academic pursuits of African American women in STEM', *Journal of Progressive Policy & Practice, 2*(3): 273–93.

Chemla, K., & Keller, E. F. (Eds). (2017), *Cultures without culturalism: The making of scientific knowledge*, Durham: Duke University Press.

Christensen, A. D., & Jensen, S. Q. (2012), 'Doing intersectional analysis: Methodological implications for qualitative research', *NORA-Nordic Journal of Feminist and Gender Research, 20*(2): 109–25.

Chua, A. (2011), *Battle hymn of the tiger mother*, New York: Penguin Press.

Cicourel, A. V. (1964), *Method and measurement in sociology*, New York: Free Press.

Clandinin, D. J., & Connelly, F. M. (2000), *Narrative inquiry: Experience and story in qualitative research*, San Francisco: Jossey-Bass.

Cochran-Smith, M., & Lytle, S. L. (1999), 'Relationships of knowledge and practice: Teacher learning in communities', *Review of Research in Education*, 24: 249–305.

Collins, P. H. (1990), *Black feminist thought: Knowledge, consciousness, and the politics of empowerment*, Boston: Unwin Hyman.

Collins, P. H., & Bilge, S. (2016), *Intersectionality*, Malden: Polity.

Conle, C. (2000), 'Thesis as narrative or "what is the inquiry in narrative inquiry?"', *Curriculum Inquiry, 30*(2): 189–214.

Conway, M. A., Singer, J. A., & Tagini, A. (2004), 'The self and autobiographical memory: Correspondence and coherence', *Social Cognition, 22*(5): 491–529.

Cooper, B. (2015), 'Intersectionality', in L. Disch & M. Hawkesworth (Eds), *The Oxford handbook of feminist theory*, retrieved from: https://www.oxfordhandbooks.com/view/10.1093/oxfordhb/9780199328581.001.0001/oxfordhb-9780199328581-e-20

Corburn, J. (2005), *Street science: Community knowledge and environmental health justice*, Cambridge, MA: The MIT Press.

Crawford, C., & Greaves, E. (2015), *Ethnic minorities substantially more likely to go to university than their White British peers*, London: Institute for Fiscal Studies.

Crenshaw, K. (1989), 'Demarginalizing the intersection of race and sex: A Black feminist critique of antidiscrimination doctrine, feminist theory, and antiracist politics', *University of Chicago Legal Forum*, *1989*(8): 139–67, retrieved from: https://chicagounbound.uchicago.edu/uclf/vol1989/iss1/8

Crossley, N. (2001), *The social body: Habit, identity and desire*, London: Sage.

D'Amato, L. G., & Krasny, M. E. (2011), 'Outdoor adventure education: Applying transformative learning theory to understanding instrumental learning and personal growth in environmental education', *The Journal of Environmental Education*, *42*(4): 237–54.

Da Silva Lopes, B., Pedrosa de Jesus, M. H., & Watts, D. M. (2016), 'The old questions are the best: Striving against invalidity in qualitative research', in M. Tight and J. Huisman (Eds), *Theory and method in higher education research* (Vol. 2, pp. 1–22), Bingley: Emerald Group Publishing.

Dasgupta, M., Gupta, C., & Teaiwa, K. M. (2007), 'Rethinking South Asian diaspora studies', *Cultural Dynamics*, *19*(2–3): 125–40.

Davis, K. (2008), 'Intersectionality as buzzword: A sociology of science perspective on what makes a feminist theory successful', *Feminist Theory*, *9*(1): 67–85.

Dawson, E., Archer, L., Seakins, A., Godec, S., DeWitt, J., King, H., & Nomikou, E. (2020), 'Selfies at the science museum: Exploring girls' identity performances in a science learning space', *Gender and Education*, *32*(5): 664–81.

Delahunty, J., & O'Shea, S. (2019), 'I'm happy, and I'm passing. That's all that matters!': Exploring discourses of university academic success through linguistic analysis', *Language and Education*, *33*(4): 302–21.

Delgado, R. (Ed.) (1995), *Critical race theory: The cutting edge*, Harvard: Temple University Press.

Department of Business Innovation and Skills (BIS) (2015), *Fulfilling our potential: Teaching excellence, social mobility and student choice*, retrieved from: https://assets.publishing.service.gov.uk/government/uploads/system/uploads/attachment_data/file/474227/BIS-15-623-fulfilling-our-potential-teaching-excellence-social-mobility-and-student-choice.pdf

Department for Children, Schools and Families (2008), *Statistical first release: Attainment by pupil characteristics, in England 2007/8 (Annex 1) SFR 32/2008*, London: Department for Children, Schools and Families.

Department of Education and Science (DES) (1975), *The Bullock Report: A language for life*, London: HMSO.

Department of Education and Science (DES) (1985), *The Swann Report, education for all: The report of the Committee of Inquiry into the Education of Children from Ethnic Minority Groups*, London: HMSO.

Devlin, M. (2009), 'Indigenous higher education student equity: Focusing on what works', *The Australian Journal of Indigenous Education*, *38*(1): 1–8.

Dewey, J. (1988), 'The quest for certainty', in J. A. Boydston (Ed.), *John Dewey: The later works, 1925–1953* (Vol. 4), Carbondale: Southern Illinois University Press. (Original work published 1929).

Dhamoon, R. K. (2011), 'Considerations on mainstreaming intersectionality', *Political Research Quarterly*, *64*(1): 230–43.

Diekman, A. B., Weisgram, E. S., & Belanger, A. L. (2015), 'New routes to recruiting and retaining women in STEM: Policy implications of a communal goal congruity perspective', *Social Issues and Policy Review*, *9*(1): 52–88.

Dimitriadi, A. (2013), 'Young women in science and technology: The importance of choice', *Journal of Innovation and Entrepreneurship*, *2*(1): 1–14.

Dixon, T. (2012), 'Emotion: The history of a keyword in crisis', *Emotion Review*, *4*(4): 338–44.

Dou, R., Hazari, Z., Dabney, K., Sonnert, G., & Sadler, P. (2019), 'Early informal STEM experiences and STEM identity: The importance of talking science', *Science Education*, *103*(3): 623–37.

Douglas, J. D. (1967), *The social meanings of suicide*, Princeton: Princeton University Press.

Duckworth, A. (2016), *Grit: The power of passion and perseverance* (Vol. 124), New York: Scribner. ISBN 13: 978-1-5011-1110-5.

Dweck, C. S. (2006), *Mindset: The new psychology of success*, New York: Random House.

Egan, C., & Gardner, L. (1994), 'Race, class and reproductive freedom: Women must have real choices!' *Canadian Woman Studies*, *14*(2): 95–9.

Environics Institute (2016), *Survey of Muslims in Canada*, retrieved from http://www .environicsinstitute.org/uploads/institute-projects/survey%20of%20muslims%20in% 20canada%202016%20-%20final%20report.pdf

Erel, U., Haritaworn, J., Rodríguez, E., & Klesse, C. (2010), 'On the depoliticisation of intersectionality talk: Conceptualising multiple oppressions in critical sexuality studies', in Y. Taylor, S. Hines & M. E. Casey (Eds), *Theorizing intersectionality and sexuality* (pp. 56–77), Basingstoke: Palgrave Macmillan.

Erikson, E. (1968), *Identity, youth and crisis*, New York: Norton.

Fadel, L. (2018), 'Being Muslim in America', *National Geographic*, *233*(5): 42–77.

Fenwick, T., & Landri, P. (Eds) (2014), *Materialities, Textures and Pedagogies*, London: Routledge.

Finlay, S. M., Raman, S., Rasekoala, E., Mignan, V., Dawson, E., Neeley, L., & Orthia, L. A. (2021), 'From the margins to the mainstream: Deconstructing science communication as a white, Western paradigm', *Journal of Science Communication*, *20*(1): 1–12.

Flap, H., & Völker, B. (2008), 'Social, cultural, and economic capital and job attainment: The position generator as a measure of cultural and economic resources', in N. Lin & B. H. Erickson, *Social capital: An international research program* (pp. 65–80), Oxford: Oxford University Press.

Fouad, N. A., & Bynner, J. (2008), 'Work transitions', *American Psychologist*, *63*(4), 241–51.

Fulbright, K. (1985), 'The myth of the double-advantage: Black female managers', *The Review of Black Political Economy*, *14*(2): 33–45.

Furrer, C., & Skinner, E. (2003), 'Sense of relatedness as a factor in children's academic engagement and performance', *Journal of Educational Psychology*, 95(1): 148–62.

Garvey, P., & Miller, D. (2021), *Ageing with smartphones in Ireland: When life becomes craft*, London: UCL Press.

Gay, G. (2013), 'Connections between classroom management and culturally responsive teaching', in C. M. Evertson & C. S. Weinstein (Eds), *Handbook of classroom management*, 353–80, New York: Routledge.

Ghuman, P. A. S. (2011), *British untouchables: A study of Dalit identity and education*, Burlington: Ashgate.

Giddens, A. (1991), *Modernity and self-identity: Self and society in the late modern age*, Stanford: Stanford University Press.

Gieryn, T. F. (1999), *Cultural boundaries of science: Credibility on the line*, Chicago: University Chicago Press.

Giordano, S. (2017), 'Who can't, teach: Critical science literacy as a queer science of failure', *Catalyst: Feminism, Theory, Technoscience*, 3(1): 1–21.

Giroux, H. A. (1988b), *Teachers as intellectuals*, South Hadley: Bergin & Garvey Publishers Inc.

Giroux, H. A. (2004a), 'Cultural studies, public pedagogy, and the responsibility of intellectuals', *Communication and critical/cultural studies*, 1(1): 59–79.

Gorard, S., Rees, G., & Fevre, R. (1999), 'Patterns of participation in lifelong learning: Do families make a difference?', *British Educational Research Journal*, 25(4): 517–32.

Gould, S. J., & King Jr, M. L. (1998), 'The Cultural Study of Science and Science Education', in Cobern, W. W (Ed.), Socio-Cultural Perspectives on Science Education: An International Dialogue 4 (p. 1), Dordrecht, Boston, London, Kluwer Academic Publishers.

Goulden, M., Mason, M. A., & Frasch, K. (2011), 'Keeping women in the science pipeline', *The ANNALS of the American Academy of Political and Social Science*, 638(1): 141–62.

Grossman, J. M., & Porche, M. V. (2014), 'Perceived gender and racial/ethnic barriers to STEM success', *Urban Education*, 49(6): 698–727. DOI: 10.1177/0042085913481364

Hankivsky, O., Vorobyova, A., Salnykova, A., & Rouhani, S. (2017), 'The importance of community consultations for generating evidence for health reform in Ukraine', *International Journal of Health Policy and Management*, 6(3): 135–45.

Hanley, P., Bennett, J., & Ratcliffe, M. (2014), 'The inter-relationship of science and religion: A typology of engagement', *International Journal of Science Education*, 36(7): 1210–29.

Hanson, S. L., & Gilbert, E. (2012), 'Family, gender and science experiences: The perspective of young Asian Americans', *Race, Gender & Class*, 19(3–4): 326–47.

Harris, A. (1990), 'Race and essentialism in feminist legal theory', *Stanford Law Review*, 42(3): 581–616. http://dx.doi.org/10.2307/1228886

Hase, S., & Kenyon, C. (2015), *Self-determined learning*, London: Bloomsbury.

Haw, K. (2010), 'Being, becoming and belonging: Young Muslim women in contemporary Britain', *Journal of Intercultural Studies*, 31(4): 221–45.

Hazari, Z., Sadler, P. M., & Sonnert, G. (2013), 'The science identity of college students: Exploring the intersection of gender, race, and ethnicity', *Journal of College Science Teaching*, *42*(5): 82–91.

Heddy, B., & Kevin, P. (2015), 'Bigger is not always better: Should educators aim for big transformative learning events or small transformative experiences?', *Journal of Transformative Learning*, *3*(1): 52–8.

Hinkel, E. (2001), 'Building awareness and practical skills to facilitate cross-cultural communication', in M. C. Murcia (Ed.), *Teaching English as a second or foreign language* (3rd ed., pp. 443–58), Boston: Heinle, Cengage Learning.

Hoffman, A. (2012), 'Climate science as culture war', *Stanford Social Innovation Review*, *10*(4): 30–7.

Homer, M., Ryder, J., & Banner, I. (2014), 'Measuring determinants of post-compulsory participation in science: A comparative study using national data', *British Educational Research Journal*, *40*(4): 610–36.

Hopkins, P. (Ed.) (2017), *Scotland's Muslims: Society, politics and identity*, Edinburgh: Edinburgh University Press.

Howes, S. S., Henning, J., Mills, M. J., & Huffman, A. H. (2018), 'Yes Virginia, there is a gender disparity problem—And it goes beyond STEM', *Industrial and Organizational Psychology*, *11*(2): 318–23.

Hussain, A. S. (2017), *UAE preschool teachers' attitudes toward inclusion education by specialty and cultural identity*, Doctoral dissertation and Doctoral Studies. 3785, Walden: Walden University, https://scholarworks.waldenu.edu/dissertations/3785

Hussain, Y., & Bagguley, P. (2007), *Moving on up: South Asian women and higher education*, Stoke on Trent: §Trentham Books Limited.

Ijaz, A., & Abbas, T. (2010), 'The impact of inter-generational change on the attitudes of working-class South Asian Muslim parents on the education of their daughters', *Gender and Education*, *22*(3): 313–326.

Illeris, K. (2014), *Transformative learning and identity*, London and New York: Routledge.

Illouz, E. (2008), *Saving the modern soul. Therapy, emotions, and the culture of self-help*, Berkeley: University of California Press.

Ireland, D. T., Freeman, K. E., Winston-Proctor, C. E., DeLaine, K. D., McDonald Lowe, S., & Woodson, K. M. (2018), '(Un) hidden figures: A synthesis of research examining the intersectional experiences of Black women and girls in STEM education', *Review of Research in Education*, *42*(1): 226–54.

Jang, S. T. (2018), 'The implications of intersectionality on Southeast Asian female students' educational outcomes in the United States: A critical quantitative intersectionality analysis', *American Educational Research Journal*, *55*(6): 1268–306.

Jensen, M., Foster, E., & Eddy, M. (1997), 'Creating a space where teachers can locate their voices and develop their pedagogical awareness', *Teaching and Teacher Education*, *13*(8): 863–75.

Keddie, A. (2009), 'National gender equity and schooling policy in Australia: Struggles for a non-identitarian feminist politics', *The Australian Educational Researcher, 36*(2): 21–37.

Kennedy, D., & Highland, A. (2007), *Writing and using learning outcomes: A practical guide*, Cork: Mimeograph, University College Cork.

King, A. (2000), 'The accidental derogation of the lay actor: A critique of Giddens's concept of structure', *Philosophy of the Social Sciences, 30*(3): 362–83.

Knapp, G. A. (2005), 'Intersectionality: Ein neues Paradigma feministischer Theorie?; Zur transatlantischen Reise von, Race, Class, Gender', *Feministische Studien: Zeitschrift für interdisziplinäre Frauen-und Geschlechterforschung, 23*(1): 68–81.

Ko, L. T., Kachchaf, R. R., Hodari, A. K., & Ong, M. (2014), 'Agency of women of color in physics and astronomy: Strategies for persistence and success', *Journal of Women and Minorities in Science and Engineering, 20*(2):171–95.

Kritskaya, O. V., & Dirkx, J. M. (1999), 'Symbolic representations as mediators for meaning construction: An exploration of transformative pedagogy within a professional development context', in A. Austin, G. E. Hynes & R. T. Miller (Eds), *Proceedings of the 18th annual Midwest research-to-practice conference in adult, continuing and community education* (pp. 184–90), St. Louis: University of Missouri.

Lease, S. H., & Dahlbeck, D. T. (2009), 'Parental influences, career decision making attributions and self-efficacy. Differences for men and women?' *Journal of Career Development, 36*(2), 95–113. https://doi.org/10.1177/0894845309340794

Leong, F. T. L. (1993), 'The career counselling process with racial-ethnic minorities: The case of Asian, Americans', *The Career Development Quarterly, 42*(1): 26–40.

Liu, J., McMahon, M., & Watson, M. (2015), 'Parental influence on mainland Chinese children's career aspirations: Child and parental perspectives', *International Journal for Educational and Vocational Guidance, 15*(2): 131–43.

Lucey, H., Melody, J., & Walkerdine, V. (2003), 'Uneasy hybrids: Psychosocial aspects of becoming educationally successful for working-class young women', in M. Arnot & M. Mac an Ghaill (Eds), *The Routledge Falmer reader in gender and education* (pp. 238–52), London: Routledge.

Ludhra, G. (2015), 'A black feminist exploration of the cultural experiences and identities of academically "Successful" British South-Asian girls', PhD Thesis, London: Brunel University.

Ludvig, A. (2006), 'Differences between women? Intersecting voices in a female narrative', *European Journal of Women's Studies, 13*(3): 245–58.

Luo, Y. (2022), *An investigation of the experience of university students and teachers with language learning and teaching mediated by mobile technologies*, Unpublished PhD Thesis, London: Brunel University London.

Maddock, M. N. (1981), 'Science education: An anthropological viewpoint', *Studies in Science Education, 8*(1): 1–26. DOI: 10.1080/03057268108559884

Malcom, S. M., Hall, P. Q., & Brown, J. W. (1976), 'The double bind: The price of being a minority woman in science', in *Proceedings of American Association for the Advancement of Science Minority Women Scientists Conference, AAAS Publication*.

Malik, S. (2012), 'The Indian family on UK reality television: Convivial culture in salient contexts', *Television and New Media*, *14*(6): 510–28.

Martino, W., & Rezai-Rashti, G. M. (2009), 'The politics of veiling, gender and the Muslim subject: On the limits and possibilities of anti-racist education in the aftermath of September 11', in J. Dillabough, J. McLeod & M. Mills (Eds), *Troubling gender in education* (pp. 111–25), London: Routledge.

May, V. (2001), *Lone Motherhood in Finnish Women's Life Stories: Creating Meaning in a Narrative Context*, Abo: Abo Academy Press.

Mazzarol, T., & Soutar, G. (2002), 'Push-pull factors influencing international students' destination choice', *The International Journal of Educational Management*, *16*(2): 82–90.

McAdams, D. P., Bauer, J. J., Sakaeda, A. R., Anyidoho, N. A., Machado, M. A., & Magrino-Failla, K. (2006), 'Continuity and change in the life story: A longitudinal study of autobiographical memories in emerging adulthood', *Journal of Personality*, *74*(5): 1371–400.

McAdams, D. P., & McLean, K. C. (2013), 'Narrative identity', *Current Directions in Psychological Science*, *22*(3): 233–8.

McCall, L. (2005), 'The complexity of intersectionality', *Signs*, *30*(3): 1771–800.

McGee, E. O., & Bentley, L. (2017), 'The troubled success of Black women in STEM', *Cognition and Instruction*, *35*(4): 265–89.

Meetoo, V. (2016), *The identities of South Asian girls in a multicultural school context: Constructions, negotiations and constraints*, Doctoral thesis, London: UCL (University College London).

Meetoo, V. (2019), 'Beyond "between two cultures": Micro processes of racialised and gendered positioning of South Asian and Muslim girls in an "everyday" British multicultural school context', *Gender and Education*, *33*(7): 864–80. DOI: 10.1080/09540253.2019.1632810

Metcalf, H. (2010), 'Stuck in the pipeline: A critical review of STEM workforce literature', *UCLA Journal of Education and Information Studies*, *6*(2). DOI: https://doi.org/10.5070/D462000681

Mezirow, J. (1991), *Transformative dimensions of adult learning*, San Francisco: Jossey-Bass.

Mezirow, J. (2000), *Learning as transformation: Critical perspectives on a theory in progress*. The Jossey-Bass Higher and Adult Education Series, San Francisco: Jossey-Bass Publishers.

Mezirow, J. (2018), 'Transformative learning theory', in K. Illeris, *Contemporary theories of learning* (pp. 114–28), London and New York: Routledge.

Mezirow, J., & Taylor, E. W. (Eds) (2009), *Transformative learning in practice: Insights from community, workplace, and higher education*, San Francisco: John Wiley & Sons.

Miller, R., Liu, J., & Ball, A. (2020), 'Critical counter-narrative as transformative methodology for educational equity', *Review of Research in Education, 44*(1): 269–300. DOI: https://doi.org/10.3102%2F0091732X20908501

Mirza, H. S. (2009), *Race, gender and educational desire: Why Black women succeed and fail*, London and New York: Routledge.

Mirza, H. S. (2013), '"A second skin": Embodied intersectionality, transnationalism and narratives of identity and belonging among Muslim women in Britain'. *Women's Studies International Forum, 36*: 5–15.

Mirza, H. S., & Meetoo, V. (2018), 'Empowering Muslim girls? Post-feminism, multiculturalism and the production of the "model" Muslim female student in British schools', *British Journal of Sociology of Education, 39*(2): 227–41.

Mirza, H. S., Meetoo, V., & Litster, J. (2011), 'Young, female and migrant: Gender, class and racial identity in Multicultural Britain', in J. Christodoulou, *Young migrant women in secondary education: Promoting integration and mutual understanding through dialogue and exchange* (pp. 143–82), University of Nicosia Press, retrieved from: http://www.medinstgenderstudies.org/wp-content/uploads/Integration_of _young_migrant_women_2011.pdf

Mujtaba, T., & Reiss, M. J. (2014), 'A survey of psychological, motivational, family and perceptions of physics education factors that explain 15-year-old students' aspirations to study physics in post-compulsory English schools', *International Journal of Science and Mathematics Education, 12*(2): 371–93.

Nash, J. C. (2008), 'Re-thinking intersectionality', *Feminist Review, 89*(1): 1–15.

Nelson, K., & Fivush, R. (2004), 'The emergence of autobiographical memory: A social cultural developmental theory', *Psychological Review, 111*(2): 486–511.

Nissen, M. E. (2006), *Harnessing knowledge dynamics: Principled organizational knowing & learning*, London: IRM Press.

O'Brien, J. M., Scheibling, R. E., & Krumhansl, K. A. (2015), 'Positive feedback between large- scale disturbance and density- dependent grazing decreases resilience of a kelp bed ecosystem', *Marine Ecology Progress Series, 522*: 1–13. DOI: 10.3354/ meps11193

Ollerenshaw, J. A., & Creswell, J. W. (2002), 'Narrative research: A comparison of two restorying data analysis approaches', *Qualitative Inquiry, 8*(3): 329–47.

Olmos-Gómez, M. D. C., Luque-Suárez, M., Becerril-Ruiz, D., & Cuevas-Rincón, J. M. (2021), 'Gender and socioeconomic status as factors of individual differences in pre-university students' decision- making for careers, with a focus on family influence and psychosocial factors', *International Journal of Environmental Research and Public Health, 18*(3): 1344. DOI: 10.3390/ijerph18031344.

Ong, M., Smith, J. M., & Ko, L. T. (2018), 'Counterspaces for women of color in STEM higher education: Marginal and central spaces for persistence and success', *Journal of Research in Science Teaching, 55*(2): 206–45.

Ong, M., Wright, C., Espinosa, L., & Orfield, G. (2011), 'Inside the double bind: A synthesis of empirical research on undergraduate and graduate women of color in science, technology, engineering, and mathematics', *Harvard Educational Review*, *81*(2): 172–209.

Opara, E. (2017), 'The transformation of my science identity', in D. Gabriel & S. A. Tate, *Inside the Ivory Tower: Narratives of women of colour surviving and thriving in British academia* (pp. 124–35), London: Trentham Books/IOE Press.

Ortony, A. (Ed.) (1993), *Metaphor and thought*, Cambridge: Cambridge University Press.

Osborne, J. W. (2009), 'Commentary on retirement, identity, and Erikson's developmental stage model', *Canadian Journal on Aging/La Revue canadienne du vieillissement*, *28*(4): 295–301.

Paa, H., & Mcwhirter, E. H. (2000), 'Perceived influences on high school students' current career expectations', *The Career Development Quarterly*, *49*(1): 29–44.

Papademetriou, D., Sumption, M., & Somerville, W. (2009), *Migration and the economic downturn: What to expect in the EU?*, Washington: Migration Policy Institute, retrieved from: https://www.migrationpolicy.org/sites/default/files/publications/EU_Recession_backgrounder.pdf

Parekh, B. (2001), 'Rethinking multiculturalism: Cultural diversity and political theory', *Ethnicities*, *1*(1): 109–15.

Park, H., Behrman, J., & Choi, J. (2012), *Do single-sex schools enhance students' stem (science, technology, engineering, and mathematics) Outcomes?*, PIER Working Paper No. 12-038, retrieved from: http://dx.doi.org/10.2139/ssrn.2153812

Patacchini, E., & Zenou, Y. (2012), 'Ethnic networks and employment outcomes', *Regional Science and Urban Economics*, *42*(6): 938–49.

Patil, V. (2013), 'From patriarchy to intersectionality: A transnational feminist assessment of how far we've really come', *Signs*, *38*(4): 847–67.

Payne, J. (2003), *Choice at the end of compulsory schooling, research report No. 414*, London: Department for Education and Skills.

Peach, C. (2006), 'South Asian migration and settlement in Great Britain, 1951–2001', *Contemporary South Asia*, *15*(2): 133–46.

Phillips, A. (2010), *Gender and culture*, Cambridge: Polity.

Phoenix, A. (2011), 'Psychosocial intersections: Contextualising the accounts of adults who grew up in visibly ethnically different households', in H. Lutz, M. Vivar & L. Supik (Eds), *Framing intersectionality: Debates on a multi-faceted concept in gender studies* (pp. 137–52), Farnham: Ashgate.

Pimpa, N. (2005), 'A family affair: The effect of family on Thai students' choices of international education', *Higher Education*, *49*(4): 431–48.

Platt, L. (2005), *Migration and social mobility: The life chances of Britain's minority ethnic communities*. Bristol: Policy Press.

Plummer, K. (2001), *Documents of life 2: An invitation to a critical humanism*, London: Sage.

Powney, J., & Watts, D. M. (2018, originally published 1987), *Interviewing in educational research*. London: Routledge and Kegan Paul.

Pritchard, P. A. (Ed). (2011), 'Success strategies for women in science: A portable mentor', Amsterdam, Netherlands, Elsevier.

Pritchard, P. A., & Grant, C. (Eds) (2015), *Success strategies from women in STEM: A portable mentor*, San Diego: Elsevier Academic Press.

Psillos, S. (2018), *Realism and theory change in science*, retrieved from: https://stanford .library.sydney.edu.au/archives/fall2020/entries/realism-theory-change/

Pugh, K. J. (2020), *Transformative science education: Change how your students experience the world*, Columbia University, New York and London: Teachers College Press.

Pugh, K. J., Bergstrom, C. M., & Spencer, B. (2017), 'Profiles of transformative engagement: Identification, description, and relation to learning and instruction', *Science Education, 101*(3): 369–98.

Puwar, N. (2004), *Space invaders: Race, gender and bodies out of place*, Oxford and New York: BERG.

Rainey, K., Dancy, M., Mickelson, R., Stearns, E., & Moller, S. (2018), 'Race and gender differences in how sense of belonging influences decisions to major in STEM', *International Journal of STEM Education, 5*(1): 1–14.

Razack, S. (2005), 'How is White supremacy embodied? Sexualized racial violence at Abu Ghraib', *Canadian Journal of Women and the Law, 17*(2): 341–63.

Reay, D. (1998), 'Always knowing' and "never being sure": Familial and institutional habituses and higher education choice', *Journal of Education Policy, 13*(4): 519–29.

Reay, D. (2004), 'Education and cultural capital: The implications of changing trends in education policies', *Cultural Trends, 13*(2): 73–86.

Reay, D., David, M., & Ball, S. (2001), 'Making a difference? Institutional habituses and higher education choice', *Sociological Research Online, 5*(4), retrieved from http:// www.socresonline.org.uk.ezproxy.brunel.ac.uk/5/4/reay.html

Reese, E., Yan, C., Jack, F., & Hayne, H. (2010), 'Emerging identities: Narrative and self from early childhood to early adolescence', in K. C. McLean & M. Pasupathi, *Narrative development in adolescence* (pp. 23–43), Boston: Springer.

Rennie, L. J. (2014), 'Learning science outside of school', in N. G. Lederman & S. K. Abell, *Handbook of research on science education* (Vol. II, pp. 134–58), New York: Routledge.

Resmini, M. (2016), 'The leaky pipeline', *Chemistry, 22*(11): 3533–4.

Rhodes, C. (2000), 'Ghostwriting research: Positioning the researcher in the interview text', *Qualitative Inquiry, 6*(4): 511–25. DOI: 10.1177/107780040000600406.

Riessman, C. K. (2008), *Narrative methods for the human sciences*, Thousand Oaks: Sage.

Rompelmann L. (2002), *Affective teaching*, Lanham: University Press of America.

Rosenblatt, J. (2015), 'Chip off the old block', *University of Toledo Law Review, 46*(2): 371–4.

Rossi, A. (1965), 'Women in science: Why so few? Social and psychological influences restrict women's choice and pursuit of careers in science', *Science, 148*(3674): 1196–202.

Roth, W. M., & Middleton, D. (2006), 'Knowing what you tell, telling what you know: Uncertainty and asymmetries of meaning in interpreting graphical data', *Cultural Studies of Science Education*, *1*: 11–81. DOI: https://doi.org/10.1007/s11422-005 -9000-y

Rugkåsa, M., Yivisaker, S., & Eide, K. (2018), 'Silenced stories of social work with minority ethnic families in Norway', *Critical and Radical Social Work*, *3*(2): 77–89.

Ruiz Castro, M., & Holvino, E. (2016), 'Applying intersectionality in organizations: Inequality markers, cultural scripts and advancement practices in a professional service firm', *Gender, Work & Organization*, *23*(3): 328–47.

Russell, K. (2007), 'Feminist dialectics and Marxist theory', *Radical Philosophy Review*, *10*(1): 33–54.

Ryan, R. M., & Deci, E. L. (2000), 'Self-determination theory and the facilitation of intrinsic motivation, social development, and well-being', *American Psychologist*, *55*(1): 68–78. DOI: https://doi.org/10.1037/0003-066X.55.1.68

Salehjee, S. (2017), *Making scientists: Developing a model of science identity*, Doctoral dissertation, London: Brunel University London.

Salehjee, S., & Watts, D. M. (2015), 'Science lives: School choices and 'natural tendencies', *International Journal of Science Education*, *37*(4): 727–43.

Salehjee, S., & Watts, D. M. (2018), 'Models of scientific identity', in P. Stffen, *Science and technology education: Perspectives, opportunities and challenges* (pp. 1–62), Hauppauge: Nova Science Publishers.

Salehjee, S., & Watts, D. M. (2020), *Becoming scientific: Developing science across the life-course*, Cambridge: Cambridge Scholars Publishing.

Salehjee, S., & Watts, D. M. (2021), 'Supporting beginning teachers in embedding scientific literacy', in S. Salehjee (Ed.), *Mentoring science teachers in the secondary school* (pp. 228–43), London: Routledge.

Salehjee, S., & Watts, D. M. (2022), 'Intersectionality as personal: The science identity of two young immigrant Muslim women', *International Journal of Science Education*, *44*(6): 921–38. DOI: 10.1080/09500693.2022.2059119

Salem, S. (2018), 'Intersectionality and its discontents: Intersectionality as traveling theory', *European Journal of Women's Studies*, *25*(4): 403–18.

Sang, K., Al-Dajani, H., & Ozbilgin, M. (2013), 'Frayed careers of migrant female professors in British academia', *Gender, Work and Organisation*, *20*(2): 58–171.

Savater, F. (1997), *Polı'tica para Amador*, Barcelona: Editorial Ariel.

Schank, R. C. (1990), *Tell me a story: A new look at real and artificial memory*, New York: Charles Scribner's Sons.

Schiffman, S. (2012), Power of Positive Selling: 30 Surefire Techniques to Win New Clients, Boost Your Commission, and Build the Mindset for Success, United States: The McGraw-Hill Companies, Inc.

Schwartz, S. H. (2009), 'Causes of culture: National differences in cultural embeddedness', in G. Aikaterini & K. Mylonas (Eds), *Quod Erat Demonstrandum: From Herodotus' ethnographic journeys to cross-cultural research: Proceedings from* the 18th International Congress of the International Association for Cross-Cultural *Psychology*. https://scholarworks.gvsu.edu/iaccp_papers/64/

Shain, F. (2003), *The schooling and identity of Asian girls*, Stoke-on-Trent: Trentham.

Shain, F. (2010), 'Refusing to Integrate? Asian girls, achievement and the experience of schooling', in C. Jackson, Carrie F. Paechter & E. Renold (Eds), *Girls and Education, 3-16, Continuing Concerns* (pp. 62–74), Maidenhead: Open University Press.

Shams, T. (2020), 'Successful yet precarious: South Asian Muslim Americans, Islamophobia, and the model minority myth', *Sociological Perspectives*, *63*(4): 653–69.

Sheafer, T. (2007), 'How to evaluate it: The role of story-evaluative tone in agenda setting and priming', *Journal of Communication*, *57*(1): 21–39.

Shields, S. A. (2008), 'Gender: An intersectionality perspective', *Sex Roles*, *59*(5): 301–11.

Shimwell, J., DeWitt, J., Davenport, C., Padwick, A., Sanderson, J., & Strachan, R. (2021), 'Scientist of the week: Evaluating effects of a teacher-led STEM intervention to reduce stereotypical views of scientists in young children', *Research in Science & Technological Education*. DOI: 10.1080/02635143.2021.1941840

Sluss, D. M., & Ashforth, S. E. (2007), 'Relational identity and identification: Defining ourselves through work relationships', *Academy of Management Review*, *32*(1): 9–32.

Smith, W. A., Allen, W. R., & Danley, L. L. (2007), '"Assume the position... you fit the description" psychosocial experiences and racial battle fatigue among African American male college students', *American Behavioral Scientist*, *51*(4): 551–78.

Smooth, W. G. (2013), 'Intersectionality from theoretical framework to policy intervention', in A. R. Wilson (Ed.), *Situating intersectionality: The politics of intersectionality* (pp. 11–41), New York: Palgrave Macmillan. https://doi.org/10.1057/9781137025135_2

Smyth, J. (Ed.) (1987), Educating Teachers: changing the nature of pedagogical knowledge, London: Falmer Press.

Social Mobility Commission (2016), *Asian Muslims and black people do better in school, worse in work*, retrieved from:https://www.gov.uk/government/news/asian-muslims-and-black-people-do-better-in-school-worse-in-work

Spaights, E., & Whitaker, A. (1995), 'Black women in the workforce: A new look at an old problem', *Journal of Black Studies*, *25*(3): 283–96.

Squires, J. (2007), *The new politics of gender equality*, New York: Palgrave Macmillan.

Styhre, A., & Eriksson-Zetterquist, U. (2008), 'Thinking the multiple in gender and diversity studies: Examining the concept of intersectionality', *Gender in Management: An International Journal*, *23*(8): 567–82.

Sullivan, M. G. (2002), 'Rapin, Hume and the identity of the historian in eighteenth century England', *History of European Ideas*, *28*(3): 145–62.

Swartz, D. L. (2002), 'The sociology of habit: The perspective of Pierre Bourdieu', *OTJR: Occupation, Participation and Health*, *22*(1): 18–30.

Syed, M., & Ajayi, A. A. (2018), 'Promises and pitfalls in the integration of intersectionality with development science', *New Directions for Child and Adolescent Development*, *2018*(161): 109–17.

Taconis, R., & Kessels, U. (2009), 'How choosing science depends on students' individual fit to science culture', *International Journal of Science Education*, *31*(8): 1115–32.

Tang, M., Fouad, N. A., & Smith, P. L. (1999), 'Asian Americans' career choices: A path model to examine factors influencing their choices', *Journal of Vocational Behaviour*, *54*: 142–57.

Taylor, C. (1992), *Multiculturalism and the politics of recognition*, Princeton: Princeton University Press.

Teranishi, C. S. (2007), 'Impact of experiential learning on Latino college students' identity, relationships, and connectedness to community', *Journal of Hispanic Higher Education*, *6*(1): 52–72.

The Lancet Digital Health (2020), 'All things being equal: diversity in STEM', *The Lancet Digital Health*, *2*(4): e149. DOI: https://doi.org/10.1016/S2589-7500(20)30067-4

The Pew Research Centre (2012), *The Global Religious Landscape. A Report on the Size and Distribution of the World's Major Religious Groups as of 2010*, Washington, DC: Pew Research Center's Forum on Religion & Public Life.

Tramonte, L., & Willms, J. D. (2010), 'Cultural capital and its effects on education outcomes', *Economics of Education Review*, *29*(2): 200–13.

Trujillo Sáenz, F. (2002), 'Towards interculturality through language teaching: Argumentative discourse', *Cauce, revista de filología y su didáctica*, *25*: 103–19.

Tseng, M. S., & Carter, A. R. (1970), 'Achievement motivation and fear of failure as determinants of vocational choice, vocational aspiration and perception of vocational prestige', *Journal of Consulting Psychology*, *17*(2): 150–6.

Turner-Bisset, R. (1999), 'The knowledge bases of the expert teacher', *British Educational Research Journal*, *25*(1): 39–55.

Tyrer, D., & Ahmad, F. (2006), *Muslim women and higher education: Identities, experiences and prospects: A Summary Report*, Liverpool: Liverpool John Moores University and European Social Fund, retrieved from: https://citeseerx.ist.psu.edu/viewdoc/download?doi=10.1.1.616.2705&rep=rep1&type=pdf

Varelas, M. (2012), *Identity construction and science education research*, Rotterdam: Sense Publications.

Varney, R. M., & Heinrich, K. K. (2021), 'A garden, not a leaky pipeline', *The Teaching Professor* (online), retrieved from: https://www.teachingprofessor.com/topics/student-learning/a-garden-not-a-leaky-pipeline/

Wagner, W., Sen, R., Permanadeli, R., & Howarth, C. S. (2012), 'The Veil and Muslim women's identity: Cultural pressures and resistance to stereotyping', *Culture and Psychology*, *18*(4): 521–41.

Wainwright, E., & Watts, D. M. (2019), 'Social mobility in the slipstream: First-generation students' narratives of university participation and family', *Educational Review*, *73*(1): 111–27. DOI: 10.1080/00131911.2019.1566209

Watkins, C., & Mortimore, P. (1999), 'Pedagogy: what do we know?', in P.Mortimore (ed.), *Pedagogy and its Impact on Learning*, London: PaulChapman/Sage.

Watts, D. M. (2015), 'Public understanding of plant biology: Voices from the bottom of the garden', *International Journal of Science Education, Part B*, *5*(4): 339–56.

Webb, O. C., Ackerly, D. D., McPeek, M. A., & Donoghue, M. J. (2002), 'Phylogenies and community ecology', *Annual Review of Ecology and Systematics*, *33*: 475–505.

Weedon, E., Riddell, S., McCluskey, G., & Konstantoni, K. (2013), 'Muslim families' educational experiences in England and Scotland: Final report', in *Inclusion and Diversity*, Edinburgh: University of Edinburgh Centre for Research in Education, retrieved from: http://www.docs.hss.ed.ac.uk/education/creid/Reports/32_MFEES _FinalRpt.pdf

Wellcome Trust (2014), 'Experiments in Engagement: Engaging with young people from disadvantaged backgrounds', *Science Beyond the Classroom*, retrieved from: http://www.engagement.manchester.ac.uk/resources/engagement/young_people _beyond/Wellcome%20Trust%20Experiments%20in%20Engagement.pdf

Wells, C., Gill, R., & McDonald, J. (2015), 'Us foreigners: Intersectionality in a scientific organization', *Equality, Diversity and Inclusion: An International Journal*, *34*(6): 539–53.

Whiston, S. C., & Keller, B. K. (2004), 'The influences of the family of origin on career development: A review and analysis', *The Counseling Psychologist*, *32*(4): 493–568.

Wilson, A. (1978), *Finding a voice: Asian women in Britain*, London: Virago.

Wilson, A. (2018), *Finding a voice: Asian women in Britain*, 2nd edn. Daraja Press. https://www.amazon.co.uk/Finding-Voice-Asian-Women-Britain/dp/1988832012 ?asin=B07FPXWHD2&revisionId=f6c0bd76&format=1&depth=1.

Wilson, A. (2022), *Being Interdisciplinary, Adventures in urban science and beyond*, London: UCL Press.

WISE (2015), *Women in science, technology, engineering and mathematics: The talent pipeline from classroom to boardroom UK Statistics 2014*, retrieved from: https://www .wisecampaign.org.uk/wp-content/uploads/2021/03/WISE_UK_Statistics_2014.pdf

Wong, B. (2012), 'Identifying with science: A case study of two 13-year-old "high achieving working class" British Asian girls', *International Journal of Science Education*, *34*(1): 43–65.

Wong, B. (2015), 'Careers "from" but not "in" science: Why aspirations to be a scientist are challenging for minority ethnic students?', *Journal of Research in Science Teaching*, *52*(7): 979–1002.

Wong, B., Elmorally, R., Copsey-Blake, M., Highwood, E., & Singarayer, J. (2021), 'Is race still relevant? Student perceptions and experiences of racism in higher education', *Cambridge Journal of Education*, *51*(3): 359–75.

World Economic Forum (2019), *Towards a reskilling revolution industry-led action for the future of work*, Centre for New Economy and Society Insight Report. World Economic Forum (pp. 91–3), Boston Consulting Group.

Yazedjian, A., Toews, M. L., Sevin, T., & Purswell, K. E. (2008), 'It's a Whole New World: A qualitative exploration of college students' definitions of and strategies for college success', *Journal of College Student Development*, 49(2): 141–54.

Zuccotti, C. V. (2015), 'Do parents matter? Revisiting ethnic penalties in occupation among second generation ethnic minorities in England and Wales', *Sociology*, 49(2): 229–51.

Index